D1555886

HITLER

AND HIS

WOMEN

HITLER
AND HIS
WOMEN

PHIL CARRADICE

PEN & SWORD
HISTORY

AN IMPRINT OF PEN & SWORD BOOKS LTD.
YORKSHIRE - PHILADELPHIA

First published in Great Britain in 2021 by
PEN AND SWORD HISTORY
An imprint of
Pen & Sword Books Ltd
Yorkshire – Philadelphia

ISBN 978 1 52677 954 0

A CIP catalogue record for this book is available from the British Library.

Typeset in Times New Roman 11.5/14 by
SJmagic DESIGN SERVICES, India.
Printed and bound by CPI Group (UK) Ltd, Croydon, CR0 4YY

Pen & Sword Books Limited incorporates the imprints of Atlas, Archaeology,
Aviation, Discovery, Family History, Fiction, History, Maritime, Military,
Military Classics, Politics, Select, Transport, True Crime, Air World,
Frontline Publishing, Leo Cooper, Remember When, Seaforth Publishing,
The Praetorian Press, Wharncliffe Local History, Wharncliffe Transport,
Wharncliffe True Crime and White Owl.

For a complete list of Pen & Sword titles please contact
PEN & SWORD BOOKS LIMITED
47 Church Street, Barnsley, South Yorkshire, S70 2AS, England
E-mail: enquiries@pen-and-sword.co.uk
Website: www.pen-and-sword.co.uk

Or
PEN AND SWORD BOOKS
1950 Lawrence Rd, Havertown, PA 19083, USA
E-mail: Uspen-and-sword@casematepublishers.com
Website: www.penandswordbooks.com

MIX
Paper from
responsible sources
FSC® C013604

Contents

Introduction

Reading back through these manuscript pages of *Hitler and His Women*, it is interesting to see how often the image of an actor and his audience comes up. Unravelling the analogy is simple. Hitler is the actor, an evil actor but still a great one; the German people are the naïve, unwitting, but oh so willing, audience.

That does not necessarily mean that Hitler, wherever he went, whatever he did, was doing nothing more than playing a part. His ideas and ideologies cannot be defended or excused. They were the driving force behind his actions; there can be no doubt about that. How those ideas were passed on to a waiting public is another matter altogether.

Hitler's control over the massed audiences, either in an auditorium or, later, around the family wireless sets which he and Joseph Goebbels had enabled almost every family in Germany to purchase, was strikingly effective. It was exactly like a skilled and politically minded Laurence Olivier, Henry Irving or even Shakespeare himself guiding, manipulating and forcing their audiences to believe every word that was uttered. Only a superb actor could have delivered his lines so perfectly and measured his success so efficiently.

For a wide range of reasons, not least his ability to act out a part and play the character that they all wanted to see, Hitler's control over his devotees was vast. That was particularly so with the women who flocked in their thousands to hear him speak or just to watch as he drove past in his open-topped Mercedes. The women of Germany loved him, hung onto his every word and he responded by making them seem special.

Not to put too fine a point on it, the women of Germany were Hitler's lovers, as he was theirs. He could not make personal contact with all of them but that simply made the relationship between them so much more special. And it made him so much more desirable:

INTRODUCTION

> Many saw him as a super-god and his public appearances were marked by thousands of often swooning women hysterically screaming his name in what was close to sexual fantasy … Newsreels of the day showed footage of pretty young blonde women waving frantically as he passed by, their faces contorted with passion.[1]

The role of women in Hitler's Germany has been discussed before. They were a crucial factor in his success and, arguably, in his failure when the bombs came crashing down onto their homes and dreams. But what has been only rarely examined are the lives and impact of the women who were close to Hitler, women who may have influenced his character, and thus his decisions, from the moment of his birth to his death in Berlin in 1945.

Adolf Hitler used his women. He used them as a sounding board, as emotional support, as red-blooded heroines and, in particular, as Teutonic images of old. In the most part they came willingly under his spell, giving their love and infatuation, their help and support, with only one expectation: that he would make Germany great again.

A man of many parts, Hitler wove a magical spell around his women and that includes – almost to the very end – those millions of adoring women across Germany who would never meet him but still revered and loved him. But it is particularly relevant for those closest to him.

For a man supposedly so pledged, so dedicated to his country and to his mission, it is surprising to realize that there were actually dozens of women with whom he had intense emotional contact and relationships. Many of these relationships were kept hidden. Even Eva Braun remained an unknown figure until the final weeks of Hitler's life.

Not all of Hitler's relationships involved sexual activity. Some of those relationships were with women who were clearly mother figures, either real or surrogate; some were simply platonic; others were not real women at all but were flitting, insubstantial creatures that clung like butterflies to the edges of his life and were little more than idealized visions from his dreams.

Whatever the basis of Hitler's relationships with women, there was always an edge of eroticism to his contact. It may never have been realized or acted upon but it was always there, powering his behaviour – sometimes flirtatious, sometimes dominant and sometimes submissive – in almost all of his interventions with women.

However, for a large number of Hitler's women, from the higher-profile adherents to the dozens of nameless brief encounters who have now faded into history, contact did indeed start and finish in a sexual encounter. Brief or extended, bizarre or natural, affairs of the flesh mattered to Adolf Hitler – affairs, that is, in the widest possible context.

Hitler was a complex man, difficult to read and understand. Even with those to whom he did not actually 'make love', there was, for both parties, the fascinating concept of being 'in love'. Eroticism without romance or sex.

Once you realize the breadth and depth of Hitler's dreams and desires, it is hard to imagine or re-imagine the traditional view of a cold, distant demagogue working alone, without female support or comfort. If nothing else this book will try to show just how much Hitler needed and obtained that comfort. To that extent he was an ordinary man with ordinary wishes and plans.

Except that he wasn't ordinary at all. As we all know he was filled with an evil that remains, even now, hard to quantify. But putting the two elements of his character together is what makes the man so fascinating.

As Dale Robertson used to say at the end of almost every episode of the 1950s *Wells Fargo* TV series: 'There's a little bad in the best of us, a little good in the worst.' Adolf Hitler never witnessed the arrival of television but he was an enormous fan of America's Wild West and an inveterate reader of Karl May's lurid cowboy books. He might well have agreed with Robertson's comment.

Chapter 1

Popular Opinion: Myth and Truth

Try this as an experiment. Stop any passer-by, any man or woman you might encounter in the street or at the bar of your local public house, and ask them for their opinion of Adolf Hitler. The vast majority of those questioned will stare at you as if you had just uttered a piece of blasphemy or a particularly unpleasant and foul word. They will then probably all agree that Hitler was one of the most sinister and evil men who ever lived.

From the inception of the Nazi Party in the early 1920s until its demise in 1945, Hitler's warped, twisted and malformed mind spawned a regime that murdered millions and terrified the whole world. He took many of his early ideas from the man he regarded as his mentor, an alcoholic right-wing theorist who lived in and around the Munich area. Dietrich Eckart was a poet and writer whose fanciful ideas and theories held great appeal for Hitler but the culminations of his plans – the death squads, the concentration camps and the gas chambers – were his and his alone.

In the years immediately after 1945, following his suicide in the besieged and battered city of Berlin, Hitler's influence remained significant. Even now, from well beyond the grave he continues to haunt and cast his malign influence across the globe.

It seems that Hitler's evil knew no bounds. Apart from ruthless military campaigns in places like Poland and Greece, the rabid desire for lebensraum in the East, vicious race laws across Germany and newly conquered German-held territory, Hitler and his Nazi Party perpetrated a series of pogroms and massacres that have remained unequalled in the history of the world. Inventing murder on an industrial scale, his name has become a byword for the cold and calculated extermination of millions of helpless and hapless groups of people.

Thousands of books have been written condemning Hitler and his actions while hundreds of films and documentaries have also been produced. There have been others, perhaps not quite as many as the anti-Hitler variety but still a significant number, which have attempted to explain away the killings and the brutality, even to deny them altogether. In its own way the denial of the Holocaust has always been a concept as evil and diabolical as anything that came out of the Third Reich.

Beyond the arguments and the debates, the sheer horror of Hitler's Holocaust remains as a programme of carefully devised and organized murder that can be glibly called man's inhumanity to man. In whichever way they are looked at and whatever they are used for, the tragic groups of innocent men, women and children who went, largely unknowing, to the gas chambers, are a wide-ranging and eclectic selection of would-be victims.

Jews, gypsies, Slavs, Jehovah's Witnesses, Quakers and communists were the primary targets of the Holocaust. They were not alone. Physically, mentally and emotionally disabled people were also caught in the crosshairs of the Nazis' all-seeing scrutiny. So, too, were intellectuals, homosexuals and even members of Hitler's own Party. The list of his victims seems at times to be endless.

At the risk of being considered fey or overly poetic, it does not stretch the imagination too much to conjure harrowing visions of Hitler's countless dead and persecuted. They range and reach far into the distance ahead of you like a faintly perceived but always remembered regiment of ghost figures. It is a fanciful and effete response, perhaps, but that is what such horror leads to in many thinking and imaginative individuals.

On a more prosaic level, what Hitler's use of terror meant to anyone who was opposed to the Nazi view of the world was a lengthy period of unmitigated horror. It was a time of such fear that it is now difficult to imagine how people felt. Trying to capture that fear is, frankly, beyond most of us.

Once in power Hitler's fury knew no bounds. Critics of the Nazi regime and members of the sects designated for destruction might all expect, sooner or later, to hear the terrifying midnight knock on their door or wake to an early morning raid by Gestapo* and SS** officers. Persecution, punishment, torture and, ultimately, death were the inevitable result for anyone who dared to voice a counter opinion or represent opposition and disagreement to the Nazis.

---

* Geheime Staatspolizei, the Nazi secret police.
** Schutzstaffel, lit. Protection Squadron, the major Nazi paramilitary, latterly military, organization.

The classic or standard image of Hitler, one that most people can recognize and possibly even relate to, comes from the 1930s. It is that of the dictator in his brown SA* uniform, designed for the stormtroopers by Party member Hugo Boss, standing in front of adoring thousands at one of the many Nuremberg rallies or election meetings. He is hurling invective, ranting and screaming himself into near-apoplexy. Metaphorically at least, the tyrannical Hitler holds the admiring host in the palm of his hand. Thousands stare at him, unblinking, unthinking but all of them in raptures and totally accepting what he says. They are mesmerized, in thrall to his words and vision of the world. No matter how many times he repeats his promises and condemns all the many enemies of the Third Reich – both of which he does over and over again, at the expense of almost any explanation or rationalization – the crowds worship and scream back their acceptance.

Under the leadership of a man like this almost anything is possible. And that is exactly what Hitler is offering: 'almost anything'. Nobody seems to know, least of all him, how he will obtain these misty, ill-defined utopian ideals for his people. That is part of the Hitler mystique. He seems to be saying that if you follow him and listen to him, if you agree with his ideas and join him, then the whole world will be open to you. But the questions have to be asked: what *are* those ideas, what *are* the ideals he is propagating?

For the non-partisan observer the ideals of the 1930s Party meetings and rallies would always remain unclear. Apart from a few lofty targets such as an end to unemployment, Germany restored to power and wealth, the ultimate realization of Aryan destiny, the ideals are little more than sketchily drawn outlines, like a child's view of the world. The audience can fill in the blanks with almost anything they might like to dream about. 'Almost anything' soon becomes 'Almost everything'. That is really what Hitler seems to be offering when he stands before his public to make his promises, almost anything they want. It is not the reality of the dream but the offer itself, made with such certainty and such violent aplomb that matters to the worshipping crowds.

Hitler screams and gesticulates, he sways and moves from side to side on the podium. His hands weave magical shapes in the air. Spittle flies from his lips and his eyes glisten with an appeal that everyone, even those hundreds of yards away at the back of the stadium, swear they

---

* Sturmabteilung, or Storm Detachment, the initial Nazi Party paramilitaries.

can see. To those not of the faith he seems a madman; to those who believe and trust in each word he utters he is nothing short of a messiah.

The one thing that no one can doubt, not his supporters, not his opponents and certainly not the representatives of foreign governments who look on in shock and horror, is that this man knows how to work a crowd. He can control them, whip them into fury and, when needed, quieten them into a menacing, sibilant hush. It is a skill practised by many but only truly gained by very few. From a faltering and stuttering start his diatribe gathers momentum. It is slowly and carefully done, even though very few in the auditorium realize it. The pattern is always the same, a gradual move from uncertainty to confidence and ultimately to a level of command that somehow manages to mirror Hitler's view of his mission.

The climax is always spectacular and eventually the crowds are treated to the howls of manic rhetoric that he famously spews out, wherever and however his speech is given. Hitler runs the crowd through every imaginable emotional gamut and they are like putty in his hands. Now, in hindsight, it is impossible not to view the performance as a public version of the sexual act, a slow and gradual build up to a cataclysmic and orgasmic climax, both for him and for the worshipping thousands. At the end both Hitler and his audience are fulfilled. The word 'audience' is used deliberately for Hitler is the player, the actor on stage. The crowd who applaud and scream are the equivalent of the spectators in an Elizabethan theatre.

Like the sixteenth-century playgoers, the groundlings who packed into the Globe, the Curtain and other theatres of London, they demand a quality performance. The subject and the content remain, very clearly, only secondary factors. And eventually they are sated. They have been reduced to sweat-soaked, exhausted, brain-washed zombies who at that moment really believe that he and they can take over and control the whole world.

That is what most observers see. Yet there is another side to Adolf Hitler, a softer, calmer and more normal side, if that word 'normal' can ever be used in regard to such an individual. It is a private side of his personality, one that he keeps carefully hidden from the world. It concerns not warfare, not German expansion and not even anti-Semitic promises of retribution. Where it is displayed and seen at its best is simply in his attitude towards women.

It is a surprising, even startling attribute but there is no doubt that once in the company of women Hitler changes and becomes a more laid-back character altogether. Almost unbelievably he becomes compassionate, caring and agreeable. Unknown to most people, he has a keen and infectious sense of humour, usually withheld from public scrutiny until he is relaxed and surrounded by women whose company he enjoys and in the face of whom he does not feel threatened or abused. Then he flirts and smiles, charms the company with his wit and knowledge. He is a skilled mimic and raconteur and he now becomes a man with whom it is a pleasure to sit, talk and spend a couple of agreeable hours.

Time and the events of history have fixed our perceptions of Hitler, the Nazis and the whole of the Third Reich. What that means is that it is now difficult to imagine him as anything other than the ranting demagogue shown in the plethora of television documentaries and films to which we are regularly subjected.

But as far as many German women of the inter-war years were concerned, this evil killer of millions was a somewhat different person altogether. They understood that when policy and the safe governance of the country demanded it, he might have to be ruthless, to be stern and even brutal. That was acceptable, that was how it had to be. But even those who had never been nearer to him than across the cavernous spaces of the Nuremberg stadium or the sawdust-covered floor of a Munich beerhall knew, truly knew, that he also had a softer side.

Apart from acceptance by his women it was an affection – an affectation almost – that was noted by very few. It is unlikely that this propensity for female company and the change in character that accompanied it was ever considered important by his acolytes and the myrmidons whose primary concern was for their own position and advancement. If it was noticed it was soon pushed away, relegated to the depths of individual memory. Hitler's staunchest allies, both within and without Party circles, saw only what they wanted to see in the man who had given them, and would continue to give them, immense power and position. Their vested interests would not allow them to take any other view.

However, for those who had no interest in climbing the Party ladder to the top, men like Hitler's personal pilot Hans Baur who was content with his position, the attraction of the Führer to what was then still termed 'the weaker sex' was obvious. Baur recorded one instance during a trip to Weimar:

> Whilst we were out Hitler turned round to Sauckel, who was walking behind us with a group of other Party leaders. 'See that we have some female companionship at table tonight, Sauckel. All day long I'm surrounded by men, and I'd like to hear women's voices for a change.'[1]

Sauckel happily obliged and dinner that night was taken in the company of a large and willing posse of enchanted young women. Such contact between the Leader, the Führer as he became universally known after 1934, and his worshipping female supporters was distant, ephemeral almost, and was limited to nothing more than his appreciation of the sound of those 'women's voices'.

Hitler knew that the press and the authorities would pounce eagerly on any dalliance he might enjoy and that while his order would lead to the arrival of twenty or thirty young girls, his words to Fritz Sauckel, as recorded by Baur, did at least reveal that he had an enjoyment in the attention and presence of women. That enjoyment was a two-way process but, as far as Hitler was concerned, it was always short-lived.

Invariably, after two or three hours, Hitler's interest faded or passed away. He was not bored, exactly, but he had a mind that was impossible to pin down to one reality. He had something of a 'butterfly brain' as it might be described. Internally, after a few hours his imagination was already wandering onto other issues and the company would be relegated to the back of his mind. Then he would slip away, sometimes offering warm goodbyes, and sometimes just exiting the room before anyone noticed. However he departed, he would leave behind an enchanted group of what might now be regarded and labelled as an early example of totally smitten 'groupies'. He would have called them soft-headed female adherents.

There is an interesting question that has to be asked. Did the feelings and reactions of Hitler's female acquaintances, of his women friends and daily companions, have any effect on his plans and policies? The answer is, in most cases at least, probably not. The women like Sauckel's 'rent a crowd' who gathered around him, happy just to be in his company, were like ships that pass in the night. They would remember the contact with the Führer; he would not.

With his long-term female friends things might have been very different. For many years people did not believe that this group of friends ever existed. Yet despite the generally perceived and widely held view of a man standing alone, married only to his country and dedicated to his mission, Hitler did actually have many intense relationships with women. Those who fell into this category could have influenced, if not his plans and policies then certainly his personal makeup and characteristics – in other words, his personality. And that personality would, of course, be essential in helping him to take decisions.

The complexities of Hitler's personality were tortuous in the extreme but, if it is not stating the obvious that what he did, what he achieved, where he succeeded and where he failed, can be related directly to his inner beliefs and feelings – not a quality that can always be attributed to every politician or statesman, either then or now.

Significant developments in his character can, at least in the early stages of his life, be linked to the women he encountered, the women he loved, used and abused. Not every one of them, of course, would leave such a rich trail of influence. A great deal would depend on the woman's own individual and collective character and personality.

Analysis is not easy. It must be remembered that for all of his political life Hitler remained the consummate actor, a man who could jump from one role to another with barely a pause for breath. This man who might be a ranting, obsessive tyrant one minute could be a caring, compassionate and supportive father figure the next. His range was wide and each part was totally believable.

How, then, can he be assessed? The answer is with difficulty and no small degree of surmise. The interested reader or student is often tempted to invoke the old variety-show comment, 'Will the real Adolf Hitler please stand up.' Even then, the man who stood for identification would depend on the audience and the purpose behind both the question and the likely answer.

One thing is clear, however: Adolf Hitler was fascinated by women; that is a recorded fact. He liked to have them around him and found great pleasure in their company. If nothing else they provided him with a relaxing, rejuvenating environment. An hour or two in the trenches, at the battle front or, in his case, scheming on the murder of millions, followed by an evening of tea and cakes and mindless chitchat, made Adolf Hitler's day complete.

That was with his women. They were a special part of his life and therefore received special treatment, even the distant ones. But with his male colleagues the evening sessions usually went on late into the night and slid into an inevitable series of harangues from the Führer. With his women Hitler was often quite prepared to let them do the talking.

All of this might be a shallow way of looking at Hitler's relationships with women but he undoubtedly compartmentalized his various interactions with the women who listened to him and adored him. All of them had their place. Their task was defined by the man himself, sometimes subliminally, often directly. The women and his relationships with them can be divided into three distinct groups which, generally speaking, were self-reliant and totally separate from the others.

Firstly, there was the great mass of women who looked on and admired from a distance. A few, like the selection from Weimar, as arranged by Sauckel and recorded by Baur, might be lucky enough to meet him, to come within the remit of his strange but compelling personality. Their moment in the limelight was short and they invariably retired to worship and admire from a distance.

Then there were those within arm's reach, women who might be called on to give comfort and comment to their Führer. They were the secretaries, cooks, pilots, domestics, actresses and photographers who played an occasional but definitive role in the life and career of Adolf Hitler.

Members of this group would be permitted revealing insights into the character of the man and, occasionally, would even be allowed to make their views known. However, it did not do to make comments that were too ideologically opposed to Hitler's views as his secretary Christa Schroeder discovered in 1942 when she took him to task over the issue of supplying cigarettes and tobacco to the troops then fighting in Russia:

> He rose quickly and took his leave 'ice cold' and with an aggrieved expression, from which I finally saw what I had done. Next afternoon when I enquired of the manservant in what mood the boss found himself today, Hans Junge gave us a long look and told us that tea would be taken today without the ladies.[2]

Hitler sulked with Christa Schroeder for several months, still using her secretarial services but treating her with cold reserve. Despite apologizing and accepting the entire fault for upsetting him, Christa Schroeder was never treated with quite the same intimacy again. She was accepted back into the fold but the young Traudl Junge, who had joined Hitler's staff not long after the outbreak of war, seemed to be granted many of the favours that had previously gone to Christa.

The final group, last but certainly not the least important, was the small number of women who were intimate with him. Intimate did not always mean there was a sexual relationship but these were women who shared his triumphs and disasters in public and in private. It was, often, something of a poisoned chalice. Three members of this group – five if you include Eva Braun and Magda Goebbels – committed suicide; such was the pressure, stress and mystique of being involved in any form of intimate relationship with Adolf Hitler.

Most of the women who became close to Hitler were physically attractive. He admired all sorts of beauty, provided it fitted with his particular choice or vision. In verse, in music, in art and in women his tastes were unchanging and remained with him to the end of his life. The women he admired most were either very young or considerably older than him. Young and old, both types were unthreatening. Both were generally supportive, but ultimately it all depended on the use to which they were likely to be put.

Whatever the relationship there was always an agenda as far as Hitler was concerned. In *Mein Kampf* he wrote about the role and position of women, using this seminal document to make clear – as it did in so many other points of intent – exactly where he stood with regard to women and what he believed:

> They feel little shame at being terrorized intellectually and
> they are scarcely conscious of the fact that that their freedom
> as human beings is impudently abused … They see only the
> ruthless force and brutality of the determined utterances, to
> which they always submit.[3]

He was later to comment, scathingly but privately, that women did not know how and when to keep their mouths shut. Always worried about the rumour machine and its consequences it was one more of the reasons that passing affairs and 'one-night stands' were out of the question. He once described the masses, those thousands of German men, women, boys and girls who hung on his every word, as feminine in their makeup – stupid and easily influenced. And this from the man who liked women and enjoyed being in their company.

Hitler may have had a poor opinion about the abilities of women in general but it did not stop him liking them. Liking and trusting were two vastly different issues. He would hardly have given any of them command of the armies on the Eastern Front. However, command of his kitchens, control over his reports and documents, the management of his various residences across Germany, these were gifts that he certainly did bestow, more than happily, on the women in his life.

The cynic might argue that these were not really important responsibilities but to Hitler they were. He knew only too well that the basic levels of existence, the physiological levels such as the need for warmth, comfort, food and so on, had to be filled or played out. Otherwise the human being, as an entity and a thinking person, would not work; and you only have to look at the concentration camp regimes to see the truth of that statement.

Apart from that his stance was simple. A woman's time should revolve around the three Ks: *Kinder*, *Küche* and *Kirche* (children, kitchen and church), their chief purpose being to provide and rear increasing numbers of perfect Aryan children to fight in the wars that would ensure the safety and continuation of the regime and the country. It was a sexist, self-interested approach but it was not untypical of German and other cultures at this time.

It has been estimated that approximately 50 per cent of the Nazi electoral vote came from women, a statement that is supported by the fact that from the beginning of the movement there had always been a large proportion of women at the Party meetings and rallies. The reason for this support remains unclear although the sexual element cannot be ignored. Many of those who watched and listened to him speak would have gone away with their minds full of fantasies and impossible dreams. Hans Baur attempted, on several occasions, to speak to these supporters to find out what they really thought about Hitler:

> I talked to the girl who was sitting beside me. She was 22 and very attractive but she told me that she was afraid

she would never get married because when she compared all the men she had ever met with Hitler, they were so far inferior to him that none could possibly satisfy her.[4]

The young women who hung on the Führer's every word, as Baur discovered, were fanatical, some even hysterical in their admiration for Hitler. It was certainly not his looks that aroused them. His physical appearance was always secondary to what he believed even though he came to appreciate the value of strong, upright bodies and smart, dazzling clothing. It was an appreciation that reached its zenith with Hugo Boss's black SS uniforms. Even then it is interesting to note that Hitler never donned the SS uniform himself, as he had done, and continued to do, with the SA Brownshirts.

Once he became Chancellor, he realized that he needed a 'makeover' and many of his more unappealing traits and looks were dropped. During his rise to power, however, he was anything but the upright example of German manhood that he so relished and adored.

Despite his piercing blue eyes – hypnotic blue eyes as they were sometimes called – Hitler cut, at first glance, an unprepossessing figure. He was below average height, slight rather than slim, with dirty finger nails and discoloured teeth. His tiny toothbrush of a moustache and the jet-black lick of hair combed across his forehead gave him a comedic rather than commanding appearance – more Chaplin than Cromwell.

Perfect looks are never guaranteed to bring a perfect response and most observers were soon to admit that they had got it wrong. But as one American writer commented after meeting Hitler for the first time:

> He is formless, almost faceless, a man whose countenance is
> a caricature, a man whose framework seems cartilaginous …
> He is inconsequent and voluble, ill poised and insecure. He
> is the very prototype of the little man.[5]

Hitler might have been many things but he was never a 'little man'. Such views rarely lasted beyond first meeting. Once unleashed, the quality of his voice and the display of raw power that emanated from him, along with the additional factor of hysteria in the audience, could well have helped create the magnetic, charismatic figure that he became. There is a modern comparison that might be useful to look at. In the 1960s, almost any concert or performance by popular beat groups like the Beatles or the Rolling Stones was accompanied by the advent of a new phenomenon: wet underwear left under the seats of the screaming fans when the concert was over. Mass hysteria had supplanted individual delicacies. Sudden incontinency and pre-orgasmic discharge were not the only issue for the over-enthusiastic girls and some fans even attempted to throw themselves from balconies or other high points when they discovered that they could not get close enough to their idols.

Hitler's adoring female audience might not have screamed in bladder-draining delight or tried to throw themselves from the top of the Brandenburg Gate whenever he stood up to address the crowd, but large numbers of them did scream his name when he appeared while some did indeed faint or swoon and some even charged the stage. The majority were content to stay in their places and keep their sexual fantasies to themselves. This was a different age, circumstances were vastly dissimilar and, above all, Hitler's intention was not to entertain but to educate and convert. It is therefore hard to know if his appearance had the same effect on his female fan base as Paul McCartney or Mick Jagger. However, if Hans Baur was right about the adulation for the Führer bordering on hysteria, then some form of sexual arousal in those who sat and watched is not only possible but highly likely.

Hitler had only a passing or peripheral interest in the women who gazed at him with such adulation. They were, in the main, beyond his reach just as any further contact with them was beyond his inclination. That was no accident. That was how he wanted it, that was how it was arranged.

His public image and persona were far more important to him than any brief physical exchanges in a hotel bedroom or on the back seat of his Mercedes. He enjoyed the company of the panting, goggle-eyed women for a short time, enjoyed enchanting and bewitching them and to that extent his interest was little more than an extension of his political programme.

Just as Jagger, McCartney and the rest were intent on selling records, so Adolf Hitler was concerned with selling his Party. His aim was to gain help in implementing his radical policies and advancing Aryan supremacy. Most times he succeeded quite easily.

It remains difficult to judge Hitler's real effect on the adoring fans once you take away the matter of mass hysteria. Most photographic records of the time were carefully controlled propaganda pieces and the roving cameras of Leni Riefenstahl, Heinrich Hoffmann and others were careful to pick up only the attractive, mesmerized faces of adoring women – mostly young adoring women.

Nevertheless, written records do seem to support the visual ones. According to those who watched, as partisan supporters or as opponents, Hitler was worshipped and much of that adoration seemed to come from women. He, of course, took it all in his stride.

Ultimately, the adulation of the women he met and charmed did little more than stroke his ego. It would have been hard for it to have done anything less and must be seen as a more private version of the acclaim he received from the large-scale gatherings like the Nuremberg rallies. If the rallies nourished him and kept him going in times of stress, the more private meetings with women who clearly adored him soothed his metaphorical brow and reinforced his opinion about himself.

*

For many years there was speculation about Hitler's sexuality. That speculation continues to this day and some of the allegations are, to say the least, bizarre.

The novelist Martin Amis has recently alleged that Hitler did enjoy the sexual act but, due to a hygiene fetish, preferred sex with his clothes on and disliked getting his underclothes messy.[6] While we do know that Hitler sometimes changed his underpants three or four times a day, it must be remembered that Amis was writing and talking as a creator of fiction which, although it may have been informed by research, was ultimately made up or invented for the purpose of audience entertainment.

At the other end of the spectrum even before the Second World War ended psychoanalyst Walter C. Langer prepared a report for the American Office of Strategic Services (OSS), claiming that Hitler was an impotent coprophile.[*] He also alleged that Hitler had feminine traits and might have been homosexual.

With or without any clear evidence, many other writers have decided that he was totally impotent, some believing that he was a voyeur and an inveterate masturbator. The claim that his right testicle was undescended

---

* Coprophilia: enjoyment and sexual pleasure gained from the sight and feel of human faeces.

not only gave rise to a ribald song but provided the base for many of the allegations about sexual inadequacy.

The medical examination he was given following the Beer Hall Putsch and his arrest in 1923 confirmed that Hitler did in fact have only 'one ball', as the song goes. There was also the rumour that he was suffering from penile hypospadias – an extremely small penis which forced him to urinate from a hole at the base of the shaft rather than from the tip.

The allegations go on and on, wide ranging and constant. If they are only half true then many of the other stories or legends about Hitler's hidden life – his love affairs with Geli Raubal and Eva Braun, for example – cannot possibly have any veracity. Hard factual proof is not available and you are left with the old adage: 'You pays your money and you takes your choice.' Even so the accusations remain. Sometimes, you feel, they will never go away.

While the most damaging of these accusations has been that of coprophilia, the most persistent has been that Hitler was a homosexual. Either practising or latent, the charge of homosexuality has been an accusation that Hitler, alive or dead, has been unable to dislodge. There has been much speculation but no evidence for this although many would say that, with regard to the accusation of homosexuality, his enjoyment of women's company could well be a nod in the right direction. It is, at best, a dubious and somewhat fragile connection.

Many of his adult friends and colleagues, men like SA leader Ernst Röhm, long-term supporter Rudolf Hess and bodyguard Ulrich Graf, were either homosexual or had gay tendencies. It was not something either Hitler or his supporters ever chose to hide.

That does not automatically place Hitler in the same section of society but for a long while homosexuality was rife, and tolerated, in Nazi organizations like the SA. The intense fury with which homosexuals were later persecuted in the Third Reich – over 50,000 eventually being sent to the concentration camps before the regime finally fell – might possibly reflect a reaction and a degree of political necessity by Hitler and his cronies.

Rudolf Hess, who was nicknamed Fraulein Anna and Black Emma by other Nazis, was alleged to have had an affair with Hitler whilst they were together in Landsberg prison. His devotion to Hitler was certainly all-encompassing but that does not prove that he and his adored Führer were lovers in the physical sense of the word.

At the same time, the perverted nature of Hitler's alleged coprophilia and sexual encounters with his niece Geli and possibly with one or two others were lurid enough to remain in everyone's memory. Party members and comrades like Ernst Röhm were even confident enough to refer to the practice, albeit in a somewhat guarded and oblique way, in Hitler's presence:

> He [Hitler] is thinking about the peasant girls. When they stand in the fields and bend down at their work so that you can see their behinds – that's what he likes, especially when they've got big round ones. That's Hitler's sex life.[7]

Hitler apparently remained tight-lipped but silent during Röhm's tongue-in-cheek tirade! His thoughts have remained unrecorded but, interestingly, it was not long before Ernst Röhm perished during the Night of the Long Knives.

Walter Langer, writing from a psychological base, has alleged that the only way Hitler could control his coprophagic tendencies was to remain aloof from deep and meaningful relationships. If so, it could explain why Hitler chose to remain distant from the majority of his female admirers, keeping them at arm's length in order to prevent intense emotional feelings: 'As soon as such feelings are aroused, he feels compelled to degrade himself in the eyes of the loved object and eat their dirt figuratively, if not literally.'[8]

It is all fascinating stuff but there is absolutely no evidence that any of this is true. Like the others, Langer is guessing, albeit making guesses that, as much as anything else, are fuelled by education and professional knowledge. The writer Ian Kershaw is just one of many historians who question the value of the stories. He argues that:

> Rumours of Hitler's sexual perversions are … based on dubious evidence. [They are] little more than a combination of rumour, hearsay, surmise and innuendo, often spiced up by Hitler's political enemies.[9]

Blackening Hitler's character, blackening the career and personality of any public figure for that matter, was a common occurrence in the wild and criminal underworld in which Hitler lived and worked. It was certainly no worse than the articles and stories that were run by the rabidly anti-Semitic Julius Streicher in his paper *Der Sturmer* or the lies and rumours that Hitler and the Nazis were soon spreading about their Jewish and Communist opponents.

In this more enlightened and accepting modern age the obvious response to all of this might be quite simple: so what? But in the 1920s and 1930s homosexuality in particular was still a criminal offence and carried the toxic stain of perversion. Adherents were considered 'less than men' and this was a smear that Hitler, both before his rise to power in 1933 and after he had become Chancellor of Germany, could simply not afford to see bandied about too freely.

Always a contradictory character, Hitler was both repelled and fascinated by sex. To him the worn-out, degraded prostitutes that he encountered or saw during his time as a down-and-out in Vienna and Munich held no sexual appeal. To him they were merely evidence of the moral decadence of the Austrian and German nations. Whether or not the pimps who matched them with clients and took their money were actually Jewish is a matter of conjecture. However, Hitler certainly believed and alleged that they were, thus adding one more prejudice to his seemingly limitless range of phobias and hatreds.

Disliking prostitution did not stop Hitler carefully observing the women of the streets as they went about their work. It was, as he tried to explain, part of his social education. There were rumours of him using prostitutes, even of his being treated for syphilis which he had supposedly caught from one of them, but yet again the accusations remain just rumours. They fascinate readers and students but cannot be proved or disproved.

Hitler certainly enjoyed being 'in the dirt', figuratively and literally. His period in the doss houses of Vienna and Munich could and should have been much shorter as he had the means and the talent to escape what others would regard as a degrading experience. He could have painted much more than the occasional postcard. There was a ready market for such art but it would have taken a degree of effort that Hitler did not seem to possess or, at best, wish to use. It was only the outbreak of the First World War that forced him out of the malaise into which he had sunk. To the end of his days he looked back, if not fondly then certainly proudly, to his time in the slums of Austria and Germany.

Hitler's time in the doss houses gave him credibility in the eyes of the labouring classes but, more importantly, allowed him to observe others at work and play, in extremis and in moments of success. However, his voyeurism – and there is really no other way to describe it – certainly did not prevent him enjoying the company of what he regarded as a 'better' class of women. At such times, when he did allow himself to subside into the soft pool of femininity that he loved so much, his behaviour was both coquettish and flirtatious. He was certainly not above remarking favourably to people like Hans Baur and his chauffeurs Erich Kempka and Emile Maurice on the appearance of young women and girls they chanced to pass in the street.

As a child and as an adult Adolf Hitler remained a man of extremes. His rages were so violent that he could easily be reduced to tears by events that others would casually dismiss. He would occasionally throw himself to the floor and foam at the mouth. Almost anything could ignite his rage. In particular if he was crossed or contradicted – a trait that grew worse the longer he was in charge and the closer he came to the end – his eyes would flash and a stream of obscenities would pour forth.

Yet once the fury had been unleashed or freed his behaviour might give way to mild and accepting moments of peace and relaxation. It hardly stopped him being a monster of depravity but it did show that there was more than one side to this man of many contradictions. His secretary Christa Schroeder has commented:

> There was not just one Hitler, but several Hitlers in one person. He was a mixture of lies and truth, of faithfulness and violence, of simplicity and luxury, of kindliness and barbarity, of mysticism and reality, of the artist and the barbarian.[10]

Some of his behaviour towards women, particularly in the early days, was decidedly odd. He was, for example, quite likely to make sudden and unexpected declarations of love to beautiful women, regardless of their station or position. It was an element of his impetuosity, something that he and many others would regard as part of his charm. It was a deliberate ploy. He was unschooled, just an ordinary working-class lad who had none of the refinements and manners of those brought up in a more privileged environment. And, of course, people loved it.

His friend and early financial supporter Ernst Puzi Hanfstaengl once entered his own sitting room and found Hitler, a regular visitor to the Hanfstaengl home, on his knees, declaring undying passion for Helena, Puzi's startlingly attractive American wife.

Puzi did a double-take but Hitler was not embarrassed to be discovered like this and Helena, who found the whole thing quite amusing, was realistic. Hitler had no interest in her: his love and his lust, she told Puzi, were reserved solely for the task of attaining power. She was correct. Such passions were not real, being little more than the mood of the moment for a young man who was always liable to undergo sudden changes of behaviour. If he ever developed emotional passions for Helena they quickly faded and it was not long before Hitler was professing a similar affection for Puzi's sister Erna.

There was undoubtedly something of the retarded or undeveloped adolescent in Hitler's sudden attractions and passions. Such moments were invariably hopeless or destined to remain unfulfilled, exactly like his adolescent infatuations back in Austria, exactly like the adolescent infatuations of almost any growing and developing boy. As Helena Hanfstaengl realized only too well, Hitler's protestations of love and admiration were just shallow statements. They were really little more than the emotional outpourings of a semi-grown man, someone still finding his way around the dangerous and threatening adult world. Hitler's protestations of love were advances that would lead him and the woman to whom they were addressed absolutely nowhere. Nor were they ever intended to. Helena found it faintly amusing but many others did not. They took him seriously and fell for the line. To some extent it was also the actor in him, that compelling, almost overpowering urge to be centre stage in everything he did. Here again he was playing the part that the situation demanded – or, rather, the part that he felt the situation demanded.

All of his life he had little ability to differentiate between what he wanted and what others either needed or wanted. His wishes and desires always came first. As the world was to discover, it was a tragic failing. Both Helena and Erna Hanfstaengl were in positions of social power and were able to help him gain access to people and places that he knew would be important in his rise to the dizzying heights of international diplomacy. Therefore, use them he would. Professing love and admiration for beautiful women like the Hanfstaengls was undoubtedly a case of Hitler operating in the microcosm, making protestations of eternal love or friendship, promises that he would not or could not ever keep. You might easily say he was practising for a performance on the wider world stage.

When he moved to the macro environment, promising rejuvenation and the reclamation of Germany's rightful position in the world, then that was something rather different. That was the moment when Adolf Hitler became considerably more dangerous.

Clearly, then, Adolf Hitler liked women. He enjoyed spending time in their company and would laugh and joke with them along with everyone else in the party. But he would also use them and maybe, on occasions, abuse them as well.

During the final epoch-ending days of the Reich, as he approached the end of his life, Hitler unashamedly used his female staff in the Bunker and the other places where he hid out in Berlin, turning them into unofficial group therapists. He was under stress and he had nowhere else to turn.

His long-time secretary Christa Schroeder was clear about the benefits Hitler gained from quiet, intimate meetings with his staff:

> Hitler happened to pass the Staircase Room at teatime, saw us sitting there and asked if he might join us. This hour of easy chatter was so much to his liking that he later came to tea almost daily. The Staircase Room was a place where he felt unburdened and I always had the impression that what he said there came from a secret memory box which at all other times he kept locked shut.[11]

As always it was Hitler's needs that were dominant, driving the burned-out dictator forward, even as his end approached. His needs demanded these idle moments away from the problems of a dying regime but no one should ever interpret his actions as displays of regret. Hitler regretted nothing he had ever done and remained practical, unrepentant and driven until his final day.

There is an obvious and perhaps unfortunate comparison to be made between the women in his life and with, of all things, his favourite dog Blondi. Blondi, a large and powerful German shepherd, was a creature that he adored and would fight to the death to defend and keep safe.

Hitler seemed to enjoy having his photograph taken but apart from formal studio portraits by Heinrich Hoffmann which were an essential element of his political profile, the best and most revealing are when he is shown posing alongside Blondi. On these occasions he is natural and very much 'at home'. And yet, at the end of his life, without any hint of regret, Hitler used the animal to test the efficiency and power of the fatal cyanide he would soon give to Eva Braun. The dog was dead within minutes, leaving Hitler unconcerned and a pragmatist to the end.

While he enjoyed being in the company of strikingly beautiful women, entertaining them and admiring their good looks, Hitler freely acknowledged that he had a preference for a somewhat different sort of girl. He always distrusted men who failed to admire a woman's beauty but he was equally as clear that there were some women you admired and others that you held close to you.

It was a degree of compartmentalization that did not stop with the women in his life but was a technique that helped him balance so many balls in the air at one time. He had no real deputy to whom he could delegate decisions or actions. Rudolph Hess was a mere cypher, at least until he decided to parachute into Scotland in a ridiculous attempt to end the war. Göring, Himmler and Goebbels were more concerned with advancing their own careers and lining their own pockets than they ever were about the future of Germany. At the end of the day everything in the running of the Third Reich emanated from Adolf Hitler. It is impossible to imagine the regime existing without him just as it is impossible to imagine him on the arm of someone like Marlene Dietrich.

In the days before he became Chancellor he and his chauffeur Emile Maurice would drive around the streets of Munich looking for attractive women. Hitler would excitedly point out those he considered beautiful. Sometimes they would stop and Hitler would treat the women to tea but that was as far as it went.

Being seen to grow close to a ravishing beauty or to hold a torch for some well-known celebrity would, he felt, cut him off from other women. Whether that was a conscious or sub-conscious decision it was still an important consideration. He needed the great mass of femininity, the German women who so adored him, to support the Nazi Party and, once he had achieved ascendency, to maintain the position of supreme power in Germany. Right or wrong, it was an attitude which meant that while he could enjoy the beauty of others, he could never claim it as his own.

Always totally sure of his political and military intentions, Hitler was less convinced when it came to personal relations.

The fear of rejection was always there, lingering like an impending abscess beneath the surface of the gum. Why bother with the unattainable when his power and position could guarantee him acceptance elsewhere: 'His personal preference was for a simpler, sweet type of girl. "I would far rather choose some pretty little typist or salesgirl as my partner," he once commented.'[12]

He did not elucidate further but it was a revealing attitude that manifested itself in the shape of two women from either end of his life, his mother and his long-time mistress. There was no fear of rejection from a Klara Hitler or an Eva Braun, both of whom were totally committed to him and to his welfare. His mother Klara had, arguably, already sacrificed her life for his sake. Eva, as his mistress and wife, would willingly do so in the years ahead.

Hitler accepted such sacrifice as his right. If they loved him as they claimed then the women he most trusted would not stop short at taking the ultimate step and putting their lives at risk, just as he had done with his greatest love of all, Germany. If he was prepared to make the ultimate sacrifice, the unspoken but still omnipresent expectation was that others would do the same. It was an attitude that did not begin and end with his women but remained with him throughout his years of power.

At the same time, it was not just great beauty that caused him to take a step backwards. He had always held a hatred for intellectuals, ever since his failure at school and in his unsuccessful attempt to gain entry to further education: 'These impudent rascals [intellectuals] who always know everything better than anybody else … The intellect has grown autocratic, and has become a disease of life.'[13]

If intellect, generally, was a problem for him, intellect in women was doubly annoying, terrifying even. Consequently, Hitler particularly disliked getting too close to women of intellect and intelligence and would avoid them if at all possible. Between them, beautiful women and intelligent women offered a threat that he neither wanted nor accepted. Non-challenging partners who would agree with his opinions and accept his dictates were more agreeable all round. Best stick to the little typist or shop assistant.

His preference for this type of woman can be seen in the first and last great loves of his life, his mother Klara, and his companion of fourteen years, Eva Braun. The former he had no option but to accept; she was his mother and he was bonded to her in a tie of affection that lasted nearly fifty years after her death but she was, and remained until her death, little more than an Austrian peasant woman with little understanding of the wider world.

The second, Eva Braun, was a deliberate choice. To most of the population of Germany she was unknown and was deliberately kept so. Many of those who were aware of her existence, intimate Party officials and staff at the Berghof, failed to see the appeal. Yet she was chosen by the most powerful man in Germany, arguably in Europe, precisely because of her non-threatening and accepting personality.

When he died Adolf Hitler had come full circle, from the close and comforting arms of a woman who loved him and nurtured him into life to the close and comforting arms of another woman who also adored him and stood beside him as he left a world and a people he had come to hate. In between the two sets of comforting arms that meant so much to him – even though he did not really know it – he had experienced beauty and passion, power and influence, in women who had helped make him the man he became.

Love, if he knew the meaning of the word, had not unduly bothered him and he had unashamedly used the women he encountered. As with so many of the relationships in his life he had taken what he needed from the encounters with little or no concern for the women involved.

Arguably the first and last loves of his life were his only true loves; everything else – including possibly his much-lauded affair with Geli Raubal – was mere experience. That at least was emotional commitment of a sort but it was hardly the deep and meaningful commitment that his soul, troubled and troubling as it was, really required.

There might well be debate about the extent to which Hitler's women influenced his policies and actions but there can be no doubt about the affection he felt for them as a gender or about the way that certain of them helped mould and develop his character.

Chapter 2

A Loving, Dysfunctional, Dangerous Family: Klara, Angela and Paula

Adolf Hitler was born at 6.30 in the evening of 20 April 1889. His place of birth was the small town of Braunau am Inn, on the frontier between Austria and Germany. Being born on the Austrian side of the divide was an annoying but not disastrous accident for the incipient German dictator. He had little time for the archaic and already tottering Austro-Hungarian Empire and from an early age had visions of the country of his birth joining with her neighbour to the north and west in a pan-Germanic state that would control the whole of Europe.

The time of his birth, with night beginning to fall, was nothing if not appropriate. Hitler was always a creature of the night, preferring to work through the hours of darkness, rise at mid-morning and stay out of the brittle sunlight of southern Germany. On a more esoteric level he was also a man who brought darkness to the world. It was a darkness so intense and malignant that its like had rarely, if ever, been seen before. Hitler's birth, at 6.30 in the evening at the beginning of a period of gathering gloom, was somehow fitting – a foreshadowing of the larger and greater darkness yet to come.

His father Alois was a customs inspector for the Austro-Hungarian Empire, a big, broad and brutal man who drank heavily and was not averse to using his fists on his wife and children. He had trained first as a cobbler and then served for a time as an NCO in the Austrian army, something that was useful in helping to progress his career with the customs service. It did nothing, however, to make his personality gentle or accommodating. Alois was illegitimate and originally known by his mother's name Shicklgruber. Despite considerable searching, the father of Alois – Hitler's paternal grandfather – remains unknown. It is a fact that has led to various speculations including the spurious and unfounded rumour that this missing grandfather might actually be Jewish.

Alois was legitimized in 1876 when his mother married Georg Hiedler, a miller's assistant from the Waldviertel region of Austria, and thereafter went by the name of Hitler. Alois was married three times, his third wife Klara Poelzl being the mother of Adolf Hitler. Twenty-three years younger than her husband, Klara was of peasant stock but spent most of her early working life as a domestic cleaner and servant. She was an accepting, pious woman and a loving mother to her children, in particular the young Adolf, as well as Alois Junior and Angela, the children of her husband by his second wife.

Klara was originally employed as a servant in the Hitler household, often being regarded and reported as a foster daughter to Alois. With Alois's second wife already unwell and, as it transpired, terminally ill, it was perhaps inevitable that she and her employer/foster father should begin a romantic relationship. When he was free from the shackles of his sickly second wife it was equally as inevitable that Alois should turn to Klara as a readymade mother and housekeeper.

Klara was related by blood to her husband. As second cousins their union was forbidden by the Catholic Church and Alois had to make a special appeal for them to marry. Dispensation was given but the fact that they were related may have affected the health and blood stock of the children from the marriage. At least three of them died when in infancy. Out of the six children that Klara bore for Alois only two – Adolf and Paula – survived into adulthood. And Paula, the last of Klara's children, was reportedly a little simple.

Adolf was a sickly child and Klara was terrified that he might, like his siblings, die young. So, she cossetted him and doted on him all her life. Hitler's half-brother Alois Junior later went on record, telling the world that Klara spoiled the 'precious' little boy and that he had been forced to underatke many of the chores that should, by rights, have been Adolf's. As Alois Junior had been replaced by the newly born child, young Adolf, in the affections of his father, it is unclear just how unbiased a record his views actually were.

During his career as a customs officer Alois Hitler was posted to various towns along the Austrian–German border. When Adolf was still little more than a toddler the family moved, first to Passau and then to Linz where the future warlord and dictator spent the formative years of his childhood and adolescence. This bustling border town was where, at least to begin with, Adolf Hitler went to school. The third largest centre of population in Austria, Linz was well equipped with theatres and concert halls. Sitting astride the River Danube, the town lay only thirty kilometres from the Czech border and was ideally placed to garner influence and interest from German, Austrian and Czech cultures.

Alois was already over 50 when Adolf was born, a man set in his ways and unresponsive to new ideas and thoughts. A monarchist and a firm supporter of the Austro-Hungarian Empire, Alois was a typical mid-range or minor official of the Hapsburg regime. He enjoyed parading in his uniform and was happy with the esteem that greeted him whenever he walked down the street or entered his favourite tavern in the evenings.

In 1895 Alois retired to Hafeld where he spent his time drinking in alehouses and keeping bees. By now, however, a gulf had opened up between Alois and Adolf. Alois wanted his son to emulate him and join the customs service: it was a good, solid profession with prospects for a young man who was educated and enthusiastic. Adolf did not know what he wanted to be but he knew that he certainly did not want to join the customs service. As he later wrote, for the first time in his life he was forced into a position of 'open opposition'. The thought of sitting chained to an office stool, spending his life filling in forms, was abhorrent to him. Perhaps, more importantly, he told his father how he felt and continued to feel. It was honest enough but it was a recipe for disaster.

Hitler dabbled with several false starts – he would join the church or perhaps enlist in the military – before, at the age of 12, deciding that he would become an artist. If Adolf Hitler was appalled by the thought of becoming a civil servant, Alois was even more enraged by what he perceived as his son's flippant, almost feminine desire to draw and paint:

> 'Artist? Not as long as I live, never!' As the son had inherited some of the father's obstinacy, besides having other qualities of his own, my reply was equally as energetic ... At that our struggle became a stalemate. The father would not abandon his 'Never' and I became all the more consolidated in my 'Nevertheless'.[1]

The resulting series of confrontations were invariably physical, violent clashes that saw the young man beaten on a regular basis. Neither party would back down but after each beating, Klara was there to soothe her boy and bathe his wounds. She tried hard to act as a barrier between the two warring Hitlers, protecting and shielding Adolf, slipping him money to take him out of the house into the sanctuary of the town streets whenever Alois's temper exploded in fury.

The beatings did eventually stop. If Hitler can be believed it came about as a result of reading in his favourite Karl May cowboy book that it was a sign of courage to bear pain stoically, without murmur or complaint:

> I decided that when he beat me next time, I would make no sound. When it happened – I knew my mother was standing anxiously by the door – I counted every stroke out loud. Mother thought I was mad when I reported to her with a beaming smile, 'Thirty-two strokes father gave me!' From that day I never needed to repeat the experiment, for my father never beat me again.[2]

Hitler by this stage was sure that he had a great destiny, a future that would reward both him and the Germanic peoples. He respected his father and, probably quite naturally, given the ferocity of his outbursts, feared him. But he did not love him. Alois was a hard man to love. Uncommunicative, gruff and brusque, he rarely spoke to Klara, let alone his son. Alois might have shown some initial degree of affection for the infant Adolf but that emotion soon vanished in the face of petulant attitudes from the spoiled – not to say ruined – little boy. Like so many precocious children Adolf Hitler simply did not know when to close his mouth, nod in agreement and stay silent.

Far more significant than any early childhood disagreements was the timing of the disputes. The gulf that opened up between father and son became particularly bitter at the onset of young Hitler's adolescence. Beginning with Adolf's reluctance to accept the customs service as a future career, the artistic and even foppish ways adopted by his son at the onset of the adolescent period infuriated Alois Hitler. Alois was not the man to understand and make allowances for emotional and physical changes in the young man. In his opinion Adolf should have been unswerving in the acceptance of his father's wishes. Klara invariably took the son's side in any almost argument or dispute, albeit silently and surreptitiously, and this simply made matters worse.

It is difficult to imagine two more diametrically opposed individuals than Alois and Klara Hitler. There must have been love of a sort, yet the antipathy of Alois was so strongly marked that one cannot help but wonder how the two of them were ever attracted to each other. She was sweet and some would say quite pretty, a quiet and conscientious housewife who took pride in her spotless house and hearth. Some reports say that she was a little simple. She was, perhaps, naïve and saw few of the problems that modern observers would identify in her marriage. Alois, the man and the breadwinner, was in charge and it was therefore Alois who dictated the rules of the family. That was how it was, she felt; that was how it would always be. It did not stop her trying to protect Adolf, the love of her life.

Alois stood in complete contrast to his wife. He was efficient at his work – although lack of formal education had stalled his career path, something that might have caused him resentment – but, like many state officials, he was very conscious of his position. He expected to be obeyed and saw little use for the social niceties in life. Short-tempered, standing on his dignity whenever there was a dispute, he was a tyrant and a bully.

Adolf Hitler was helpless and unable to respond to his father's brutal behaviour in any way other than maintain a proud and dignified silence, à la Karl May. He was himself the main target for the violence and was not yet strong enough to respond in a similar fashion. On at least one occasion, while still very young, he was beaten senseless by his irate father. He put up with it, enduring the violence with a combination of stubbornness and pride. Only when the violence and the anger were turned against his mother did he become really upset – even if he could not do anything much about it.

Despite what might appear as a loveless marriage, Alois and Klara had six children: Gustav, Ida, Otto, Adolf, Edmund and Paula – but, as was so often the case at the end of the nineteenth century – few of them made it to adulthood. In addition, the children from Alois's previous marriage, Alois Junior and Angela, also helped fill up the house.

In complete contrast to his feelings for his father, the young Adolf certainly loved his mother. Like all spoiled children he was sometimes off-hand with her, expecting and getting what he wanted, when he wanted it and how he wanted it. Now, in hindsight, it is easy to see how this annoyed and even infuriated the thwarted Alois who must have sat and fumed at what he perceived as the soft handling of his wayward son. His only consolation was the beer he drank each night in the local tavern.

Adolf Hitler was 13 years old when his father suddenly died. Apparently in robust health, his death was a surprise to everyone. A stroke took him painlessly and quickly, thereby eliminating the father figure at the head of the family but also removing the conflict in the Hitler household.

Ever afterwards, in the wake of her husband's tragic death Klara stuck rigidly to the view that she and Alois had had a good marriage. To the end of her life – in public at least – she regretted his passing, believing that the children had suffered emotionally because of his absence from their lives.

Whatever she felt for her husband, her love for young Adolf never faltered. She had spoiled him before Alois died but after the bereavement Adolf became her whole world. His care was her guiding principle: she would sacrifice anything to keep her son safe.

As a pampered child, Adolf Hitler had resented the attention Klara had to give to her younger children, of whom only Paula survived infancy and childhood. He hated seeing her give help and comfort to a sibling, even though all of the time he knew that her love for him was still there and would, in due course, be focused solely on him once more. It taught him a hugely important lesson, however. The knowledge that Klara's love would soon, once again, be focused on him alone had not stopped him storming off in temper whenever his desires or plans were thwarted. He learned early in life that rage – or, better still, assumed rage – could be a powerful tactic.

The death of Alois in January 1903 might have been hard for Klara but it provided an unexpected opportunity for Adolf. He said nothing, at least not while his mother was still grieving, but soon resolved that the death of his father would relieve him of the great weight that he had been carrying on his shoulders: studying for entry into the civil service. At first Klara saw no alternative. She would stick to the plans Alois had always had for Adolf and, without too much thought on the matter, attempted to encourage the reluctant youngster to continue studying for the civil service examinations. It was, she felt, no more than her duty as a wife and widow to follow the desires of Alois. Adolf, always the stronger willed of the two, had other ideas. The young man kicked and protested and, eventually and as always with Klara, got his way.

Between them Hitler and Klara agreed that he would leave the Realschule in Linz which was preparing him for the civil service and enrol, instead, at another school in Steyr. The curriculum at this second school was reportedly easier and, with less emphasis on the sciences and technology, was better geared for a would-be artist. That suited the embryonic painter and, for a while, it seemed as if Adolf Hitler had cleverly exchanged the rigours of an environment he hated for something far more palatable.

Steyr was too far away from home to allow daily travel and Hitler had to lodge in the town during the week. He found accommodation with an official of the local court but, even so, he tried to get back home to Linz – the family had moved there after Alois's death and where conditions were that much more homely – whenever he could.

There have been rumours that Hitler was forced to leave the school in Linz because of some indiscretion with a female student. The claim has never been substantiated and must, therefore, be relegated to the scores of other unproven legends associated with Hitler. Regardless of this, he looked forward to his change of school, viewing it as a new opportunity.

Inevitably, there came a harsh meeting of dreams and reality. Formal education held little interest for him and he did no better in this new school than he had done in the old one. It was not long before he was paying scant attention to his studies. He sat in class with his nose buried in the cheap, second-rate cowboy books of Karl May that he kept concealed in his desk. Anything was better than reading the texts that were set for him by his teachers.

He did not get on with his teachers, most of whom he regarded as stupid, even moronic. Similarly, he despised the majority of his peers. Pampered and spoiled, he demanded attention and wanted to be regarded as the leader amongst the group rather than earn such dues in a more subliminal manner. His classmates resented and ignored his directions but Hitler failed to see their reaction and refused to back off.

Despite his lack of effort, his avowed aim now was to try for a place in the Academy of Fine Art in Vienna. Not for an instant, either in his mind or in his mother's, was there any thought that the Academy might reject him. He was talented, they both knew, and so he deserved the place that would certainly be offered when the time came.

Hitler continued to do badly in school and finally, in 1905, he stopped going altogether. Klara did not raise too many objections and in

Mein Kampf he cloaked his decision to drop out by claiming a sudden and debilitating illness that seriously affected his lungs. The illness, Hitler later wrote, required rest of at least a year away from school and from any form of serious study:

> What I had secretly desired for a long time, and persistently fought for, now became a reality. Influenced by my illness, my mother agreed that I should leave the Realschule ... Those were happy days which appeared to me almost as a dream.[3]

Hitler was only too well aware of his mother's paranoia over his health. He knew exactly how to play her and he did so without compunction. Whether his illness was real or invented, in hindsight for the benefit of his readers, he was determined to leave school. The worry and pain that this caused Klara was never considered – these were his 'happy days'. It was a technique he was to come back to many times in his career.

The idyllic paradise of these post-school years was made up of long dreamy hours in the countryside or idly roaming through the streets of Linz. He was supposed to be preparing his art work, making sketches and working out compositions ready for the entrance exam at the Academy. In reality he did little more than sit in street cafés, swan around and dream.

Arguably, without the restrictions of attending and working in school, Hitler became an independent and freedom-loving young man. In particular he was free to study and read whatever he liked. He now began to fully develop the interests that were to consume him in later life – German nationalism, the study of history and a passionate love of music, particularly the symbolic and powerful operas of the German composer Richard Wagner.

Shortly after the death of Alois, Klara had sold their house in Hafeld and moved back to Linz where the family took up residence in a small apartment that was cramped but cosy. Linz meant something special, both for her and for her family, and the cramped conditions in the apartment were more than compensated for by the pleasures of the town and the surrounding countryside.

Alois Junior had left the family home when he was just 14, not long before his father died. Driven out by the anger and intolerance of

Alois Senior, he had begun a wandering and wayward life that took him, amongst other places, to England and to several local prisons where he served time for theft. As far as Adolf Hitler was concerned, it meant one less body in the apartment and one less person to compete for Klara's attention.

There was little money in the Hitler household as Alois's Austrian government pension was small and barely enabled the family to survive. Hitler did nothing to help ease the strain on Klara and the rest of the family. As he was no longer attending school he could and should have taken a job of some description and brought into the home some much needed cash. That was unthinkable for him. Why should he demean himself by a thing like work? Klara was there to provide whatever was needed. She did so willingly and Hitler's demands for money – the inevitable demands of a spoiled and over-protected child – were nothing if not constant.

Financial restrictions did not worry him and for some time Adolf Hitler was supremely happy. The idle life of dreaming, some might say planning, and living at leisure in a style he could ill afford, suited him perfectly. It was, in many ways, a perfect preparation for the doss house days that were soon to come. Nothing, it seemed, could prick his bubble until, early in 1906, disaster struck.

That year Klara Hitler discovered a lump in her breast. At first, convinced that it was nothing serious, she ignored it but soon the pain became intense and in January 1907 she was forced to consult Dr Bloch, a local physician. She was diagnosed with breast cancer.

Hitler, who was now spending several weeks at a time in Vienna, supposedly studying art in the galleries and museums but really wallowing in the sub-culture of the Austrian capital, was called home. He was astounded when Dr Bloch informed him that Klara had not only contracted cancer but had left it too late for treatment and that her condition was now terminal. As with any child or young person who is told of the impending death of a loved one, Hitler was distraught. He might have sponged on Klara, abused her love and generosity, but there was no doubting his affection for her. She had become the one constant in his life and the prospect of losing that supportive presence was hardly to be borne.

His sisters were of little use to him in this time of trouble; they were as upset as him. The one person who was able to offer support of any kind was the family doctor. Even so, Dr Bloch surprisingly left it to him to tell Klara of his diagnosis. In itself that was a huge emotional blow and it shocked Hitler out of his selfishness, at least for a while. He even took on some of the household chores, caring for Klara and tending to her needs.

Dr Bloch continued to make regular visits to do what he could for Klara and the family. He watched the concern and compassion shown by the young Adolf and commented that he had never seen anyone so overcome with grief as Hitler, not just at Klara's deathbed but in the long and harrowing months leading up to it.

In a last attempt at saving Klara's life, she was persuaded to undergo the horrendous ordeal of a double mastectomy. The operation took place at the Sisters of Mercy Hospital in Linz but it was too little too late as the cancer was already eating into the pleural tissue of her chest. In constant pain, Klara soon required daily injections of morphine to make her comfortable. They did little good. With no health service then available, the treatments had to be paid for and all they managed to achieve was to deplete the meagre financial resources of the family.

In October 1907 Klara's condition deteriorated sharply. Confined to bed, she lay in agony, knowing that it was only a matter of time before the end. On a regular, desperate basis, she was now receiving treatments with iodoform, an early type of chemotherapy. The treatment involved re-opening the mastectomy cuts on her chest and inserting massive wads of gauze that had been soaked in iodoform into the wounds. Cancer treatment was still in its infancy, medical practitioners having neither the skill nor the equipment to offer what was really no more than experimental and ad hoc processes that might or might not work. The use of iodoform was an attempt to burn out the cancer cells, a brutal last-ditch attempt to save Klara's life and it failed.

The treatment was incredibly painful but Klara bore it stoically. Her throat became paralysed, she was unable to swallow and it was obvious to everyone that she was slipping away. She died on 21 December 1907 from the toxic side effects of the iodoform. Adolf Hitler was beside himself with grief. He had never before lost somebody he cared about and such torment ripped at his heart. To experience such emotional pain was a unique emotion for him.

Hitler was never to forget his mother and the love she naturally bore and gave to him. In the face of her death a huge pool, a deep well of love, affection and compassion for the woman who had given birth and reared him, began to develop in Hitler. It was a love that never died but only grew in power and complexity over the years.

Klara had given her love unreservedly, asking for nothing in return. And now, only now when his mother had gone, was Hitler able to see that. He had taken everything for granted, loving her admittedly, but only rarely allowing her to realize that his love was also strong. Although they had always been close, it is possible that Hitler did not realize quite how much he loved Klara until the diagnosis of terminal cancer. By then, of course, it was too late to do anything more than grieve.

It is all too easy for any writer or historian to fall into the trap of becoming an amateur psychologist and conclude that Hitler grew into a disturbed adult because of his upbringing. Discussion on that particular issue comes down to nature or nurture: was Adolf Hitler born bad or was he made bad? You pay your money and take your choice on that one.

Many writers have bandied about theories like the Narcissus or Oedipus complexes. However, it is more than likely that young Adolf Hitler was no more disturbed than many teenage boys who have endured a traumatic experience in their lives. Even a statement like that cannot be proved, one way or another. The last laugh on that particular issue remains with Hitler.

Nevertheless, he did have all the credentials for those labels that psychologists and social workers love to attach to their clients. On the one side there was a father he feared and possibly hated. On the other was a mother he adored but whose role in the family was that of an oppressed and downtrodden partner of a man who was both brutal and bullying. Losing both parents in quick succession would have caused any adolescent pangs of regret and sorrow.

Klara was buried on Christmas Eve in Leonding, her last wish being to rest alongside Alois. It was a painful and emotional ceremony, Hitler standing alone at the grave after everyone else had left the cemetery. Dr Eduard Bloch had taken an unusual but genuine interest in the case and it was entirely appropriate when family members called at his surgery to express their thanks and gratitude:

> Although his sisters came to Dr Bloch a few days after the funeral and expressed themselves fully, Adolf remained silent.

As the little group left he said, 'I shall be grateful to you forever' ... The bottom had obviously fallen out of his world.[4]

In 1934 Hitler honoured his mother's memory by naming a street in Passau after her. As Chancellor of Germany it was a posthumous gift well within his power to bestow.

Probably more significantly, in 1940, with the persecution of the Jews escalating, Hitler gave a personal order allowing the part-Jewish Dr Bloch and his wife to emigrate from Austria to the United States. It was an unusual but significant gift, a form of gratitude to the man who had tried, albeit unsuccessfully, to save his mother. Klara was Hitler's first love. It was a platonic and all-consuming affection and was arguably the greatest love of his life.

Hitler's childhood and adolescence probably seemed to him to be full of women – women who fawned on him, spoiled him and helped to give him an inflated view of his own skills and abilities. It is perhaps an obvious statement to make but to a large extent the members of his family were the people who helped form and mould his adult personality – and in Hitler's case those family members were women. Apart from his mother, the other women in the home were his two siblings – his half-sister Angela and full sister Paula.

Angela was born in 1883, the second child of Alois Hitler and Franziska Matzelsberger, then Alois's second wife. Angela's mother Franziska died the year after her daughter's birth and Angela and her brother, also confusingly called Alois, were brought up by Klara Poelzl – Klara Hitler as she soon became.

Adolf Hitler was born six years after Angela. As often happens with children who suddenly acquire a baby brother or sister, she and her new half-brother were thrown together and became quite close. He always remembered her with affection – indeed, she was the only member of his family, apart from his mother, to be mentioned in *Mein Kampf*.

A beautiful girl, high spirited and full of life, Angela had been strictly supervised by her father who carefully controlled and regulated the boys from the town who were soon calling on his daughter. It was something that she resented more and more the older she became.

Despite thinking that her mother overindulged and spoiled Adolf, Angela took a leaf out of Klara's book and fussed and petted her baby brother who was happy to be mollycoddled in this way. As he grew from infancy into childhood, the fussing continued. It was, Adolf felt, no more than his due.

Paula Hitler was six years younger than Adolf and the youngest surviving child of Alois Hitler. Unlike Angela, she and Hitler did not get on particularly well during their childhood years. They might have been too alike in their characters or, more likely, Adolf resented the sudden appearance of a new baby who demanded the attention that he was sure should have been his and his alone.

Whenever he spoke about Paula to his friend August Kubrizek he always referred to her as 'the kid', a dismissive but not totally unpleasant description. Given some of his more colourful comments about teachers, politicians and peers, made at around this time, it could have been a lot worse.

Despite what was reported as a strong filial affection between them, Adolf and Paula apparently quarrelled regularly during their childhood years. They were constantly bickering with each other, arguments and spats that often ended in blows. Paula later recorded that she could still feel her brother's slaps across her face. Alois Junior invariably took Paula's side in the arguments, something that only made the situation worse. Paula and Adolf may well have argued but mostly she was a quiet, passive girl who was easily led by her older brother and half-brother. Hitler undoubtedly had a degree of innate affection for his sisters, Angela in particular, but it was only to a limited degree. He was never overly fond of either of the two girls, at least not in any demonstrative way. He called them 'stupid geese' and held a low opinion of their intelligence.

But whatever he thought of them, his sisters did provide a solid framework for his childhood, offering comfort and support when Alois was at his most unbearable and violent or when Klara was engaged on other tasks. If he could not get comfort from Klara, Hitler knew that his sisters would provide surrogate affection.

Spoiled, fussed over, argued with and battled against – that was Hitler and his youthful relationship with his sisters. And yet, with Klara Hitler always there, always overseeing and indulging, it was a relatively close-knit family. Klara might have received little in the way of affection from her husband but she was always able to pour her emotions into the care and safety of her children. If they could find the time or the inclination, the siblings might just give it back.

Klara had lost so many of her children, Gustav and Ida dying in the diphtheria epidemic of 1887/8, Otto perishing within days of his birth and Edmund dying from measles in 1900. Adolf was 'her pet' as everyone remembered and Klara was damned if she was going to lose him. Paula, her only other remaining natural child, inevitably suffered in the face of such devotion. The family was effectively welded together by Klara. As a unit it had inevitably begun to disperse as the children reached adulthood but Klara's death at the end of 1907 – just two years after her husband – finally broke up the family. The offspring of Alois and Klara each quickly went their own separate ways.

Alois Junior had gone off to train as a waiter and begun a peripatetic life style that saw him working in England and marrying an Irish girl before finally returning to Germany where he opened a restaurant in Berlin. It apparently became a popular drinking and gathering place for members of the SA.

In September 1903, eager to be away from her father's strict regime, Angela had married Leo Raubal, a tax officer, setting up home not far away from Klara in Linz but out of the immediate reach of her father. Adolf Hitler and Leo Raubal did not get on. He was, after all, a member of that despised clique, a civil servant. Perhaps as a consequence of this, Hitler had limited contact with Angela for several years after her marriage.

Leo Raubal died in 1910 and Angela moved, with her three children, to Vienna. There she worked as manager of the Mensa Academia Judaica, a hostel for Jewish students. Decent and hardworking, she physically defended her Jewish students against attacks by mobs during racist rioting in the city, barring their entry into the hostel with her body. Despite being in the same town as Hitler for several years, the pair lost touch and did not re-establish contact until after the war in 1919. Angela had been Hitler's favourite sibling but the struggling artist had no interest in rekindling old dreams and feelings. In the days before the First World War he probably did not even know that Angela was in the same city.

By 1919 things had changed. He was now a decorated war hero – proudly wearing his Iron Cross First Class – and was already on the first rung of the ladder that would lead him, finally, to the very top. He had moved his base and was now a resident of Munich, an altogether more cosmopolitan environment than Vienna.

In 1924 Angela also moved to Munich. Her daughter Angelika, Geli as she was known, went with her. Geli was an attractive girl who immediately caught Hitler's eye, even at this early stage, but at the time of the reconciliation of brother and half-sister she was too young to unduly bother his libido. That would come later.

In due course Angela became Hitler's housekeeper at the Obersaltzberg near Berchtesgaden, a post she held for several years, and Geli again accompanied her mother. Inevitably the young girl was thrown more and more into Hitler's company.

Things did not end well for Angela. By 1935, Hitler was seeing a great deal of Eva Braun, much to the disgust of Angela. Hitler took no notice of his sister's disapproval, even granting Eva a position of honour on the platform at that year's Nuremberg Rally. Angela, who was also there, protested and told Hitler that Fraulein Braun, as she always called Eva, had deliberately drawn attention to herself.

Hitler immediately hit back and within a very short period Angela was dismissed from his service. There was no doubt that by this time Angela was unwell and the rift with Eva Braun gave Hitler the excuse he needed. The rigours of keeping house, welcoming foreign diplomats and running a large establishment were now beyond her. Family loyalty clearly meant nothing to him.

Angela's heart had been causing her problems for some time and in 1936, after leaving her brother's employment, she 'took the cure' at Bad Nauheim, a renowned health spa. There she met Professor Hammitzsch of Dresden University and married him. After that, contact between Hitler and his half-sister was limited to visits on his birthday and the occasional letter. On her brother's birthday Angela was forced to suffer the humiliation of standing in line like others who had come to extend their best wishes to the Führer.

Paula seems to have disappeared from view soon after her mother's death. She was just 11 years old and was placed with an aunt who would look after her and help bring her up. How long Paula remained there is not known; where she went or what happened to her in her teenage years remains a mystery but it was, presumably, a normal healthy adolescence. In the early 1920s Paula resurfaced, also having moved to Vienna where she, like Angela, ran a hostel for students. Having had no contact with him, she believed that her brother had been killed in the war. So many had died and she had received no word of him, either from the authorities or from Hitler himself. Believing him to be dead was not an entirely unusual emotion, many other Austrian and German women feeling the same way about relatives and friends.

It was therefore a total surprise when Paula began seeing his name in the papers as a political agitator on the streets of Munich and in Bavaria. Even so, to begin with she made no attempt to get in touch with him. Paula and Adolf finally re-established contact in the late 1920s when she pushed her reticence to one side and travelled to Munich to see him. By now she was living under the name Hiedler, to distinguish her from the notorious politician. She had been the subject of considerable persecution from his political opponents and was soon to adopt the name Frau Wolf – Hitler's pseudonym or nom de plume in his early days of political activity.

Despite being pleased to see her brother again, Paula remained a peripheral character in his life. She never joined the Nazi Party and never tried to make capital out of the connection even though Hitler did support her with a monthly allowance out of Party funds.

*

The period between the death of his mother and his newfound fame as a politician and agitator had not been easy for Adolf Hitler. At the same time, it had not been an entirely unwelcome respite, a sort of gestation period that ultimately made him the creature that he eventually became.

Back in 1907, with the earth barely sprinkled on his mother's grave, Hitler himself was about to take his first real steps into the dark confines of the Vienna back streets. He had failed to gain a place at the Academy of Fine Art, although he told no one of this disaster. His pride would not allow him to admit what had happened and 'come clean' about his failure.

Failure had been a bitter pill to swallow. He had plotted and planned all his life to become an artist but inability to gain a place at the Academy destroyed his dreams at the first hurdle. More than that, it confirmed his father's opinion that he would never make the grade as a creative artist.

He might curse and fume at the intellectuals and members of the intelligentsia who had denied him his rightful prize but alone, in the depths of the night, rage could do nothing to assuage the thought that, beneath it all, he was just not good enough. Perhaps his father had been right all along. Now all that was left to him was the Viennese underworld.

Looking at it from the outside, away from the reality of the situation, the anonymity of Vienna seemed to be an attractive proposition for the failed and thwarted artist. In the city, surrounded by other dropouts and dead-end characters, Hitler had nothing to prove. He could paint and sell his art to earn a few pennies but nobody there knew him as Adolf Hitler, the boy from Linz who had made such a fuss about gaining a place at the Academy. He was free to do as he wished.

However, as he was to quickly discover, the doss houses of the city were a very different proposition from the warmth of a home where his mother and sisters could always make problems disappear and enable the world to feel all right again. He might be free but there were also times when he was lonely and afraid, when there was no one there to comfort and console. That was the major problem that faced Adolf Hitler in these years in Vienna. There was nobody to soothe him, to ease his worries and concerns; there was nobody there, nobody who without reason and motive was simply there to care. All that he had to take and to hold were the memories of how his family had loved and cherished him in the past, his mother in particular. He always kept them close to his heart. And yet, despite every bitter disappointment or setback he encountered, when Hitler did finally plummet to the lows of Vienna life, he was to find that he actually quite enjoyed them. In the shadows there were no worries, no concerns apart from finding ways to survive another day. The feelings of trepidation as he made his first genuine individual moves must have been vast. Adolf Hitler, on the brink of adult life, knew that the halcyon days were over. It was time, now, to make it on his own:

> With my clothes and linen packed in a valise and with an indomitable resolution in my heart, I left for Vienna ...
> I was determined to become 'something' but certainly not a civil servant.[5]

Despite his noble words, Hitler actually had no choice. He had outgrown Linz. His failure to gain a place at the Academy was like a burning torch in his belly. He knew that he could not face the people of his home town and admit that all his dreams had come to nothing. The only hope now of making something out of his life lay in the big city of Vienna. He would try again for the Academy, this time specializing in architecture but, again, he failed to make the grade. It was another bitter blow.

Whatever else could be said about the Austrian capital it was anonymous and people who did not want to be found could blend easily into its back streets and alleyways. That suited Hitler perfectly.

He had no desire to maintain contact with friends and acquaintances back in Linz and even his two sisters meant little to him. He would wrap his bitterness and his failures around himself, use them as a shield to keep away the world.

What was left of his family could make do without him. Klara had been the mainstay of them all, his love or affection for his sisters being fairly minimal, at least in the grand scheme of things. Without her there seemed to be little point in maintaining the family unit. The one thing of note that the two Hitler boys, Adolf and Alois Junior, did for their sisters was to sign over to them the small pensions they had been given by the Austrian government on the death of their mother. It was little enough but it was at least some sort of gesture.

With Angela's husband Leo Raubal having died in 1910, she was left her to bring up three children on her own. She was a little better off than Paula as Leo had left a small pension but it was minimal. The two pensions from Alois and Adolf, tiny as they were, provided only the most basic income the two sisters had.

So ended the early life of Adolf Hitler. In many respects he had been smothered by the love of his mother but the warmth and comfort he had gained from that love were to remain with him for the rest of his time on earth. Arguably that love and compassion were elements that he was to look for all his life. He would never have admitted it – Vienna was where he was grounded and steeled; Linz was just a phase in his life. It was safer that way. It may have been a rationalization but Hitler clearly remembered his days in Vienna as the very opposite to those easy but perhaps cloying Linz days:

> I am thankful for that period in my life, because it hardened me and enabled me to be as tough as I now am. And I am even more thankful because I appreciate the fact that I was thus saved from the emptiness of a life of ease and that a mother's darling was taken from tender arms and handed over to Adversity as to a new mother.[6]

New mother or old, Klara had helped formulate the man Hitler became. She would hardly have recognized his description of himself as a 'mother's darling' and would have undoubtedly wept bitter tears at the situation in which he now found himself. Surely, she had done no more than love the boy, as any mother would? Klara had no intention of bringing up and developing a monster and it was perhaps lucky that she did not survive to see how he eventually turned out. She had done her best and that was all that could be hoped for, given the situation. Arguably Adolf Hitler spent the best years of his life trying to recapture the feelings of emotional security and compassion that his mother Klara had created in their home in Linz. Wherever he went, whatever he did, Klara Hitler proved to be a hard act to follow.

Chapter 3

Dreams of Love: Stephanie Isak and Charlotte Lobjoie

The first two early and extra-familial loves in Adolf Hitler's life are little-known affairs that are not really understood and appreciated. Both of them follow bizarre and highly unusual lines of progression. Both of them have questionable elements – one perhaps more than the other – but they still manage to fit with the personality of this highly dangerous and contradictory man. Both are, in parts, deniable but both present a fascinating angle from which to study Hitler as an adolescent and young man.

As with any early love, any adolescent infatuation, Hitler found his first loves particularly painful. He was hardly the most sociable of people and found mixing with members of the opposite sex difficult. And yet he still had dreams and desires – unusual dreams and desires maybe but still emotions that troubled him and propelled him forward. How formative those loves – the first one in particular – might have been remains open for debate.

Adolf Hitler certainly loved his mother but he was not *in love* with her. There is a difference and the point in a boy's life when he looks beyond his mother's restricting arms needs careful handling by both parties. First loves are always difficult for any boy; mother love is something that has to be understood and then stored in the right place, leaving space for that sometimes painful, sometimes glorious first infatuation.

All of which brings us to Adolf Hitler's first love. That somewhat dubious honour rests with a girl from Linz, a golden-haired beauty by the name of Stephanie Isak. The only first-hand evidence about Hitler and Stephanie comes from the pen of Hitler's friend August Kubrizek who wrote about the relationship – if relationship is the right word – in his book *The Young Hitler I Knew*. It is admittedly a one-dimensional view, told from Kubrizek's memories and interpretation, but it is entirely plausible. If only half of what he wrote is true then it remains a remarkable account of first love and Adolf Hitler's experience of it.

With a lack of corroborating evidence some historians have dismissed the claim that Hitler was ever in love with the previously unknown Stephanie. The fact that he conducted his 'affair' with her in such a very unusual manner is often used to support the negative view. And yet many other writers have accepted it as a genuine recollection, acknowledging what was clearly a major infatuation on the part of Adolf Hitler. It may or may not have been life changing but his infatuation with a distant and untouchable vision certainly helped to reinforce Hitler's view of women. Kubrizek's report is fascinating and certainly seems to fit with our knowledge of the character of Hitler as an adolescent. It also paints a colourful and dynamic picture of life in an Austrian town at the end of the nineteenth century.

That there was a girl by the name of Stephanie Isak living in Linz at the time is a known fact and the romantic Adolf Hitler, always full of the idea of idealized German womanhood, undoubtedly noticed her. The rest is down to Kubrizek and if it was not a story that concerned Adolf Hitler it would probably have been forgotten or dismissed out of hand.

His behaviour during the strangely distant, almost antiseptic 'courtship' was apparently not dissimilar from that of many other adolescents in Austria at that time. The concept of worshipping from afar, it seems, was a common one. From the moment he first saw her, Kubrizek says, Hitler was impressed by her looks, her bearing and her personality. His feelings were intense but they were kept at a distance. We will come back to that – for the moment the story rests with Kubrizek. His account of the 'love affair' is a significant part of his book and, true or invented, smacks of reality. This, you feel, is exactly how the adolescent Hitler would have behaved.

August Kubrizek's early life mirrored Hitler's. Three of his sisters died young and his mother was terrified of losing August. Like Klara Hitler, she spoiled, protected and overindulged her son. He disliked school but loved music. A gifted violinist, financial and economic circumstances forced him to work as an upholsterer in his father's struggling business. He hated it, hated the dust and dirt that got onto his lungs. He knew that he wanted to make a living as a musician.

Kubrizek's part in the pantomime of Adolf Hitler and Stephanie Isak is not insubstantial. Even the way he and Hitler met smacks of the bizarre world that the future dictator wove around himself in those adolescent years. Kubrizek fitted easily into that world, a needy youth who was, in his own way, as inadequate as Hitler. They were well matched.

Kubrizek and Hitler first encountered each other at the theatre in Linz. They were both huge lovers of music, of opera in particular, but neither of them ever had much money. That meant they could get into the theatre but they had to stand throughout the performance. The area on the ground floor of the auditorium was large and spacious but the open space in front of two pillars supporting the royal box offered the best acoustics in the hall. The position could never replace the sheer delight of sitting through a performance but opera-goers with limited funds, like Hitler and Kubrizek, would stand with their backs propped against one or the other of these stanchions and drink in the music and the words.

One evening just before All Saints Day in 1904, Kubrizek arrived to find the right-hand pillar, his favourite spot, already taken by a pale, skinny youth of a similar age to him. It was Adolf Hitler. They glared at each other, then Kubrizek went to stand against the left pillar. The two music lovers did not speak until the interval. They had no money for refreshments like the rest of the audience and were almost forced into conversation with each other while most people were at the bar. The two boys were waiting for the performance to start again and conversation seemed to come easily. They quickly discovered points of mutual agreement. In particular, both of them were critical of the performance by one of the singers in that evening's production.

After that Hitler and Kubrizek often met at performances of various operas and were soon taking evening strolls together. They became friends; in fact, they became the only friend that either of them seemed to have. Kubrizek did not fool himself, however. He knew that there was an ulterior motive and rationale behind Hitler's offer of comradeship:

> Soon I came to understand that our friendship endured largely for the reason that I was a patient listener ... He [Hitler] generally lacked money for food. But even if he had it, he would prefer to starve and spend it on a theatre seat.[1]

Kubrizek's ability as a listener was particularly useful when, in the spring of 1905, Hitler became obsessed with Stephanie Isak. Almost immediately he told Kubrizek that he was in love with a girl in town, his declaration taking his friend totally by surprise. But after that it seemed as if every minute of the day was taken up with Stephanie.

Hitler was a demanding comrade, unashamedly dragging Kubrizek out of his place of work in the upholstery business if he was late for a meeting or assignation. He had little care or concern that his friend's hours of work had not been completed. In the main Kubrizek was not unhappy to be kidnapped in this fashion. Unlike his friend, patience had never been one of Hitler's great qualities and if Stephanie Isak was involved, somewhere, in that day's programme of planned events he was doubly anxious and likely to demand the immediate presence of August Kubrizek. Even if she wasn't, Hitler still needed an avid listener as he walked and talked incessantly about his love.

Hitler's infatuation with Stephanie, Kubrizek states, lasted a surprisingly long time and was a period of unrequited love for him. It was unrequited because Hitler never spoke to her, not once in the four years that he was obsessed by her. They were four years when the sight and even the thought of Stephanie caused him such pangs of heartache that he more than once declared that he would kill himself as a gesture of his love. They were theatrical claims and not even Kubrizek was taken in. The next evening Hitler would be there at the appointed hour, ready and all too willing for the nightly parade.

The evening walk – parading as it has also been called – was one of the traditions of Linz and many other Austrian garrison towns. Every Sunday and sometimes in the week as well young army officers would sweep along the streets, flirting with and attracting the attention of the carefully chaperoned girls of the town. Stephanie was one of those girls. She was tall and slim, unaffected and pretty with bright, expressive eyes and a glorious mane of thick blond hair that she usually wore swept back into a bun. Hitler was enchanted with her and thought her appearance made her ideal for the part of Elsa in *Lohengrin*. His ideal vision of her, as he described it to Kubrizek, was to picture her riding on a white steed through fields of flowers, dressed in a long, elegant velvet gown. Her hair would be flowing out behind her and she would be the picture of innocence. As ever she would be pure and untouched. The picture he painted for Kubrizek could have come straight out of a Bavarian fable or folk opera.

Hitler even wrote poetry about his love. It was always dedicated to Stephanie but none was ever delivered and none has survived. The verses invariably had titles like 'Hymn to the Beloved' and, if Kubrizek is to be believed, it is not too difficult to imagine the content.

Two or three evenings a week Stephanie promenaded, invariably with her widowed mother and sometimes her brother as well. Almost every time she stepped out onto the streets of Linz, Hitler would be there on the sidewalk to watch her walk past. His constancy was noticed by Stephanie but no further advances were made by either side. Hitler knew that as a young, immature and unprepossessing adolescent he could not compete with the officers of the Empire in their beautifully cut and startlingly colourful uniforms. By contrast he was just a pale, skinny civilian. Very often Stephanie passed him by without even realising he was there. When this occurred, Hitler was furious although his anger was directed not at the girl but at the officers. 'Conceited blockheads' he called them as he waxed lyrical about the soldiers' perfumed bodies and the fact that they all wore corsets to keep their bellies in tight control.

No amount of persuasion would convince Hitler that he should speak to Stephanie. When Kubrizek suggested it, Hitler was furious and retaliated with the comment that his friend simply did not understand the extraordinary love that existed between him and the girl. He was convinced that she shared his views on all things and therefore simply did not need to speak to her. She would know what he felt and thought. He would worship from afar.

Even so he would erupt into fits of raging jealousy if he saw her talking too animatedly or flirting too openly with an officer. After a while he would change his attitude – her behaviour, he said, was deliberate, a ruse to hide her own feelings for him. Then, if she happened to ignore him, things would change again – then he would be ready to destroy himself. There was even another change in his repertoire – he would kill himself by jumping into the river, he declared, but only if Stephanie was prepared to die with him.

When Stephanie did occasionally acknowledge him, Hitler was beside himself with joy. In June 1906 at the annual flower festival in Linz, she leaned out of her carriage and threw him a flower as she passed by. It was no more than a happy, spur-of-the-moment gesture but Hitler's interpretation was very different. 'She loves me,' he declared, 'she loves me' and folded the flower away to be kept and gazed at for years afterwards.

Hitler's fantasy world was clearly the product of a mind that was already unbalanced. Arguably such fantasies and dreams are not always a major issue; many eager adolescents go, quite successfully, through such angst and emerge on the other side as well-balanced individuals. Very rarely do the problems of teenage years linger long into adulthood when matters like starting a career, marriage and rearing children tend to take first place in the priorities of most people.

With Hitler, however, his depth of feeling was vast. Even at this early stage of his life he was unable to separate fact from fantasy. His dreams of success, both with Stephanie and with his career, were bound up in the one long-held idea of a life in art. If that failed to materialize he had nothing to fall back on, not even the girl he adored. His life was a fantasy but he had neither the power nor the ability to turn that fantasy into reality. That sort of power came much later in his life.

A madcap scheme to kidnap the girl and then kill her along with him was, at least for Stephanie, mercifully dropped. Hitler had to content himself with standing on a street corner watching and waiting for his beloved vision of loveliness to pass by.

His infatuation began when he was 16, just at the point where he dropped out from formal schooling. It overlapped with his first tentative explorations of the art scene in Vienna, both of his passions welding themselves together in what must have been a boiling fury in the belly of a young man not really equipped to deal with either. He would not declare his love for Stephanie, Hitler said, until he had gone through the Academy in Vienna and received a formal qualification. Then he would return to Linz to claim his prize. She was loyal and honourable; she would wait for him and they would be married.

When he was away in Vienna, supposedly preparing for his entry to the Academy, Hitler charged Kubrizek with watching Stephanie's movements. Operating as something of a stalker, Kubrizek duly followed her and reported back to Hitler, telling his friend where she had gone, the people she had met and what she did for leisure. One of Stephanie's great loves, he reported, was dancing. Perhaps learning to dance would be a way of making contact? Hitler's response was predictable. No way would he learn to dance; it was a decadent pastime and of no interest to him.

His protestations undoubtedly concealed a weakness in him. Despite his love of opera, he had no real ear for music and certainly a very limited understanding of rhythm. To be watched on the dance floor would have been agony for him but, more significantly, he believed that Stephanie's love of dancing was little more than social etiquette: 'Stephanie only dances because she is forced to by society on which she unfortunately depends. Once she is my wife, she won't have the slightest desire to dance.'[2]

Despite his objections Kubrizek harboured a sneaking belief that Hitler practised dancing at home with his sister Paula. It is possible although neither Hitler nor Paula ever commented on any dance lessons or practice sessions.

Meanwhile the dreams persisted. He would build Stephanie a house, renaissance style, where they would live together in a Wagnerian paradise and he would worship her for the rest of his life. She was never out of his thoughts, not even during the agonizing months around his mother's death – indeed the thought of Stephanie probably helped keep him going during the most traumatic period he had ever known.

Hitler's infatuation lasted until he was 20 years old. By then he was deeply into the mire of Vienna's back streets and all dreams of passing through the Academy before returning to claim Stephanie as his bride had been exposed as exactly that – dreams, mere dreams.

Stephanie Isak did not know of the passion Hitler held for her. When interviewed about it many years after the Second World War she expressed surprise but did admit to having once received an anonymous letter from someone asking her to wait for him until he had finished his studies at the Academy in Vienna. Not knowing to whom or where she should reply, nothing further was done.

Stephanie married one of 'her officers', Maximillian Rabatsch, who did well and rose to the rank of colonel in the Austrian Army. Hitler, meanwhile, went off to Vienna where he held Stephanie's memory as a talisman. To him she was always an idealized image and although his adolescent infatuation did eventually fade, he never forgot his blonde beauty and the way she made him feel.

If there was one lasting effect of the infatuation it was the picture that she lodged in Hitler's mind of the ideal Teutonic woman. That image was one that would never go away. Stephanie was tall and graceful, untouchable and pure, someone to be worshipped from afar and, if necessary, a creature for whom he and every other German man should be willing to sacrifice their lives. This reflected the soul of Germany and Stephanie Isak was the epitome of what the German or Aryan race would soon be fighting to protect and defend.

Like so many of Hitler's ideals it was all a myth, in the same way that Stephanie, at least as Hitler saw her, was a myth. That was why he never spoke to her, never attempted to make contact. That way the myth, the dream, could never be broken.

*

Move forward, now, to the horrors of the First World War. The causes of the war were many and varied. They ranged from Germany's desire to gain a place in the sun alongside the empires of Britain and France to the domino-like series of alliances which ensured that the path to violent conflict was inevitable once the first of the 'big' nations declared war on each other. Whatever the causes, within a few months of the war's outbreak in the summer of 1914 millions of men were doing their damndest to kill each other in what quickly became the world's first truly global conflict. All of them fought with, as they saw it, 'God on their side' and Adolf Hitler was no different from thousands of other eager conscripts.

By the summer of 1917 he had been fighting almost constantly against the British and the French for nearly three years. Austrian he may have been but he had enlisted in a German regiment, surviving and battling in the mud and the blood of the Western Front.

He had moved from backstreet Vienna to backstreet Munich some time before war broke out, believing implicitly in the strength and might of the German Empire as opposed to what he saw as the degeneracy and rottenness of Austria. As far as Hitler was concerned, Austria was the past; Germany represented the future.

The theory might have been right but life in the Munich slums was very similar to life in the Viennese ones. Hitler lived in doss houses, painted small watercolours and sold them to tourists in order to survive. He lived on handouts and frugal meals, shuffling around the streets in a huge, engulfing overcoat. He met and was familiar with all elements of lower German society, everyone from prostitutes, pimps and thieves to Jewish traders and the owners of run-down pawn shops.

When war erupted in 1914, he immediately enlisted in the German Army. His enlistment was not achieved without difficulty as he was still technically an Austrian citizen. While the Central Powers, surrounded on all sides by the Allies, were happy to make use of his services, the first thought was that he should be fighting for Austria. He managed to convince the authorities that Bavaria was now his home and went on to serve in the 16th Bavarian Reserve Regiment, usually known as the List Regiment after its first commander.

After basic military training he served as a front-line soldier, acting as a runner taking messages to and from regimental headquarters and enduring assault by rifle fire, artillery shelling and hand grenades on a daily basis. It meant that he spent time in the trenches of the front line and back at regimental HQ, always within range of enemy fire.

Hitler's war was a dangerous and difficult one but he carried out his duties efficiently. There were no complaints either about the way he served or his courage. As a reward for his bravery he was initially awarded the Iron Cross Second Class and then, to his unutterable joy, the Iron Cross First Class.

It was rare for any man in the ranks – Hitler never rose above the rank of Gefreiter (lance-corporal) – to receive the higher award and for this he had to thank his company officer, a Jewish lieutenant by the name of Hugo Gutmann. Impressed by Hitler's courage, Gutmann lobbied his seniors long and hard on behalf of his company runner. The irony was not lost on the world's press or on Hitler himself who may well have helped to save Gutmann's life after the passing of the severe anti-Semitic laws of the 1930s.

In the early summer of 1917 Hitler and his unit were out of the trenches on a rest period. After the continuous frenzy of fighting, Hitler now had free time and spent it, sketching, in the area around the French village of Fournes-en-Weppe. It was there that he supposedly met the 16-year-old Charlotte Lobjoie. According to the legend she and other girls were hay making outside the town when they saw a solitary German soldier sitting quietly on the edge of the field. It was Adolf Hitler. He was gazing into the distance and drawing or writing in a sketch book. They became intrigued and Charlotte, the most forward of the group, went across to ask him what he was doing. The story of what happened next has been told by Charlotte's son, Jean-Marie Loret. According to him the young German soldier and his mother took a liking to each other and became friendly. Later that first evening they took a walk together. It quickly became a regular habit and after what Jean-Marie called a tipsy evening in June 1917, they ended up having sex.

Nobody seems sure how long the relationship lasted but it could not have been for very long. German troops, like their British and French counterparts, were too valuable to be left idly twiddling their thumbs and the List Regiment would have been back in the lines after just a week or two out at rest on recuperation and reorganization.

Similarly, no one knows how many times Hitler and Charlotte engaged in the sexual act but, from the way the story has been recorded, it seems to have been only once. That was if the story of the relationship were true and there are many reasons to doubt its veracity. All of this, Jean-Marie claimed, had been told to him by his mother shortly before her death in 1951. The German soldier, she said, was the German dictator and Jean-Marie, the product of that romantic evening, was Hitler's illegitimate son. If the story is true, a few days after the sexual union Hitler returned to his unit, unaware of any potential consequences of the brief encounter. Charlotte did not know quite where he had gone or what might have happened to him and so contact ended once Hitler returned to the ranks. That, at least, was her story.

The birth registry for the St Quentin area does in fact state that an illegitimate son was born to Charlotte Lobjoie in March 1918. The father was reported to be an unknown German soldier. There is, however, no mention of Adolf Hitler – nor should there be as, if Charlotte's story is true, she was unlikely to know more than his first name. It was not for some time after he went back to the trenches that she realized she was pregnant.

There have been several other variations of the story which was taken up and given some degree of credibility by German historian Werner Maser in the 1970s. In one version Hitler and Charlotte met first in Wavrin, a town which was located in German-occupied France. She then followed Hitler around the front to various postings like Seboncourt and Fournes-en-Weppe. After the war Charlotte moved to Paris where she became a dancer and then married a lithographer by the name of Clement Loret. He duly gave Jean-Marie his name. The boy, who had originally been put up for adoption, later joined the French Army and during the Second World War served with the police. He may well have had connections with the Gestapo but no charges were ever brought or, more significantly, no unofficial 'tar and feather justice' was ever meted out to him in the wake of the German defeat.

According to Jean-Marie little packages of money were often delivered to Charlotte during the war, presumably sent by Hitler to keep her financially secure. These, Jean-Marie claimed, were carried and given to his mother by German officers or soldiers. The Führer had, it seemed, discovered the truth about Charlotte and her son when, now in the role of conquering hero, he had visited the areas where he had been billeted in the earlier war. It is scant confirmation but Hitler's valet Heinz Linge, who was with him, reported the Führer talking to several local people and coming away very thoughtful. Following the visit, on Hitler's orders Himmler and the Gestapo then tracked Charlotte down to her house in Paris.

Jean-Marie Loret went into business after the war but became insolvent and died in 1985. Before that he had married and fathered nine children. One of the children, Phillippe, recently went public to claim that he was Hitler's grandson. He has made no move to prove the claim but believes it implicitly, just as his father believed in the tale of his parentage.

Like so much of Adolf Hitler's early life the story is full of half-truths, wishful thinking and a great deal of circumstantial evidence. There is no firm proof either way and the interested bystander is left thinking, perhaps as the participants in the tale were thinking when the story originated: wouldn't it be great if this all happened to be true?

Hitler, out of danger for a while and perfectly relaxed in the French countryside, may well have taken a fancy to the young Charlotte. However, as several of his comrades from the trenches later confirmed, he was violently opposed to any sort of relationship between German soldiers and French girls, and any connection between him and Charlotte remains an unlikely prospect.

In the dugouts and in rest periods out of the lines Hitler often ranted about German manhood and the Aryan future which were too important to be polluted by mixing with people of an inferior race. Men who did that type of thing, he stormed, had no sense of German honour. With views like that, so publicly and vehemently displayed, it is unlikely that he would then have fallen into the very trap he so despised.

On the other side of the coin, Hitler may have been lonely and needed the company of a pretty country girl. Such things have always happened in wartime and the soldiers of the First World War were no different from any other young men whose life expectancies were short and for whom a brutal and painful death was always waiting.

Against all the odds relationships between ideological opposites were often formed regardless of nationality and opportunity. But with Hitler, his ideas about race and the purity of blood stock already formed, it is at best unlikely.

There are several other drawbacks to the premise. Firstly, there was Hitler's character. He was hardly the sort of man for whom a 16-year-old girl – and an enemy 16-year-old girl at that – would have fallen. He was, his comrades testified, taciturn and distant. He was certainly not good looking in the accepted fashion of the time and was far more concerned about the future of Germany and its empire than he ever was with personal relations.

He did not smoke and rarely drank or swore. He was shy, particularly in the company of women, so it was hardly likely that he would respond to the advances of an intrigued and impressionable girl. And then, still at that time a practising Catholic, he believed in the value and importance of the sexual act – but inside marriage.

If events did unfold as Charlotte and Jean-Marie suggest, it is impossible not to wonder how Hitler managed to keep such a relationship secret from his fellow soldiers. In packed dugouts, in situations where tension and stress were high and confidences easily exchanged, it would have been almost impossible to keep such news from the curious attention of bored, frightened and gossip-seeking soldiers. The process of 'walking out' with someone was, by its nature, a public event. Even if he and Charlotte had not been seen together by his comrades, the village of Fournes was invariably full of German soldiers at rest or on leave. Somebody would have talked and the news would have got back to his unit where it would have been devoured as keenly than if the pair had been observed by his comrades when they were out on their supposedly regular evening walks.

As neither Hitler nor Charlotte spoke each other's language, one obvious problem is how they managed to communicate. Sex needs no verbal interchange but in Jean-Marie's story the sexual act came only at the end of a period of 'walking out' and some form of dialogue would surely have been required during that time.

As for Charlotte, the idea of moving in Hitler's wake from posting to posting like some twentieth-century camp follower is preposterous. In 1917 free movement in German-occupied France was severely limited, as it was throughout the war. Perhaps if Hitler had been a general it might have been possible but as a humble lance-corporal the idea falls at first base.

DNA testing and genetic certification from the University of Heidelberg in order to back up the claims of Jean-Marie have proved inconclusive:

> Jean-Marie had the same blood group as Hitler; he had the same handwriting and his features were similar to the dead dictator. All this was, however, circumstantial. It was later proved by geneticists that he could have been Hitler's son, but it was not proved that he actually was.[3]

The sister of Charlotte Lobjoie has agreed that she did walk out with a German soldier in 1917 and the result was an illegitimate child. But when shown a picture of the young Adolf Hitler, she did not recognize him and was adamant that this was not the man.

The matter was left in something of a limbo state. As with Stephanie Isak we know that there was definitely a girl by the name of Charlotte Lobjoie in Fournes-en-Weppe and that she gave birth to an illegitimate son. The connection with Adolf Hitler, however, remains open for discussion. Charlotte may well have met Hitler, possibly even walked out with him for a while but the story of the illegitimate son seems a little too pat, too precise to be taken at face value.

Like the Hitler Diaries which were 'discovered' in the 1980s and were eventually found to be forgeries, most historian and writers would dearly love the story of Hitler having an illegitimate son to be true. Unlike the Hitler Diaries, we will probably never know.

*

Hitler's two early loves – one of them certainly, possibly both – reflect the strange nature of the man or, rather, the man he was slowly becoming. He followed the pattern already set in childhood and in adolescence, as someone who was distant, reserved and self-contained. If he had been less interested in himself, less interested in the world as he wanted to make it, he may have spoken or made direct contact with Stephanie Isak. That would have been a momentous step for him and then the events of the twentieth century would have taken a very different turn.

If that had happened Charlotte Lobjoie, who may or may not have borne him an illegitimate child, was someone who would hardly have featured in his story. She was, at best, a fleeting character, a spear carrier rather than a main player, but still someone who might have fulfilled a need in a lonely and unfocused man. Did she and Hitler have a brief affair? The jury is still out on that but, after careful consideration, the general consensus would be probably not.

Christa Schroeder, one of Hitler's long-serving secretaries, met with Charlotte's son Jean-Marie Loret some years after the Second World War and wrote about the encounter in her memoirs. They were the recollections of an old woman but Christa Schroeder was as vibrant and alive in 1979 as she had been during her days with Hitler in the Berlin Bunker and her words ring true. Jean-Marie was hoping that Schroeder might help confirm his claim to be Hitler's son but the events in Picardy had taken place many years before her involvement in the Hitler story. The difficulties with language also hindered any real progress. Her comment on the meeting probably sums up the attitudes and thinking of many people: 'While out walking with him in the Blumenau, when he went ahead of me, I think I saw a similarity to Hitler in the gait and posture, but it is easy to deceive oneself in such things.'[4]

Hitler's days of idleness in Linz and his months in the trenches of Flanders and Picardy were as important for his education as a course of studies at university or college. When looked at dispassionately, the women he loved during that time, admittedly in his own, rather different and unusual way, were an integral part of his studies. Just like his mother and family before them the two women, peripherally or directly, played an important part in making the man.

It may sound disingenuous but, apart from the dictatorship, the mass killings and the crimes against humanity, what sort of man did Hitler become? That is not a rhetorical question but one that needs to be asked and answered if we are ever to understand the mind of Adolf Hitler. We know that as time went on, he grew increasingly psychotic and undoubtedly led Germany on a path to destruction. However, the events and cruelties that he initiated do little to reveal the inner man – and we need to know what sort of human being could possibly envisage and then put into place such instruments of evil as those seen in Nazi Germany.

All of his life Hitler was a dreamer, someone with a self-imposed mission that he saw as being light years beyond the capabilities of many other, ordinary men. The dreams and visions did not always fit easily together but his idyll of a Germanic utopia complete with pure Stephanie-like heroines persisted right to the end of his regime and his life. If anything, it was that idyllic dream, that vision of Stephanie on her horse, gown and hair flowing freely behind her as she rode across the inner eye that provided the fuel to the Nazi fire. Understand that vision, that ideal, and you are some way to understanding Hitler the man. The Nazi ideologues, the 'thinking men' of the Party rather than the thugs who manned the gates and the ovens of the concentration camps, saw the possibilities of Hitler's vision. They may not have been able to conjure such visions themselves but they were certainly able to pick up his dreams, pick them up and run with them.

Despite popular belief, Hitler's romantic inclinations did not stop with the traditional view of him as a platonic lover wedded only to Germany. He was someone with sexual desires and needs, just like any other man. The difference was that he had learned to control those needs so that Christa Schroeder's words might well have a degree of truth: 'He was erotic with the women by whom he surrounded himself but never sexual.'[5] If Hitler did have sexual relations with Charlotte Lobjoie in 1917 you do wonder if it was physically and emotionally fulfilling for him. If not, would it be pushing credibility too far to suggest that the encounter in the fields of Picardy might have nudged him into some of the bizarre behaviours that were later talked about in post-war Munich?

All of his life Hitler was a ditherer, a man lacking in decisiveness. That might seem strange for someone who is often described as 'the great gambler' but how else could he spend four years dreaming of Stephanie Isak and at the end of that period still do nothing. This lack of purpose is demonstrated time and again in his career. His inability to take decisive action during the Beer Hall Putsch, his unwillingness to order the execution of Ernst Röhm in 1934, holding back the panzers when the British Army lay at his mercy in Dunkirk – the list of indecisive action goes on and on. They are all moments when advice from others was simply ignored.

The enormous successes of his military campaigns and political manoeuvrings in the late 1930s and early 1940s, a period when fate seems to have dragged him along in its wake, has tended to hide the fact that, like many gamblers, Hitler would always prefer to do nothing rather than take an unequal chance. He needed space and time to think things through before he would take action.

The other side of his character was that he was also a user who would seize his opportunities as and when they came – as, perhaps, he did with Charlotte Lobjoie. Put the two together, the ditherer and the chancer, and you get a complex personality that was constantly pulling at itself and occasionally getting things very badly wrong.

When he got it right – the invasion of France and the Low Countries in 1940, for example – his winnings were spectacular; when he got it wrong, as in the snows of the Soviet Union in 1942/3, he very quickly, to use a gambler's analogy, was broken and went bust. It was the same with his personal life. The early infatuations and the resulting encounters set a pattern that says a lot more about Hitler's desires and plans for the future than almost any other action he might have taken.

With Stephanie his performance was that of the unsure man, not willing to risk rejection and suffering as a result – the ditherer personified. Stephanie was an ideal, an ideal that was as much a dream as reality. She was, at the time and in hindsight, a creature of the brain and the heart. Viewed now, from a distance, she does not seem to be a creation of flesh and blood at all.

Charlotte, well, Charlotte was not even a gamble. Whether she was real or symbolic, she was a sure thing and when her use was over she could be rejected or dropped as soon as Hitler wished. If she does fit somewhere into the picture – and that remains a very large 'if' – Charlotte Lobjoie was simply there to be used, to be taken as a representation of a conquered people. She was disposable.

One other point needs to be made about these early relationships. The youth of the girls is significant. Stephanie Isak was 17 when Hitler saw her for the first time, just one year older than him. Charlotte Lobjoie, if he did actually meet her, was only 16 and he, as a serving and experienced soldier, was 28.

Hitler's interest in young women that he felt he could influence and control undoubtedly set a precedent. He had older admirers, too, but these were women who could help him, financially and politically, in his rise to control in Germany. With young women Hitler could well be interested, physically and sexually. If not, as with Stephanie Isak, there was the delicious prospect of fantasy love and contact. Perhaps, in a way, Hitler enjoyed that even more. Sometimes the youth of his young women rejuvenated him, filled him with hope when times were desperate. At other times he just enjoyed looking at them. For all of that, it is hard to know if they should be blessed or cursed.

Chapter 4

Women of the World:
Society Ladies at Large

When the Armistice of November 1918 brought a stop to the fighting on the Western Front, Adolf Hitler was in hospital at Pasewalk. He had been gassed in one of the final Allied attacks of the war as the British, French and American forces steadied themselves for the final push into Germany. The gas itself did little damage but as with so many casualties, the side effects of the weapon were almost as deadly and Hitler was blinded just a week before the end of hostilities.

His gassing and subsequent blindness were minor injuries and would normally have needed just a few days' rest and regular bathing of his eyes to enable him to see again. And yet his blindness continued. His state of being unable to see what was in front of him and around him was as much an emotional problem as a physical one. It was effectively a mental breakdown. Hitler could not see simply because he did not want to see, did not want to admit to the reality of the situation in which he and the rest of the Germany now found themselves. He was devastated by the sudden collapse of the country and could find no rational reason for it.

Lying in his hospital bed, mind in turmoil, he eventually decided on the cause of Germany's defeat. It was the same answer that so many German soldiers came up with: Germany had not been defeated at all, her armies might be retreating but they were intact, no enemy soldier had set foot on home soil and the morale of the German soldiers was good. Not defeated then but stabbed in the back by the politicians and financiers at home. In particular, they had been betrayed, let down by the Jews and the Marxists.

The myth of the November Criminals – the men who had signed the Armistice with the Allied powers, forced the abdication of the Kaiser and set up the Weimar Republic – was born. For Hitler it was a lifeline.

He recovered his sight, remained in the army for a further two years and went back to Munich where, amongst other activities, he was charged with attending meetings and reporting on the activities of various fringe political groups.

The story of how Hitler stumbled across the German Workers' Party and realized its potential for a would-be right-wing politician like him is well known. He found a political mentor in Dietrich Eckart who helped him in his thinking – the creation of a right-wing programme of nationalism blended with the left-wing socialism that most workers demanded.

The socialist aspect of the Party was, as it turned out, a fallacy that was never more than a bald and neglected statement in the Nazi manifesto. The changing of the Party name from the German Workers' Party to the National Socialist German Workers' Party (NSDAP) was, like the manifesto, little more than a sop to the labouring classes of the country. All of that, however, was a matter that no one knew or even believed at the time.

Enthusiasm for a cause, Hitler soon discovered, was all very well but political parties could not survive on the good will of their members. The NSDAP needed patrons and Adolf Hitler, with his silver tongue and burning ambition, was just the man to find them.

One of his earliest patrons was Frau Hermione Hoffmann. The widow of a head teacher who had died in 1907, she was not as rich or as well connected as Hitler's later supporters but she was comfortably off and she provided invaluable help in the early days when the Party was fighting to survive in Munich. She had helped Hitler during the war, having been one of many women who offered comfort and assistance to the troops at the front. Her role was limited, consisting of knitting socks, of providing food parcels and, sometimes, giving people like Hitler, without parents or family, a roof over their heads when they were back in Germany on leave.

A friendship gradually developed between the shy corporal and the enthusiastic and tireless widow. That friendship became particularly strong when they realized that both of them supported the same end of the political spectrum. Even so, contact was fragmented due to the nature of war and the various postings of the List Regiment.

After Hitler's return to Munich, Frau Hoffmann was keen to renew the friendship, despite being thirty years older than him. She was obviously fascinated by Hitler but there was nothing sexual or erotic about her interest. She clearly cared about him and agreed with his ideas. Hitler, for his part, liked her and was grateful for the support she now gave to him.

Frau Hoffmann enrolled as an early member of the Party and later became Chair of the Nazi Women's League in Bavaria. On a more practical level she helped Hitler by giving him food and money, even providing clothes. Perhaps even more telling, she made her apartment in Solln outside Munich open to all Party members, not just Hitler. This was particularly useful while he was incarcerated in prison for leading the Beer Hall Putsch. It provided a focus, a physical base for men whose leader had been suddenly taken away, leaving them rootless and isolated.

Known throughout Munich as 'Hitler Mum' tales abounded of Hitler sitting on the floor at the feet of Hermione Hoffmann, head in her lap as she stroked his head. It was a pose or position that he was later to adopt with other supportive older women, each of them being perfect surrogate mother figures.

Affection between Hitler and Hermione was a two-way process. She obviously cared about him and to begin with he gave her affection and mother-love. However, Frau Hoffmann's direct involvement with Hitler gradually fell away as he was taken up by the richer Munich matrons and the need of her help decreased. Even so, her support for the Party and affection for Hitler never wavered.

As time went on and the Party grew, Hitler may not have needed so much direct support but he maintained contact with her, visiting whenever possible, even if that involved him travelling from Berlin to deliver birthday wishes. Despite being well over 70, Hermione Hoffmann remained an active member of the Nazi Party until the end. She co-founded the Solln group of the NSDAP and even managed to outlive Hitler by several months, dying in October 1945.

After Hitler's involvement began in 1920, the embryonic Nazi Party quickly found much of its support in the demobbed soldiers, men recently discharged or, as they would have it, cast aside from the armies of the now exiled Kaiser Wilhelm. But it soon became clear that, given the correct support and led in the right direction, the Nazi Party might just offer a way forward for the disaffected upper classes of Bavaria.

The Nazi's failed coup of November 1923, the Beer Hall Putsch as it was known, showed Hitler that the way to power did not lie simply with the gun and the jackboot. For Hitler and the Nazis, it was a lesson that was hard earned. Hitler had modelled his putsch on Benito Mussolini's earlier march on Rome', without realizing that the Italian dictator had never actually marched into the Italian capital but had stopped several miles short of the target. The success of Mussolini and his Blackshirts had depended more on other factors such as support of the Italian king, the Church and the bitterness of the common people than it ever did on the bullet and bayonet.

In contrast to the 'March on Rome', Hitler's Beer Hall Putsch was a total failure. Sitting in prison, analyzing and trying to rationalize the reasons for the failure, Hitler was able to see that he would now have to turn to a more universally acceptable route to power. What was required was a veneer of respectability so that the German people would voluntarily vote the Nazi Party into the Reichstag and, ultimately, into power. Thuggery could be reserved for the city streets and back alleys where the battle for supremacy between the communists and the Nazis would be continued. The real battle, however, would now lie in the ballot box and the various political forums.

In order to fight that fight the Party needed considerably more financing than it was currently receiving and it needed a high profile – not just any old profile but a politically correct high profile.

Hitler found these in the form of well-off members of Munich and Bavarian society, many of whom were women. Just as he had a liking for young girls, it seemed that older women – most of them well over 50 – found something very interesting and attractive in the young revolutionary. Hitler was happy to play on this aspect of his appeal.

Dietrich Eckart was largely responsible for introducing Hitler into society. Eckart, as a right-wing activist, often found it diplomatic to absent himself from the attention of the authorities. He had soon realized that one of the safest and most enjoyable places to keep himself out of the limelight for a brief period was fifty miles away from Munich on the Obersaltzberg. Eckart might have been a revolutionary and a political activist, but he was also a poet with a love of beauty and the natural world. He came to love the Obersaltzberg area and introduced Hitler to several of the householders on the mountain. One of these was Frau Helene Bechstein, wife of the famous piano maker. An anti-Semitic speaker on behalf of her family firm, Helene's public pronouncements of the Jews caused many musicians to boycott

Bechstein products. It made no difference to Helene; she continued airing her views as she saw fit.

Helene Bechstein and Hitler had first met in 1921 at a villa she owned at Berchtesgaden on the Obersaltzberg. Each of them had heard of the other's reputation and at Eckhart's prompting, Helene found that she rather liked the young Austrian rabble rouser.

As the months passed feelings went beyond liking; Helene became inordinately fond of Hitler and bestowed the nickname Wolfchen (Little Wolf) on him. She gave him gifts and donations of money for the Party, all of which Hitler eagerly accepted. Even his famous open-topped Mercedes – the car which met him at the gates of Landsberg Prison when he had served his time for the attempted Beer Hall Putsch – arrived curtesy of Helene Bechstein at a cost of RM 26,000.

That, however, was about as far as it went. Helene may well have wanted greater intimacy but to Hitler she was not a sexual object, simply a surrogate mother – just like Hermione Hoffmann. She did make the comment that she would have liked Hitler to be her son and secretly harboured desires that he would marry her daughter Liselotte Bechstein, Lottie as she was known. Lottie was not a pretty girl and as far as Hitler was concerned good looks in his younger women friends were very important. Helene's dreams of a union between her daughter and her protégé therefore came to nothing, although legend declares that Hitler did once propose to Lottie but was turned down. If this is true it was probably no more than Hitler trying to keep the Bechsteins sweet and the cash flow flowing. It is difficult to know quite how close Hitler and Lottie really were. He presented her with one of his water colour paintings, inscribed with his love and signed 'Your Wolf'. In itself that meant nothing but whether or not it signified something to Lottie is a rather different matter.

After Lottie's death her husband stated that she had told him she and Hitler had been sexually involved. Once again there is no proof but Hitler was more than capable of using his contacts in this way. If all that it took to keep the Bechstein support and cash flowing into Nazi coffers was a little matter of copulation then that was what he would provide. Like Charlotte Lobjoie before her, Lottie would have been cast aside when she was no longer useful.

Perhaps Helene Bechstein's greatest value to the Nazi Party came not in monetary gifts but in the society contacts she was able to put

Hitler's way. After the failed putsch of 1923 Hitler was arrested and incarcerated, briefly as it turned out, in Landsburg Prison. Helene Bechstein visited him there, even claiming that he was her adopted son in order to gain admission. Greater and longer contact with Hitler in his room at Landsberg Prison – technically a cell but far more palatial and well equipped than that – convinced Helene that this was indeed a great man but one who needed to be taken in hand and improved upon. Still very much an old soldier, a down and out, a country yokel or a street-corner activist, he needed the rough edges of his personality chiselled off. It was inevitable that on his release, after serving only a few months of a five-year sentence, Helene quickly introduced Hitler to Munich society.

One of the most important people he now met was Elsa Bruckmann. The wife of publisher Hugo Bruckmann, Elsa was the daughter of a Bavarian prince and, more importantly for the aspiring politician, she oversaw a regular salon where, each Friday, the cream of Munich society gathered to talk and discuss matters of the day. Writers like Rainer Maria Rilke along with leading architects, scientists and painters were regular attendees. Dietrich Eckart had already been accepted by this circle; now it was Hitler's turn.

Between them Bruckmann and Bechstein – Bruckmann in particular – moulded Adolf Hitler into someone who would grace the dining room of any middle-class home. The raw material was there but it was instantly obvious that there was much to be done and that Bruckmann would have her work cut out if she was going to make Hitler acceptable to the upper reaches of society:

> She groomed him for success, teaching him how to behave
> at the dinner table, how to eat individual dishes such as
> lobster, what clothes to wear for each occasion and even
> how to kiss a lady's hand.[1]

Elsa Bruckmann and Helene Bechstein were both drawn towards Hitler, not just by his personality and the raw power he exuded but by the policies he preached. They wanted to see Germany great again, taken out of the control of the Jewish and Marxist financiers who, as they saw it, were in control of the Weimar Republic – at the expense of traditional grandees like themselves. Hitler was their great hope for the future.

Bruckmann joined the Nazi Party in June 1932 but, on Hitler's orders, the date of her joining was backdated to 1 April 1925. Strangely, although she was awarded the Golden Party Badge in 1934 Helene Bechstein did not join the Party until 1944. That seems a very late date with the war as good as lost and Hitler's future uncertain, to say the least. From the beginning of their contact, however, she and her husband did fund the publication of the Nazi paper *Volkischer Beobachter*.

Both Bechstein and Bruckmann were anti-Semites whose support Hitler greatly valued. They were not alone. Soon a large portion of Munich society – rich men and women who believed that by pumping money into the Nazi Party they could achieve their dreams of renewed power – were gathering around Hitler like moths around a candle flame. The Nazis were a means to an end for these people. They had a clear agenda and felt they could control Hitler and his cronies, who were after all just a collection of ruffians and ex-soldiers. The elite of Bavaria were soon talking openly about the prospects for the future – prospects that Hitler would open up for them. Let him do the dirty work, while they would be content lurking in the background, pulling strings and waiting for the moment to rip the rug from underneath the feet of the little Bavarian corporal. Bruckmann, Bechstein and all of the others were to learn, at their cost, that they did certainly not control Adolf Hitler. On the contrary, he controlled them, happily playing them with his newly developed charm and exploiting their dreams of glory. When the time came, he would make his move and it would not require the grandees of Bavarian society to help him.

Two of his most important early supporters – two without any significant secret agendas – were Ernst 'Puzi' Hanfstaengl and his American-born wife Helena. Hailing from one of the most prominent and richest families in Bavaria, Puzi was educated at Harvard in the USA where he apparently wrote several valedictory songs for the college football team. He might have remained in America but was fond of his German heritage. As a consequence, he married Helena and returned to Germany in 1922. He first met Hitler at a political gathering in a beer hall just under a year later. He was immediately attracted by what Hitler had to say and by his powerful personality. He became a member of the Party.

Puzi later claimed that the Sieg Heil chant so beloved by the Nazis originated with him, something that might have been true given his familiarity with American football songs and chants. Either way he was a gifted pianist who could rouse Hitler to heights of passion or soothe his boiling spirit according to the tunes and songs he played for his Führer.

Hitler developed a brief but headstrong infatuation with Puzi's wife, Helena Hanfstaengl. He was a regular visitor to their house at Uffing just outside Munich, yet another home where he was able to rub shoulders with the elite of Bavarian society. Helene also performed a more practical duty for the battered revolutionary in November 1923. The Beer Hall Putsch was a Nazi attempt to seize power in Munich and then march on Berlin. Badly organized and naive, the Nazis were duped by Bavarian politicians and leaders like Gustav von Kahr, von Seisser of the police and General von Lossow.

Together, the triumvirate completely out-foxed Hitler. He trusted them and allowed the three men to leave the Beer Hall where he had established his headquarters. Unfortunately for Hitler, Kahr, Seisser and Lossow were as unscrupulous and two-faced as him.

Hitler became increasingly desperate and disillusioned as the rising progressed and the promised support from the police and army did not materialize. Knowing that things were going badly wrong, he decided to lead a last-ditch attempt to snatch victory by marching his SA troops through the streets of Munich. When they came up against a police cordon, shots were fired, twelve Nazis were killed and Hitler, who was dragged to the ground by the dead body of his colleague Max Scheubner-Richter, dislocated his shoulder. The march and the Putsch had ended in disaster. Putzi Hanfstaengl, who had been marching in the column, fled to Austria and Adolf Hitler fled to Puzi's house in Uffing.

Helena gave Hitler shelter, tended his injury and tried her best to console him after the disaster of the Putsch. When police arrived outside the house Hitler promptly brandished a pistol and declared that he would kill himself rather than be arrested. Helena managed to persuade him to put down the gun and the daring revolutionary went meekly into police custody.

During the pre-Putsch years and for some while afterwards Hitler also received guidance and help from Puzi's sister Erna. Both Helena and Erna were young, intelligent and emotionally and physically desirable. Simply the fact of their youth made them very different from Hitler's usual society patrons and that, in turn, enabled him to make contact with younger – but still influential – supporters. His infatuation with Helena could obviously lead nowhere and Hitler soon seems to have switched his attention to Erna. She was beautiful, charming and cultured and for many years there were rumours that she and Hitler had indulged in sex while he was hiding out in Puzi's house. They were just rumours, no proof positive having been uncovered. There were further whisperings that the pair had gone a stage further and were planning to be married. These were stories without foundation that had probably been put about by the Nazis. Munich's leading newspaper even published an article announcing the forthcoming wedding but it was all utter nonsense.

For her part Erna was embarrassed by Hitler's attentions rather than stimulated and did her best to keep him at arm's length. According to some sources she did not even like to be left alone with him in the same room. Her friends teased her about her would-be suitor and Erna was suitably chastised. Even so, she was concerned for Hitler, as a friend of her brother, and it is quite possible that Hitler mistook her courtesy for a romantic interest. Erna, coming from the Hanfstaengl family, was wealthy in her own right. She could, and probably did, help Hitler with the occasional handout but in reality, her support was in the area of connections rather than financial aid. Erna was, like most of Hitler's other patrons at this time, decidedly right wing in her beliefs and attitudes. Regardless of how she felt about him on a personal level, she actively helped her brother and Helena ease Hitler into Munich society and, in particular, assisted him in making useful contacts with young people of disposable wealth and position. The Hanfstaengl connection was a useful addition to the help Hitler received from his elderly matrons.

The Hanfstaengls could do little more. After the introductions had been made it was up to Hitler to make them a success or a failure. He had learned well and from the beginning, the vast majority of these introductions were a resounding success.

Erna, like Puzi, eventually fell out of favour with Hitler. In both cases the split was bizarre and complicated. Puzi's demise, in particular, had more than a touch of black comedy about it.

Puzi, who had been head of the foreign press bureau in Berlin and become something of the court jester in Hitler's entourage, quarrelled with the jealous Dr Goebbels. The little minister of information and propaganda undoubtedly saw the rich and cultured Bavarian as a rival for position in the Party and, more importantly, for Hitler's affection. Puzi described Goebbels as 'a satanically gifted dwarf' and eventually found himself with no recourse but to flee Germany.

In 1936, with the Spanish Civil War at its height, there had been a weird and confusing episode when it was apparently planned to drop Puzi by parachute over communist-held parts of Spain. It was something that may or may not have been an elaborate joke by Goebbels and other high-ranking Nazis. Whether it was a joke or a real attempt to kill him off, Puzi saw the writing on the wall, fled to Switzerland and, eventually, to America.

He and Helena were divorced that same year. By then Helena had done her work for Hitler and there had been no further contact between her and the Führer for some time. There appeared to be no regret from either party.

Erna was, at one stage, involved in a plot against the Führer but nothing came of what was a typically grandiose and complicated scheme involving the purchase of art galleries and shops in Paris. She had been friendly with Unity Mitford, the British heiress and Hitler devotee, but the two women fell out and Erna's star, which had continued to fly high, promptly self-destructed.

By far the longest lasting and most influential of all Hitler's early female patrons was Winifred Wagner. She was the daughter-in-law of Richard Wagner, the internationally famous composer whose booming and portentous operas had symbolized German life and history for many years. Hitler's love of Wagner and all that his music represented is well known. To him Wagner was Germany, Germany was Wagner.

Born to an English father and German mother, Winifred was orphaned at the age of three and spent her early years in a children's home in south London before being sent to live with a distant relative in Germany. She met and married Siegfried Wagner, son of the composer, more for the Germanic atmosphere of the family and their home in Bayreuth than for any particular feelings of love.

Siegfried was a homosexual and a man about whom all sorts of rumours regarding weird sexual propensities were rife. But, for the Wagners the marriage was a matter that stood above personal feelings and emotions – put simply, it was important that the name and the line continued:

> Relations with Fidi [Siegfried], twenty-eight years her senior, gradually declined into a marriage of convenience. Once the family bloodline had been secured, the spouses went their separate ways.[2]

Siegfried died in 1930. As the son of the great Richard, he had held an honoured place in German society. They may have lived different lives but between them Winifred and Siegfried worked hard to ensure that the annual Bayreuth Festival where Wagner's music was performed and celebrated became one of the foremost cultural events in Germany. After Siegfried's death Winifred continued to labour long and hard to see that the festival would continue.

The music brought huge feelings of patriotism to the German people and the audiences at Bayreuth thrilled to the display of German courage and history as depicted in Wagner's operas. Hitler was cannon fodder for such emotions, the music transporting him into a world of Teutonic legend where victory and defeat, death and noble sacrifice mingled magnificently with the dramatic deeds of the gods and superheroes of this mystical world:

> Listening to Wagner meant to him not a simple visit to the theatre, but the opportunity of being transported into that extraordinary state which Wagner's music produced in him, that trance, that escape into a mystical dream world.[3]

Despite her part-English parentage, Winifred Wagner was like so many of the more elderly patrons of Adolf Hitler, a devout German nationalist and a stalwart right-winger. In the best traditions of her father-in-law and the folk historians of the country she had become fascinated by the concept of 'blood and soil'.

To these historians, and to Winifred, a nation like Germany grew and developed out of the earth. People and the soil, they were the same and could never be separated, despite the attempts of the capitalist Jews to destroy the concept and the race. Industrialization was an irrelevance, what really mattered were the people of Germany and the soil that fuelled and fed them.

Winifred's husband, the direct link to Richard, felt the same. It was inevitable, therefore, that they became interested in the rise of the Nazi Party and, in particular, its young and enthusiastic leader.

Helene Bechstein arranged the first meeting between them all, a dinner party during the Bayreuth Festival of 1923. It was a successful meeting and, in the months and years to come Hitler was a regular visitor to the Wagner family home, the Villa Wahnfried. He even spent several Christmases there and was regarded by everyone in the family as a sort of benign uncle.

Winifred became a member of the Nazi Party in 1926 and was one of the few people in Germany to be allowed to address Hitler by the familiar *du*. Even old Party comrades like Göring and Himmler were not accorded such a privilege.

As a regular visitor to the Wagner home, Hitler came into close contact with Winifred's three children. They, like their mother, adored him and called him by the nickname 'Wolf' – another rarely bestowed honour.

Hitler felt so safe and secure at the Villa Wahnfried that on several occasions he even stayed there without his bodyguard, much to the concern of Himmler and his SS colleagues. Their protestations came to nothing. Hitler knew he had nothing to fear in the house of Winifred Wagner.

For many of those who watched from outside this cosy family circle it seemed that after Siegfried's death a marriage between Adolf Hitler and Winifred Wagner was very much on the cards. Such a union would have been hugely popular amongst the German people but it was not to be. Hitler may have been attracted to her while Winifred was unrepentant, right to the end, about her relationship with him. But marriage was out of the question. In his mind, Hitler needed to be seen as a man wedded to Germany and to the German people – at the expense of putting his own desires 'out of bounds,' at least for the time being. Even a union with someone from the Wagner circle, someone as wrapped up in German culture as Winifred, would have been impossible. That, of course, did not make his friendship with Winifred any less important to him or his love of Wagner's music any less significant. They were both an essential part of his being.

Hitler continued to frequent the Bayreuth Festival until 1940. After that running the German war machine took up more and more of his effort and energy. Despite repeated requests from Winifred he simply did not have the inclination or the time to drop everything and head for Bayreuth once a year. For her and for many stalwarts of the Nazi Party it was a great shame.

The Nazi Party and the Bayreuth Festival had, by the early years of the war, become synonymous. What it symbolized was as much a representation of the Third Reich as the enormous but featureless government buildings in Berlin or the vast crowds of worshipping thousands at Nuremberg: 'Under the Third Reich Bayreuth had become a temple of socialist art although the regime was not monolithic in this respect.'[4]

Despite increasing shortages and other problems such as finding quality musicians, Winfred Wagner continued to run the Bayreuth Festival throughout the war years until 1944.Then, with the Third Reich rapidly disintegrating around her, Winifred called a halt. The audience during those final years were not so much enthralled partisans or music aficionados as wounded German soldiers and airmen. It was war work of a sort but certainly nothing as vile as the persecution of the Jews, something that Winifred always declared that she deplored.

Knowing the importance of Wagner and his music to the members of the Nazi Party it was inevitable that once peace returned to Europe in 1945, Winifred Wagner's activities and motivations would be closely examined. Even to the uninformed outsider it was clear that Wagner's music was more than just a series of dramatic tunes – they were a part of the soul not just of the Nazi Party but of all Germany and the German people. As Winifred told the De-Nazification Tribunal to which she was summoned, all she had done, as far as she was concerned, was to simply run a music festival. Where was the fault in that? She had not urged mass killings or demonstrations; the music was her life.

Not only that, she told the tribunal, she had tried to protect and defend Jewish musicians during the danger years of the Third Reich. It did not take much imagination for the judges to see that such benevolence and care was more about her partiality for certain performers than it ever was about philanthropy or attempting to thwart an evil national policy. After receiving a fine and a suspended prison sentence Winifred Wagner was allowed to go free, provided she had no further connection with the Bayreuth Festival. The annual festival began once more in 1951 – again on the understanding that Winifred would have nothing to do with its organization or production. However, the Wagner family, her sons Wieland and Wolfgang in particular, took on the festival. They ensured that Winifred had no involvement in any aspect of the event ever again.

She died in 1980, unrepentant to the last and declaring that she would happily stand to greet the Führer if he should, at that moment, come into the room. As she said in a TV interview in 1975, 'To have met him is an experience I would not have missed.'[5]

Winifred had been hugely effective and important as a patron for Hitler. She gave him money and regular hospitality but her real benefit for the Nazi Party in general and for Adolf Hitler in particular went considerably deeper. Like the other older but influential supporters who were so crucial to his political career and the rise of the Nazi Party, she had an immense effect on how he presented himself in public. And yet, assisting with Hitler's social standing was only one of the many gifts Winifred Wagner was able to bestow on the young man who became something of a protégé to her.

Above all she had provided him with a veneer of respectability and gone some way to establishing him as a man of cultural intelligence. The memories of the violent street fights between the SA and the communists that had so marked the 1920s had not died easily and by this clear love of Germanic music and tradition Hitler was proving that he was a man of taste and artistic sensibilities. What everyone seemed to forget or ignore was that Hitler's love of Wagner went beyond the music. What that music symbolized for him was Aryan and Teutonic superiority, the concept of blood and soil that Winifred and Siegfried had identified many years before.

As a rallying cry for the Nazis and as a motivation for ordinary German men and women who might love their country but have little time for the Nazis, the music of Richard Wagner was felt in the immediate post-war years of the 1920s and in the troubled 1930s, to be hugely dangerous. It was a situation that was reflected again in the post-1945 era.

The strident chords and melodies were enough to raise the hairs on many a scalp; the themes of the operas harked back to the Teutonic legends that might conceivably lead to a renaissance of Germanic passion. And that, as far as the victorious Allies were concerned, was to be avoided at all costs.

During Hitler's rise to power the strength and significance of Wagner's music was an important factor in German nationalism. Germany had just lost the Great War, her people were angry and humiliated. They needed rejuvenation. Hitler instinctively understood and was able to use that hidden message as a rallying cry to his waiting millions.

Chapter 5

The Silver Screen: Renate Müller, Leni Riefenstahl and Others

A life-long lover of opera, Hitler was more than familiar with artistic life, albeit from a distance. He might never have trodden the boards but he certainly knew the value of a good performance when he saw one. He had witnessed so many good and bad depictions on the stage that he had an almost innate appreciation of what an audience wanted. He knew what made them happy and he knew what made them turn away in disgust – a more than useful understanding in the career of any embryonic political agitator.

In particular Hitler realized how the physical appearance of the people 'on stage' could influence any of those who stood and watched. He saw and appreciated how an audience thrilled at the warlike masculinity of Siegfried, how they cringed or quailed at the sight of the giant Fafner. Physical beauty, he realized, was crucial. It caught the eye of both the devotee and the occasional viewer. It was not by chance that Hugo Boss's SA and, in particular, SS uniforms were so startling and dramatic in their appearance. Regardless of anyone's political stance, the black-coated legions invariably caught the eye as they marched past, exactly as they were supposed to do.

On a more personal level, although he cared little about his own clothes and appearance, Hitler did have a liking for certain props that he could use to reflect his power and dynamism. Arguably his dog Blondi was one such prop, a symbol of German strength and loyalty, but his love of whips was perhaps the most noticeable of all his many affectations. He had a large collection of leather-thonged whips, mostly given to him by admirers, and in his early days he was rarely seen without one as he strode around the halls of the Chancellery or along the balconies of the Berghof. He would use the whip to emphasize his point, slapping the handle against his leg or brandishing it in the air. Only rarely did he crack it or hit out at objects.

A whip was theatrical, as powerful as a sergeant-major's pace stick: it reinforced his manhood and was an important part of the role he was playing. That was the crucial point – whether screaming on the podium, marching through the streets or engaging with friends and enemies in intimate conversation, Hitler was always playing a part.

He was happy in the company of performers – other performers, he might have said – particularly attractive female ones. He, of course, was an actor of some standing and undoubtedly saw himself as the leading man in the grandest and most significant drama of all time. The ability and opportunity to mix with others of similar talents was something he could not resist. One great appeal of mixing with actors and theatre people was that they were not usually political in any way. They were egotistical, as he was egotistical, but they had little inclination to discuss the great events of the day, things with which he was constantly dealing. Their latest performance, their costumes, the number of lines they had been given – these were their concerns, as they were Hitler's when he switched off his political antennae.

By nature inherently slothful, Hitler was a gossip. He loved nothing better than sitting idly with a group of women such as his secretaries, eating cream cakes and enjoying the latest tittle tattle. As he quickly discovered, female actors, especially beautiful ones, were the biggest gossips of all. They loved putting in the knife to everyone and anyone – just like Hitler.

In his early days as a rising politician in Munich, Hitler's chauffeur Emile Maurice was often dispatched to find beautiful women, preferably actresses, who would then spend the evening with the Führer. They would watch a film – most evenings Hitler could be found in front of the silver screen watching two or even three movies – and then talk until the early hours. Maurice was clear that sometimes Hitler and whichever lady with him at the conclusion of the evening would engage in sex. The sexual act, he said, was an end in itself. Hitler wanted no lasting relationship, just the release of pent-up feelings and emotions. Maurice told the secretary Christa Schroeder that he would be sent off to drive around whichever town they were in and gather girls while Hitler was working. They would be ready for the Führer when business was finished.

In most cases neither Hitler nor Emile Maurice ever recorded the names of these women. If the motive was sex nobody, apart from Maurice, has ever said so outright. Schroeder is clear that Hitler used eroticism rather than sex but she, like so many other witnesses, was partial in her views and loyal to her chief right to the end.[1] We have, therefore, no corroborating evidence, only Maurice's memories and statements. There is nothing to prove that he was or was not telling the truth.

It is entirely possible that the word 'actress' was simply a euphemism for women of the streets. Hitler had known – and possibly used – such professionals in Vienna and Munich and for the previous hundred or so years the term 'actress' had been taken to mean someone of low moral standing. His penchant for genuine or would-be actresses, however, has been well recorded.

Walter Langer in his book *The Mind of Adolf Hitler* had no doubt about Hitler's motives and commented on the long list of screen and stage stars that he encountered. The process was proactive – he would simply send a note or dispatch an adjutant to the film studios and before the hour was out, he would be entertaining two, three, maybe half a dozen eager young actresses. He would, according to Langer, offer to put in a good word about them to the studio chiefs and promise them better roles in the future. In general, he was always able to impress the women with his power and charm: 'On the whole he seems to feel more comfortable in the company of stage people than with any other group and often went down to the studio restaurants for lunch.'[2]

It was inevitable that people began to talk about Hitler's trysts. Their very nature – secretive, sordid, occasional – lent itself to gossip. Sometimes his meetings with starlets were real enough, they had actually taken place; at other times they were just extensions of people's imaginations, encounters that they wanted to believe had actually occurred.

Pola Negri was one such example. The Polish actress had starred in the 1936 version of *Mazurka*, one of Hitler's favourite films and Negri, with her stunning looks and temptress eyes had an immediate appeal for Hitler. She was one of the first European stars to hit the big time in Hollywood where she became something of a vamp, both on and off the screen, having engaged in scandalous affairs with Charlie Chaplin, Rudolf Valentino and many others. Negri had worked in Germany before Hollywood claimed her but when she came back to Berlin in 1937 to make films for the German-based UFA studios, she found herself feted and honoured wherever she went. Treated like royalty, her every wish was granted and it did not take Negri long to realize that she was under the 'special protection' of her admirer Adolf Hitler. The rumour machine was soon in full operation, an article about an affair between the two even appearing in the French magazine *Pour Vous*. Unfortunately, the magazine had got it very wrong. Pola Negri and Hitler had never even met. She promptly sued *Pour Vous* and won her case. Hitler simply shrugged – it was, for him, almost an occupational hazard.

Another entertainer rumoured to be close to the Führer was the Swedish singer and actress Zarah Leander. The highest-paid actress in Germany during the 1930s, she was a particular favourite of Propaganda Minister Joseph Goebbels. A rather naive young woman more interested in being a star, with all of the benefits that such a position brought, than in the political ramifications of her film making and connections, Zarah became the voice of the Third Reich. Whether or not she knew just how effective her act had become, she cannot have been blind to the fact that she had acquired immense popularity amongst the German people who flocked to see her films or to listen to her in person. Zarah Leander, despite being Swedish, truly was synonymous with the power and the glory of the Third Reich. To the people of Germany and many film buffs in the West she was Hitler's mouthpiece or, as she has been called, 'the great diversion'.[3]

Taking people's minds off the horrors of the war that was raging or about to rage was as much state-induced indoctrination as any of Dr Goebbels's propaganda films. Zarah could not or would not see it but it was inevitable that many believed her to be having an affair with Hitler. In fact, Leander met Hitler only twice during all the years she was making films for UFA. Her account of one of those meetings, a première of her 1937 film *Song of the Desert*, gives an interesting view of the Führer who, in Zarah's view at least, appeared to have a human face. She was a confident girl and despite warning looks from his entourage, she teased Hitler about his signature lock of hair, the way it fell over his forehead. After an initial momentary stab of anger, she was, surprisingly, treated to a normal, low-key response from Hitler:

> He describes in detail his struggle with the errant quiff. 'You have no idea all the things I've tried – oil, hair cream, wax and all sorts of strange concoctions. But nothing helps. The hair keeps falling over my forehead. It's simply hopeless.'[4]

On one level the encounter was nothing more than a piece of idle chitchat; on another it shows Hitler's approachability, at least with beautiful young actresses. If he could somehow have allowed himself to let down his guard and permit a relationship to develop then he and the world would undoubtedly have been much happier. But he could not do it; that was his tragedy.

He could, however, laugh at the antics of the film stars and their performances. Traudl Junge once commented on how Hitler played with Blondi, his German Alsatian, and got her to perform tricks. In particular the dog would sing with him:

> Sometimes her voice rose too high, and then Hitler said, 'Sing lower Blondi, sing like Zarah Leander.' Then she gave a long low howl like the wolf that was certainly among her ancestors.[5]

Zarah Leander was a woman who had the power and the opportunities but not the inclination to help the thousands oppressed by Hitler and the regime. So many of her songs could be interpreted, in particular, as anthems for homosexuality but it was her lyricists who were making a statement, not Leander. It would not have taken much of a leap for her to use her popularity with Hitler and influence his decisions. It was a leap she chose not to take.

Hitler and Goebbels had quickly realized the power of film as a tool. Only very few German citizens had either the money or the opportunity to attend the theatre but the cinema was open to everyone. Admission was relatively cheap; all towns of any size could boast a movie house and an evening watching the latest release was a guaranteed way of forgetting the world for a few hours.

In the 1920s and 1930s cinema was still a new medium but by the time talkies arrived in the late 1920s, the two propaganda experts had realized that movies, not religion or literature, were now the opiate of the masses. They actively encouraged the German people to go along to the cinema whenever they could. It did not matter if they were viewing an outright propaganda film or something more esoteric, attendance and subliminal indoctrination were the key things.

Hitler set the example for his people, watching movies every night. Even though he spoke only German he enjoyed films from countries like the US, Britain and France. *Mickey Mouse* cartoons were a particular favourite. One of his staff would have to provide him with a synopsis before each film – the great mass of German people did not have such luxuries but that did not stop them flocking to the cinemas in droves. What they saw, however, was heavily censored and nothing that was even remotely critical of the Third Reich or of Hitler would ever be shown.

From the moment Hitler came to power in 1933 the Reich Chamber of Film, under the direction and guidance of Dr Goebbels, began to actively purge the German film industry of all 'undesirable' elements. These elements included Jews, communists and anyone who did not adhere to Nazi philosophy and ideals. It meant that there was soon an enormous exodus of creative artists from Germany. Whether this was a matter of expulsion or of people seeing the writing on the wall and taking the decision to jump before they were pushed, matters little. The policy meant that Germany was denuded of some of the most expressive and talented artists of their generation. The exodus included writers like Herman Hesse and Berthold Brecht, composers such as Kurt Weill and, in particular, a huge swathe of men and women who had previously been employed in the German film industry that included directors such as Fritz Lang, screenwriters like Billy Wilder and hugely popular actors like Peter Lorre and Conrad Veidt.

Two of the most spectacular female stars to decamp for the US and Britain were the Austrian Hedy Lamarr and Germany's favourite screen star Marlene Dietrich. Both of them went on to enjoy lucrative and fulfilling careers in Hollywood. Dietrich, in particular, soon became a vitriolic critic of what was going on in her homeland. As she said, she had not turned her back on the country of her birth but only on what it had become under Adolf Hitler and the Nazis. Goebbels and Hitler would have dearly loved to lure her back to Germany but it was a hopeless task. She was, to the Third Reich, totally unattainable.

Hitler's sexual or erotic conquests within the acting fraternity were, mainly, amongst the rank and file of the profession. There were the occasional stars whose fame and success were already assured but mostly they were women who were on the first rung of the ladder. While not viewing Hitler's bed as a 'casting couch' they probably all hoped for some preferment because of their involvement, short as it might be, with the Führer.

He was particularly attracted to actresses like Olga Tschechowa and Brigitte Horney, relatively big names in the German film and theatre world of the Weimar Republic years. He would often, through intermediaries like Maurice, invite them to come with him to the theatre. Contact probably ended there but with lesser-known actresses what went on in the post-event hours was often the highlight of the evening.

One person who did not quite fit this bill was the beautiful Renate Müller. Already a successful German actress, she was Nordic, slim and blonde. She was, in fact, exactly the type of woman for whom Goebbels was searching to star in his burgeoning series of films to promote the Third Reich.

In the autumn of 1932 while she was filming near the Dutch coast, Goebbels introduced Renate Müller to Hitler and for the next few years the pair became something of an item. Their relationship was not exclusive but they were certainly close. The meeting was, perhaps, in keeping with the bizarre nature of Hitler's personality. According to Müller herself and to Adolf Zeissler, who was directing the film, it was a strange meeting. Zeissler later wrote a magazine article on Hitler and his star, commenting that even at that early stage the behaviour of the Nazi leader was decidedly odd.

According to Zeissler, who was busy on the set when the meeting took place, he was told about this episode by Müller and reproduced her words in his article. Hitler had been given a chair at the outer edge of the film set and the young starlet was led across to meet him:

> He sat there, not moving at all, looking at me all the time and then he'd take my hand in his and look some more. He talked all the time – just nonsense.[6]

The picture Müller and Zeissler paint is that of an excited, even besotted, devotee who has difficulty controlling his emotions, even at the most basic level. The phrase 'star struck' would not be out of place, hence the babbling that so concerned Renate. The full intensity of the relationship is not known but by Müller's own testimony we know that Hitler gave her presents, including an expensive diamond bracelet that was worth considerably more than anything he gave to either Geli Raubal or Eva Braun. Again, the impetuosity and intensity of sudden infatuation appear to rear their heads.

There are two ways of looking at what came next. The simple version is that Müller appeared in the film *Togger* which was blatantly and unashamedly anti-Semitic. Always a nervous character she had recently become addicted to heroin which may or may not have been supplied to her by Hitler's physician Dr Morell. As a result of her addiction and in a reaction against the anti-Semitic violence of *Togger*. Renate Müller had a nervous breakdown and was admitted to a sanatorium. A short while later she died after throwing herself from a third-floor window of the sanatorium building. That was the version which Hitler and Goebbels wanted the world to believe.

The other view of events is more complex, far darker and involves Adolf Hitler in considerably more detail. A number of times Müller had been to the Chancellery as a personal guest of Hitler. On these occasions he openly boasted and went into great detail about Gestapo tortures. They were mediaeval in nature, he assured her, and were highly effective. The conversations left her uneasy but she continued to see Hitler on a regular basis. One particular evening matters took a rather different turn, so much so that the next day Müller relayed the story to Zeissler who was again directing her current film. He was concerned about her dishevelled and distraught appearance on the set, had called a halt to shooting and had asked her what the trouble was. Müller replied by stating that the previous evening she had been in Hitler's rooms. From the way things were developing she believed that they were about to go to bed together and so both of them undressed. Then it all began to go wrong:

> Hitler fell on the floor and begged her to kick him. She demurred but he pleaded with her and condemned himself as unworthy, heaped all kinds of accusations on his own head, and just grovelled in an agonizing manner. The scene became intolerable to her, and she finally acceded to his wishes and kicked him.[7]

He then demanded that she beat him with his whip and hurl obscene words at him. Not knowing what else to do she obliged and at this Hitler became very sexually excited. He began to masturbate. After he had achieved orgasm, he and Müller put on their clothes, had a glass of wine and he thanked her, very civilly and very pleasantly, for an enjoyable evening.

The events had clearly left Renate Müller hugely upset and, if true, would gel with the stories of Hitler as a sexual pervert of the sadomasochistic kind. True or not, after that evening the relationship between her and Hitler certainly seemed to cool.

The story does not end there. Within a relatively short time, Renate Müller applied for permission to visit London, an appeal that Hitler rubber-stamped. Even so she was supposedly watched by the Gestapo during her time abroad although how viable this would have been remains imponderable.

During her visit Müller spent time with her former boyfriend Frank Deutsch, a Jewish actor who, because of Nazi persecution, had left Germany and was encamped now in England. On her return to Germany, Müller found that she had been blacklisted from her profession, allegedly because of her contact with Deutsch but more probably driven by Hitler's concerns about what she might say regarding their infamous night together.

The word on the street was that she was about to be arrested for 'race defamation' In 1930s Germany that was a serious charge, one that would inevitably lead to a period of incarceration in a concentration camp. It might even have led to execution. Faced with a potential criminal charge and a career that was now in ruins, Müller resorted to heroin. It was not long before she was addicted but, as often happens with addicts, she became increasingly depressed and was eventually admitted to a sanatorium for treatment. In desperation Müller appealed to Hitler. He refused to see her. Whether or not her fears were real or imagined, Müller believed that the Gestapo were keeping a close watch on her and when a car containing four black-coated agents drew up in front of the sanatorium, she panicked, threw herself from the window and was killed. It was 1 October 1937.

Suicide or murder by the Gestapo in order to get her out of the way, Müller's death was certainly very timely and convenient for Adolf Hitler. He had become increasingly conscious of public opinion and the workings of the dreaded rumour mill, having fallen victim to many bogus and partly true accusations over the previous few years. And yet, despite everything, rumours about the evening of sexual depravity soon got about. They were backed up by comments from people like Puzi Hanfstaengl and Hitler's old Party comrade Otto Strasser who had narrowly avoided arrest and shooting during the Night of the

Long Knives. Both claimed that Hitler, when attracted to a woman, tended to grovel at her feet:

> He insists on telling the girl that he is unworthy to kiss her hand or to sit near her and that he hopes she will be kind to him ... From this we see the constant struggle against complete degradation whenever affectionate components enter the picture.[8]

Hanfstaengl and Strasser, previously firm supporters of Hitler, had both fallen out of favour with the Führer and sought refuge in the US. Strasser was luckier than his brother Gregor who died in Hitler's 1934 purge, the Night of the Long Knives as it is known, despite the fact that it lasted for several days, even weeks. The purge was a ruthless culling of opponents and potential opponents, eliminating people like Ernst Röhm, his old adversary Gustav von Kahr and previous Chancellor of Germany Kurt von Schleicher.

Hitler's success on the political stage in the years leading up to the Second World War meant that his popularity in Germany soared to unbelievable heights. Stories about the more dubious side of his character went underground for a while. Only when the OSS commissioned Langer to compile his study did tales like Renate Müller's night of anguish resurface.

Both Hanfstaengl and Otto Strasser willingly contributed to Langer's *The Mind of Adolf Hitler*, the OSS study of Hitler's personality, and were highly critical of the man and the regime he had created. Living as they did in the US such a response from both men was not unexpected. The two ex-Nazis were right to be critical but in light of their dismissal by Hitler and the whole purpose of the study, the veracity of their statements has to be questioned. On the other hand, Renate Müller's account, as told to Zeissler just hours after the event, smacks of reality.

*

The filmmaker Leni Riefenstahl was, for many years, a close friend and intimate contact of Adolf Hitler. Originally a dancer and actress, this beautiful and striking woman quickly realized that her future within the artistic profession was better served behind the camera than in front of it. She directed and filmed several highly successful documentary films, focusing on the mountain scenery that she loved. Even her narrative or story films tended to focus more on the glaciers and mountains than on the words and actions of the actors. Script was decidedly secondary to location or environment.

The photography was undoubtedly stunning but it was also relentless, coming perilously close to cliché. It was exactly what the leaders of the Nazi Party wanted to see and project to the world and it was inevitable that Leni Riefenstahl would come to the notice of Joseph Goebbels and Adolf Hitler.

In a relatively short period of time Riefenstahl fell under Hitler's spell, admitting that his words had a hypnotic effect on her. Leni met him for only the second time in 1935 when she willingly admitted to him that she was astounded by all he had achieved during the two years he had been in power. She flattered him, flirted with him and fawned on him.

Hitler, for his part, accepted it as his due. He was keen to make use of her talents and immediately set her to work making films that would astound the world and establish the Nazi Party as an all-powerful accessory to his will. *Triumph of the Will*, her film of the 1934 Nuremberg Rally, glamourized the Nazi Party, portrayed it as it had never been shown before. Riefenstahl's artfully manufactured distance shots, combined with sudden and dramatic closeups of fanatical faces, managed to turn Adolf Hitler into something of a god-like figure. Hitler was eternally grateful to her and she went on to make several other 'tribute' films, notably her masterpiece *Olympia*, her version of the 1936 Berlin Olympics. Viewed in hindsight the films are, perhaps, overblown and without a central coercive aim or plan. But at the time they were considered to be magnificent depictions that caught a rapturous and dynamic people at the beginning of a march back to glory.

It was inevitable that the press would seek to join Riefenstahl and Hitler together, posing them in a romantic union. Leni was quite capable of playing up to such beliefs – after all, they pushed her career as well as that of her beloved Führer into the limelight.

By her own admission Leni Riefenstahl was desperate for an intimate relationship with the Chief, as she and many others called him. However, for whatever reason, it was Hitler who refused to take matters further. It was a strange decision on Hitler's part. Leni had all the credentials necessary to attract the Führer – she was young and beautiful, clearly fascinated by him and, above all, eminently available. She was regularly in his presence in Berlin and at the Berghof, often stealing the show from the other 'groupies' because of her extravert and outlandish ways.

The only possible reasons for Hitler's avoidance of an affair were his relationship with Eva Braun and the fact that Leni Riefenstahl was an exceptionally talented and clever woman. By 1934 Eva was well established as Hitler's mistress, although few people outside Hitler's intimate circle knew anything about her. She was jealous of exotic creatures like Leni and was quite capable of creating a scene if she thought things were getting a little beyond propriety. Eva had a wide range of techniques to fall back on; she had used them before, very effectively. They ranged from suicide attempts to sulking, and if they failed then the gentlemen of the press were always available, should they be needed. Leni Riefenstahl was a public figure and, as Hitler had already learned, too much exposure over matters like this was undesirable.

Hitler's dislike of clever women has already been noted and Leni could well have frightened him off by her knowledge and her ability as one of the premier filmmakers in the country. She had succeeded with a career in the arts – he had signally failed to do the same. As far as he was concerned, his success as a politician did not begin to equal her many artistic achievements.

A strikingly attractive woman, there was something of the Nordic goddess in Leni's appearance and images of the distant, idealized Stephanie Isak might also have interfered with any physical needs Hitler may have harboured. Whatever the reason, Leni's relationship with Hitler was, as someone once remarked, that of a bride without sex. Leni Riefenstahl continued making her films during the Second World War. Despite what she later claimed, they were clearly propaganda pieces, albeit more subtle than many of Goebbels's more flagrant anti-Semitic outbursts.

She was not above using Polish prisoners as extras in her film *Tiefland*, knowing exactly what their fate would be when their usefulness expired. To her the creation of a piece of filmic art was what mattered most; the deep-rooted passions and prejudices that it dredged up were, perhaps, of little consequence.

After the war Leni was hauled in front of a De-Nazification Tribunal. Given her career and the help it had provided for the Nazi Party, some form of judgement was inevitable. She claimed to know about concentration camps like Dachau but nothing whatsoever about the death factories such as Auschwitz and Treblinka. She was duly labelled as a 'fellow traveller' – someone who had collaborated with the

Nazi Party: 'Frau Riefenstahl furthered the Nazi tyranny in ways other than working in the Party or its organs … she emerged as a beneficiary of that tyranny.'[9]

She was incarcerated for some months and charges of war crimes against her were made by the West German government which in the late 1940s was running its own campaign against Nazi criminals and perpetrators of race hatred. They came to nothing.

After 1945 Leni Riefenstahl made no more films but pursued an active programme of legal action against anyone who accused her of holding or adhering to the right-wing beliefs of the Nazi Party. She lived to see in her 100th birthday and died, unrepentant and proud of her achievements.

The relationship between Riefenstahl and Adolf Hitler remains something of a mystery. At first sight she would have seemed the ideal partner for the dictator and there is no doubt that her superbly shot films helped establish the popularity of both Hitler and his murderous regime.

To many in Germany a marriage between Hitler and Leni would have been as appropriate a match for the Führer as one with Winifred Wagner. They might have been at different ends of the artistic spectrum – Leni would have disagreed with that – but to the German people the dramatic cadences of any Wagner opera and the soaring images of Germany's hills and mountains as shown in the Riefenstahl films were on the same emotional level.

It was, many felt, his duty to take someone – Winifred Wagner or Leni Riefenstahl, it did not matter which – to the marriage bed; others disagreed – his duty was to stay married to Germany. It remains an intriguing prospect, Leni and Hitler, one of the great 'what ifs' of modern history. Of course, it never happened. Like so much of Hitler's life the failure to exploit this potentially eye-catching partnership remains a mysterious failure. It is, ultimately, part of the Hitler mystique, one that he – and certainly not Leni Riefenstahl – could ever really explain.

Even so, the tiny glimpses that we are given by Leni and others make the whole relationship tantalizingly and frustratingly fascinating. According to Leni, on one occasion when they were alone together, walking in the country, Hitler embraced her and then stopped himself. For her it was like a slap in the face. Hitler was stoic, trying to control his emotions. He was, he told her, married to the state – the classic excuse – but as far as a public figure like Leni Riefenstahl was concerned it was probably a true enough statement. True or false, it was all she was ever going to get.

Chapter 6

Young Love: Mitzi and Henny

Apart from his numerous one-night stands – consummated or not – there were always romantic and rather more consistent figures in Hitler's life. These ranged from actresses like Renate Müller to the patient and ever-present Eva Braun. But in particular there were two early passions that, for a while at least, seemed to consume him – Mitzi Reiter and Henny Hoffmann.

Adolf Hitler returned from the Great War heartbroken, adrift and rootless. The formation of the NSDAP gave him a focus, the help of his elderly patrons provided security. But he needed more. He needed young women who would give him emotional and physical relief either as Christa Schroeder believed as an erotic stimulation or, as far as Emile Maurice and many others were concerned, at a far more basic sexual level.

Maria 'Mitzi' or 'Mimi' Reiter was born in December 1911. The daughter of an official in the Berchtesgaden Social Democratic Party she was forced, by the death of her mother, to leave school at the age of 16 and help out in the family drapery business in Obersaltzberg. It was there in 1925 that she met Adolf Hitler.

Mitzi told her story to *Stern* magazine in 1959 when, according to her, it was dogs that brought them together. Early one morning Hitler was standing outside her shop dressed in typical Bavarian style – breeches, grey stockings, the inevitable whip in his hand – and with his Alsatian dog at his side. Mitzi and her sister already knew that this was the infamous Adolf Hitler, a man who had been in prison for trying to overthrow the Bavarian government, and they were fascinated by the whiff of rebellion he represented.

Hitler, vain enough to adopt a 'pose' as he stood outside the shop, noticed the interest of the two pretty girls and introduced himself. Mitzi complemented Hitler on the beauty of his dog; they began to talk and it was clear that he was just as captivated by her. She was 16, he was 37. When Hitler suggested she might like to walk his dog with him, Mitzi agreed. She could take her sister's animal, she declared, and that would mean there would be two dogs. And so, the friendship began. They went on several walks on the hills around the area and, eventually, he asked her if she would like to come to dinner. Mitzi, already half in love with this famous and deliciously dangerous man, happily agreed. At the end of the meal they kissed and he apparently made some sort of sexual advance to her. She never went into details about what she called the 'coarse' advance which she rejected out of hand but it was clear to Hitler – Wolf as he insisted she call him – this was not the loose sort of girl he had previously met in the Vienna or Munich slums. If he wanted more out of the relationship than mere kissing, she would have to be very carefully handled.

One evening as they walked out with their dogs the two animals suddenly flew at each other. Hitler took his whip and beat his dog unmercifully – this wonderful dog that he always said he could not live without. Mitzi was shocked, appalled at what she saw as outright cruelty, and protested.

'Why did you do it?' she asked.

Hitler's response was simple: 'It was necessary.'

That could have been the end of the friendship but it was not. Hitler continued to see Mitzi. On one occasion she even accompanied him on a visit to Munich but it was a chaste relationship that did not go beyond kissing. Hitler gradually became more and more interested in the young woman, declaring his love on several occasions. It was an emotion that she fully reciprocated. According to Mitzi, he was seriously attracted to her:

> He said he wanted to marry her and produce 'lots of blond children together', but at that moment he was too tied up with politics to commit himself. He explained that he had an important mission to accomplish first and perhaps she could wait for him.[1]

She did wait – for days, weeks and months. He went back to Munich and the months turned, slowly, into a year. Sometimes it seemed to Mitzi that the waiting would never end. To begin with he wrote her love letters and even sent her two leather-bound copies of *Mein Kampf* with the request that she should read them and so understand him better. She tried but like most people found it hard to get past the first few paragraphs and pages. Then – nothing. Hitler, it seemed to Mitzi, had forgotten her.

Maybe – but not quite. There is a possibility that Hitler was being blackmailed over Mitzi. She was, after all, a minor and although there appears to have been no sexual contact between them, Hitler was still technically committing an offence. He was a perfect target for any informed blackmailer.

And now the dark and dangerous name of Emile Maurice surfaces once again. One of Maurice's former girlfriends, a woman by the name of Ida Arnold, was considered the most logical suspect for the blackmail attempt. The evidence, such as it was, might have been circumstantial but word within Nazi circles was that Ida was indeed the culprit. Having been tipped off by Maurice, she had taken Mitzi out for coffee and 'pumped her' for information just before the first blackmail letter arrived.[2]

Hitler was certainly frightened enough, in the summer of 1928, to visit Mitzi and persuade her to sign a formal statement saying that there was no relationship between them – and never had been. He took the statement to the police and the blackmail threat simply died away. Emile Maurice, having presumably warned off Ida Arnold, continued to serve in the SS and retain Hitler's favour.

With the statement signed and delivered, Mitzi was, to begin with, comfortable with the outcome. If nothing else, it had meant that she had seen her beloved Hitler. And then, once again, the only message from Munich was a reverberating emptiness that left Mitzi staring into a pit of silence once more. For weeks on end she received no contact from Hitler, nothing whatsoever.

In despair she took a length of clothes line, wrapped one end around the door handle and the other around her neck. Then, in her words, she glided to the floor and lost consciousness. Her brother-in-law arrived in the room a few moments later, untied her and saved her life.

Despite what seems to have been abandonment on his part, Hitler certainly felt deeply about Mitzi Reiter. She had, he once told her, eyes like his mother but his duty was to Germany and the Party and nothing must be allowed to get in the way of his mission.

Mitzi eventually gave in to the inevitable. She realized Hitler was beyond her reach, turned her attention elsewhere and within a few

Above: Hitler and Eva Braun pose for a photograph together at the Berghof.

Right: Klara Hitler, mother of the future dictator, taken not long after her marriage.

Above: Angela Hitler, Adolf's half-sister, in old age.

Left: Geli Raubal, Hitler's niece and, arguably, the love of his life.

Hitler and his comrades during the First World War. Hitler sits on the extreme right of the middle row. The dog, a stray picked up in the trenches, was Hitler's only true friend at this time.

The Berghof Set, men and women keeping strict distance from each other.

Above: Hitler
sleeping, Geli Raubal
gazing in admiration.

Left: Stefanie
Isak, a rather
faded photograph
from the early
twentieth century:
she never faded in
Hitler's dreams.

Hitler had always had a liking for young girls. This shows him, a man in his thirties, with Mitzi Reiter, one of his early infatuations, a girl only just into her teenage years.

Elegant and refined, Winifred Wagner, the heart and soul of Germany.

Hitler's' sister Paula, a formal studio portrait.

Adolf Hitler and Unity Mitford, an unlikely but lasting pairing.

Unity Mitford fawns in the presence of an SS guard.

Hitler and Eva Braun at dinner, an unusual photograph – Eva was normally kept at a distance during public gatherings like mealtimes.

Two views of Eva Braun in relaxed mood.

Hitler's favourite pilot, Hanna Reitsch, seen here in the cockpit of a glider

A group photograph, Henny and Heinrich Hoffman Junior seen here with Eva Braun

Hitler's adoring public.

Women from the League of German Girls preparing to work the land.

The first lady of the Reich, the elegant Magda Goebbels.

Above: German girls prepare for a gymnastic performance.

Left: Mitzi Reiter when Hitler met her again in the 1930s.

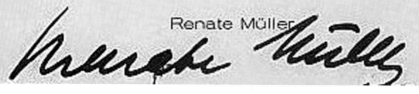

The glamorous actress Renata Müller – before Hitler made her acquaintance.

Above: Dance, like gymnastics, was considered an ideal way to keep fit and healthy – for the good of the Reich, of course.

Left: An advertising poster for Leni Riefenstahl's *Triumph of the Will*.

years she had married a local innkeeper from the Obersaltzberg area. She always retained a flame for Adolf Hitler and the marriage was not a success; she left her husband in 1931. Within a few weeks Hitler's deputy and errand boy Rudolf Hess appeared at Mitzi's door. Hitler, he told her, was still interested in her and hoped that she felt the same. Mitzi immediately left for Munich. That night she and Hitler slept together for the first time. She was older now, more experienced in the ways of the world than she had been when his advances had so appalled her back on the Obersaltzberg. Her words, brief but succinct, sum up the moment: 'I let everything happen. I had never been so happy as I was that night.'[3]

Mitzi's joy was not to last. He wanted her to remain with him as his lover. She wanted marriage. Hitler, however, was unsure. A marriage with a woman who had just left her husband, he said, might be damaging for the credibility of the Party. And so, once more, they agreed to separate. It was an amicable parting and Hitler even instructed his personal lawyer, Hans Frank, to handle Mitzi's divorce for her. Whatever else the Jew baiter Frank might have been, he was a good lawyer and the divorce went through easily enough.

Hitler and Mitzi Reiter met again in 1934. By now he was Chancellor of Germany, a man of power and destiny. On the worldwide stage and at home he was beginning to flex his muscles. He felt bold enough to ask her, again, to be his lover. Again, she refused – it was marriage or nothing. Hitler simply shrugged and got on with running the country.

Soon afterwards, in 1936, Mitzi met and married SS Hauptsturmführer Georg Kubisch. He was killed in the attack on Dunkirk in 1940, leaving Mitzi alone once more. Hitler sent her 100 red roses as a mark of his esteem and sorrow. That was their last contact. Hitler's sister Paula later stated that Mitzi Reiter was the only woman who might have been able to curb her brother's murderous instincts. She was sure that he loved her but that his duty, as he saw it, kept them apart. There was undoubted affection between them. He called her Little Mitzi, she called him Wolf and the letters he wrote to her show an unexpected tenderness and passion:

> He wrote her these emotion-filled words: 'My Dear Child, I wish I had your lovely little face before me … I would so love to be near you and to be able to look into your sweet eyes and forget everything else … Your Wolf.'[4]

Whether the words were genuinely meant or part of the standard Hitler-act, they are still startling in their intensity and in the fact that they were written by the butcher of millions. There is, you feel, real longing in the lines.

Hitler's second infatuation in those early years in Munich began at more or less the same time his relationship with Mitzi Reiter was coming to an end. It is entirely possible that he was trying to convince himself that he was not in thrall to Mitzi; equally as possible, his infatuation with the one was fading as his interest in the other grew in strength. Either way, Henny Hoffmann became, for a short but intense period, the central love interest in Hitler's life.

Henrietta 'Henny' Hoffmann was the eldest child of photographer Heinrich Hoffmann and his wife Therese, a former actress and dancer. He had been a war photographer and had always been a vicious anti-Semite. He had joined the NSDAP in 1920, almost as soon as it was founded and quickly became a friend of the Party's main speaker and prime mover, Adolf Hitler.

There was no doubting Hoffmann's ability as a photographer. He was the man who had taken the photograph of the adoring crowd in Munich's Odeonsplatz on 2 August 1914 as news of the declaration of war was announced. By pure chance the rapturous face of Adolf Hitler was caught, mid-frame. The authenticity of the image has since been questioned, many believing that Hoffmann 'doctored' the photograph but despite this, the image was taken by the Nazi Party and used in their publicity material. Called up in 1917, Hoffmann went on to photograph various aspects of the war before returning to Munich where he became involved in the anti-Bolshevik demonstrations of the time. He even published a book of his images depicting the violence and brutality that had shaken the whole of Bavaria in the immediate post-war years.

Hoffmann was a rough, beer-drinking, party-loving sort of a man, exactly the type of person who gravitated to the ranks of the SA. Now he took up the cudgel with a vengeance. He was present in the Nazi ranks at the Beer Hall Putsch but seems to have avoided prosecution and imprisonment. It did not stop him being one of the men waiting outside the gates of Landsberg Prison on Hitler's release, ensuring that his camera caught the Party leader in the best possible light as he left in his new Mercedes.

Henny and Hitler met for the first time in 1922 when she was just 9 years old. He was soon a frequent visitor to the Hoffmann apartment, situated above Heinrich's photographic studio in Munich. It was a place where he could always be sure of a warm fire, satisfying company and a good meal – important issues at that time of Hitler's life and career. Heinrich Hoffmann's wife Therese was yet another woman who mothered him and fussed over him, making sure he had warm clothes to wear and food to put in his belly. Hitler loved the ambience of the house – and there were always the Hoffmann children to play with and amuse.

As the 1920s unfolded, Hitler saw less and less of the Hoffmanns, his work commitments keeping him busy in Munich and, as his fame grew, across the country. By 1930 Henny was attending the University of Munich and had not seen Hitler for quite some time but when they did meet again that year she was, initially at least, unimpressed:

> He gave himself great airs, with his dark leather coat, his whip and his Mercedes, whose driver waited for him in front of the door. After dinner – at that time he was still Herr Hitler to us – he sat down at the piano and played some Wagner followed by some Verdi.[5]

Whether or not Henny was allowing her memory to delude her about Hitler's piano playing, it was not long before his charm had taken her in. Soon she was working for him, part-time, as a secretary, while still studying at university.

Therese Hoffmann had died, suddenly and unexpectedly, in 1928. It was a terrible blow for the family and for Hitler who had become increasingly fond of the retired actress – the theatrical appellation yet again. Heinrich Hoffmann remarried soon after the death of Therese and, as many people later saw it, the moral standing of the house took a sudden turn for the worse. There was a great deal of drinking, with ad-hoc parties being held when students and young people from the city poured into the apartment to take advantage of the liberal, party flavour of the place.

These were the final years of the Weimar Republic: across Germany it was a time of decadence and excess. In the Hoffmann house sexual activity was common and there were rumours that Henny, without the controlling influence of her mother, had now become little more than a whore who could apparently be bought by the almost penniless students for just a few marks a time. True or not, Hitler grew very close to her and was a regular attendee at the parties when, more than probably, he availed himself of her services.[6] When, one night, a drunken and loose-lipped Henny announced to the family what she and Hitler had been doing, Heinrich Hoffmann was furious. He may have been something of a drunken lout but he had his standards and the thought of his friend and Party leader playing loose and fancy-free with his daughter was beyond the pale.

Hoffmann immediately confronted Hitler. There was an argument, Hoffmann threatened to withdraw from the Party and Hitler suddenly realized that he could not afford to lose the services of such a quality artist. He had previously always been reluctant to have publicity photographs taken, preferring to remain something of a mystery man. Now he had reversed his position. He made Heinrich Hoffmann the official Party photographer, granting him exclusive rights to photograph him and, more importantly, to publish the results. Over the next ten to fifteen years the arrangement saw thousands of images of Hitler and the Party – some records say as many as 2.5 million – reproduced on postcards, in books and in newspapers. It made Hoffmann into a multi-millionaire. After the war it also bought him a four-year stint in Spandau Prison as a war criminal and profiteer whose work had aided the growth of the Nazi Party.

All of that was in the future. Back in 1930 the friendship between the two men was renewed. In the late 1930s, until war broke out in 1939, Hoffmann became a regular visitor to the Berghof. And there, of course, more photographs were taken. After the quarrel and rapprochement there seems to have been little more contact between Hitler and Henny Hoffmann, at least not of a sexual kind. However, Henny was not quite out of the picture as far as the Nazi Party was concerned.

In 1931 Henny Hoffmann met Baldur von Schirach, the youngest of Hitler's top officials and a rising star in the Third Reich. By now, Henny, like her father, saw her future linked firmly to the burgeoning Nazi Party and if she could not have Hitler then Baldur von Schirach was the next best thing. They were married on 31 March the following year. Von Schirach's parents and extended family objected violently to the match. Henny was not good enough for him, they felt. There were many reasons: to begin with there were the now-legendary stories of debauchery and bacchanalian-style antics in Henny's Munich home. For upper-middle-class Bavarians – the 'von' in their name gives everything away – her past was chequered, to say the least. As far as the von Schirachs were concerned, Henny came from a much lower social class than their family. Her father, regardless of his skill and talent as a creative artist, was in their eyes little more than a tradesman.

Hitler insisted, however, that the wedding should take place. He was clearly thinking that the joining of the man who would soon become leader of the Hitler Youth and the woman who had given the Führer more than a few nights of pleasure was a good move, both for the couple and for the Party. Hitler and SA leader Ernst Röhm were 'best men' at the ceremony.

Over the next ten years the newly wed von Schirachs were regular visitors to Hitler's gatherings at the Berghof. Henny became friendly, first with Geli Raubal and then with Eva Braun and always seemed to have Hitler's ear. She also found time to present Baldur von Schirach with four children.

In 1937 von Schirach was appointed leader of the Hitler Youth, a seminal position in the Party. The youth of Germany was its future and von Schirach was the ideal person to take charge of their education – perhaps manipulation would be a better description.

Von Schirach went on to win the Iron Cross fighting against the British and the French during the invasion of the Low Countries in 1940 and later became Gauleiter of Vienna where he oversaw the removal of over 50,000 Jews from Austria. 'Removal', as von Schirach knew, was a euphemism for the inevitable death warrant.

As the nominated leader of the Hitler Youth – and thereby all youth groups and organizations within Germany – Baldur von Schirach had complete control over the country's educational system. Henny, never backward in anything she either said or did, undoubtedly played her part in advancing the policies and plans of the Nazi Party. Baldur von Schirach was a good front man; Henny was something of the power behind the throne. A clever and calculating woman, Henny certainly knew when she was well off. By the late 1930s it seemed as if the Nazi Party would rule in Germany for many years to come and, for good or ill, Henny Hoffmann had aligned herself to the top brass in the organization. It was unfortunate for her and for von Schirach that she had a mind of her own.

Helping her husband in his job was not the end, not as far as Henny was concerned. She was in the Netherlands on an official visit during the early years of the war when, one night, screaming from outside her hotel disturbed her. She went out to see what was going on and ran into what, at first, appeared to be a riot. It was the forcible removal, along with much violence and brutality, of dozens of Jewish women and children. Instinctively Henny guessed at the fate of the people before her.

'We shouldn't be doing this,' a soldier whispered to her as she watched. 'All it does is to turn the people against us. Tell that to the Führer next time you see him.'

Henny was appalled by what she had witnessed and agreed with the words of the anonymous soldier. She went back indoors and telephoned, asking for an immediate meeting with Hitler. It was agreed and took place at the Berghof. Henny, because of the close relationship she had always had with Hitler, felt that she could speak freely and now she protested vigorously about what she had seen. Such treatment of the Jews was wrong, she insisted, it was barbaric.

Much to her amazement Hitler leapt to his feet, his face scarlet with fury. 'You are sentimental,' he declared and went on to scream about 10,000 of his best soldiers perishing every day on the battlefield. That was something to complain about, he said. Then he stormed off. Henny and her husband were never invited to the Berghof again.[7]

Henny hardly had time to ponder her 'banishment'. For Hitler and for Germany the war was beginning to take a turn for the worse and within a few months the days at ease in the Berghof were over. Henny left behind a warm and pleasant memory in the hearts of those, like Traudl Junge, who had encountered her: 'She was a nice, natural Viennese woman with a delightful flow of talk.' Frau Junge was wrong about her being Viennese but the rest of her judgement was accurate enough.[8]

After the war Baldur von Schirach was sentenced to twenty years' imprisonment as a war criminal. He was lucky to escape the hangman's noose but was sent to Spandau where, along with Rudolf Hess and Albert Speer, he eventually became one of the longest-serving Nazi prisoners.

The marriage between Henny and von Schirach had never been easy, von Schirach having been rumoured to be homosexual, and Henny filed for divorce while he was still in prison. She had formed a new relationship with Peter Jacob, the former husband of Leni Riefenstahl. The divorce did not stop her petitioning the British government – unsuccessfully as it turned out – for a reduction in von Schirach's prison sentence. Almost to the last, it seemed, she was loyal and caring, even if that loyalty was sometimes misplaced. Henny went on to write about her memories of life in the Third Reich and the people she had encountered. Her writings, such as *Price of Glory*, became bestsellers. She died in 1992.

Mitzi Reiter and Henny Hoffmann/Schirach are women who, since the end of the Second World War, have warranted little more than footnotes in the story of Hitler and the Third Reich. They were vastly different in character but if things had been different, both had the power and influence to have altered the course of history.

Mitzi might well, as Paula Hitler believed, have been the one true love of her brother's life. There are, however, many candidates for that appellation, not all of them welcome. He certainly never forgot her and thought fondly of her to his final days. Her gentle nature might well have been sufficient to change his mind on many things and, more importantly, alter the course of his more vicious, self-destructive policies.

Henny was always a more forceful character than Mitzi and had the courage to challenge what she did not think right. She would rarely back away from a problem, preferring to face it head on, and was a determined and dynamic opponent to anyone with whom she disagreed.

It is all supposition, of course but if both, or either of them, had remained in Hitler's life the world might have been a very different place. The dilemma for the historian is simple: did Hitler realize this and deliberately back away or did that fickle finger of fate decide an alternative route? It is an interesting question, probably rhetorical but well worth considering.

As a footnote to this aspect of the story, Henny Hoffman, by her challenging of Hitler's policy on the Jews, was one of the few people to stand up to him. Regardless of her past and what she had been, that at least is a fine accolade.

Chapter 7

A Forbidden Affection: Geli Raubal

Apart from Eva Braun, Hitler's niece Geli Raubal is the one woman whose name actually means something to those people who have a genuine or passing interest in the Third Reich. She was, people will tell you, his first love, his only love and she died in tragic circumstances. That is correct but there is more, much more, to the story of Adolf Hitler and Geli Raubal.

Their affair remains cloaked in mystery. Loving, abusive, perverted, dictatorial, paternal, platonic – all the options are there and have all been believed, ignored or discredited over the years. There is very little hard evidence to back up any of the possibilities and we still do not know exactly what went on between them. What we do know is sketchy and is directed as much by half-truths and legend as it is by our own desires and wishes. The manner of Hitler's feelings for Geli and the direction they took varies according to the sources of information and the intention of the writer but one thing is abundantly clear – he cared about her very deeply.

Angelika Maria Raubal was born on 4 June 1908 in the Austrian city of Linz. Always known as Geli, she was only a few years old when her father Leo Raubal died. Her mother, Hitler's half-sister Angela, brought up Geli and her siblings on her own, having no contact with Hitler or any other member of her extended family until after the First World War. The 1919 meeting of Adolf and Angela, though pleasurable, was as much a surprise to her as it was to her children. After the war Angela Raubal moved her family to Vienna, a city that was on the face of it a far more cosmopolitan environment than Linz. She maintained her contact with Hitler, even travelling to visit him while he was incarcerated in Landsberg Prison. There are various versions of how things developed from that point and there remains some confusion with dates but for several years the lives of Adolf Hitler, Angela Raubal and her daughter Geli were intertwined.

Confusion or not it seems that in 1924, after his release from prison, Angela became housekeeper for her half-brother at his apartment in Prinzregentenplatz 16 in Munich. Her two daughters, 18-year-old Geli and 12-year-old Elfriede, went with her. It was a mutually beneficial arrangement – Hitler got himself a housekeeper, Angela got herself a home.

Hitler's Munich apartment had been donated to him and furnished by Helene Bechstein. It provided him with a base in the city, somewhere comfortable but, as Frau Bechstein insisted, it was also a respectable and upmarket address. To employ his half-sister as housekeeper was a move that would have suited Hitler's patrons very well – another addition to the veneer of respectability that Frau Bechstein and Frau Bruckmann were working hard to develop and create around the Nazi leader.

After his purchase of the Berghof, a house outside the village of Berchtesgaden on the Obersaltzberg, large numbers of staff were needed to run what was intended to be a country retreat. It was clear that change was in the air. Consequently, Angela moved to the area and took command of the mountain house while the apartment in Munich was placed into the hands of the elderly Frau Anni Winter and her husband.

Another version of events comes to us courtesy of Christa Schroeder. She has stated that Angela Raubal never ran the apartment in Prinzregentenplatz and that from the beginning it was always under the control of Frau Winter. The tenancy of the original Berghof property was in Angela's name and only legally transferred to Hitler in 1927. That presupposes she had been installed at the Berghof long before 1927.

Either of the two options is a possibility. Hitler would have required someone to run the Berghof even while he still rented it, keeping the house aired and clean, ready for him when he wanted to use the place, and Angela seems the logical choice. Geli, naturally, went with her mother. The idea of spending her days in the quiet isolation of the Berghof held little appeal for the young, fun-loving Geli Raubal. She wanted excitement, she wanted to enjoy life in Munich. Above all she wanted to bask in the fame of her uncle's rather notorious name.

Geli and Hitler had become really very close, taking long walks in the hills around the Berghof, picnicking amongst the woods of the Obersaltzberg and spending more and more time in each other's company:

> Geli was a most attractive young lady and she made quite an impact on Hitler … a confident young woman, easily able to use her charm on all the men she met, including her uncle … When Angela hinted that her daughter should move to Munich to progress her education Hitler readily agreed.[1]

The apartment in the Prinzregentenplatz was relatively small, consisting of just two bedrooms and five rooms in all, but Hitler actually had two apartments side by side and so there was space enough for Geli to have her own things about her. In 1929 she enrolled as a student of medicine at the Ludwig Maximilian University – a course she did not complete – and settled down to her real role in Munich, enjoying life in the city.

If Hitler and Geli became close, the same can be said about Hitler and his housekeeper Frau Winter, albeit in a clearly platonic way. Another of his 'older ladies', she was a methodical and capable manager who was scrupulous about keeping the apartment clean and in order. But she was so much more than a simple duster and sweeper. Anni Winter was a friend, a comrade in arms who had apparently known Hitler for several years, and was the medium through which he got to know all of the city gossip. Well established in Munich, she had an ear for tittle-tattle and for ferreting out facts, for separating the truth from misinformed opinion. Anni was a respected and respectable lady – more good marks on the Bechstein/Bruckmann scale – and soon became a key figure in the Hitler entourage. Hitler valued her opinion and often asked for her views on topics or on individuals who had come to interest him. Gradually people began to realize that Frau Winter was not just a simple servant but someone who could provide a direct pipeline to Hitler. If you wanted a matter dealt with urgently, forget the formal apparatus and lines of communication, go to Frau Winter.

Meanwhile, Geli Raubal was basking in the joy of any high-spirited teenage girl suddenly let loose in a big city. She went shopping, sat in the coffee bars and mingled with the younger echelon of Hitler's retinue. The Café Heck, a popular venue for SA and Party members, soon rang with her laughter and empty chatter. She was hardly the brightest of girls but she was spirited and gregarious. She was a lively, attractive character and men were drawn to her quite naturally.

Hitler, while initially happy to let her hog the limelight, was soon glaring at those who feted and fawned on her. Geli, caught up in the romance of it all, did not realize the extent of her uncle's disapproval. She was so wrapped up in her new life that, to begin with, she also failed to realize that her Uncle Alf, as she called him, was beginning to exercise strict control over almost every aspect of her existence. It was slowly but steadily done and before she knew it, Geli Raubal was as trapped as any butterfly or moth in Hitler's web of control. After a while she found that freedom in the city of Munich was nothing more than an illusion and that she was effectively Hitler's prisoner. Soon she was not even allowed out unless he accompanied her or organized a chaperone. Increasingly confined to the apartment, she could do almost nothing without Hitler's tacit approval.

He paraded her, clothed her, showered gifts upon her and just as his patrons had done with him, he told her how she should behave in public. On the one hand it was a pampered, idyllic lifestyle but on the other, when Hitler was away campaigning or dealing with Party business, Geli was alone, bored and frustrated, staring at the four walls of the apartment. It was infuriating when all the pleasures of Munich were waiting just outside her door.

Never an intellectual or a particularly well-read woman, Geli did enjoy music. She accompanied Hitler on his regular visits to the opera, which they both loved, and after a while he convinced himself that she had a future on the stage, as an opera singer. She had a nice voice but it was never going to be strong enough for the professional stage. Nevertheless, Hitler encouraged her to take singing lessons, even though her interest was in lighter styles of music. She found the lessons boring but she demurred to him, as she did in most things – at least in the beginning. Uncle Alf knew best and Geli was not going to upset the apple cart over something as trivial as singing lessons.

And then acquaintances, friends, members of the Party in particular, began to question what was going on. Geli was, after all, Hitler's niece but here he was, treating her more like a courtesan than a relative. It was not proper, it was not done, certainly not in the refined and delicate confines of Munich society.

The two Strasser brothers, Gregor and Otto – ever internal opponents and critics of Hitler within the Nazi Party – were particularly harsh in their views. At their urging Hitler was called to account by the Party management on several occasions. Nothing happened – the upper ranks of the Nazi Party needed Adolf Hitler far more than he needed them.

The Strassers felt that Hitler's flaunting of Geli was poor publicity and Otto Strasser in particular, always virulent when it came to matters relating to Herr Hitler, was sure that he was paying for her new clothes and her various jaunts out of Party funds rather than his own pocket. Whether Hitler was creaming off Party money has never been proved but the longer he and Geli were together the clearer it became that this was no ordinary uncle–niece relationship.

Within a few months of installing Geli in his Munich apartment Hitler had become so obsessed with her that it was an almost pathological attraction. He needed to know her every move, assigned watchers to monitor her movements if he could not do it himself and decided who was or was not a suitable companion for her. And the more stringent he became the more she resented it. Sooner or later there was bound to be a reaction on her part.[2]

How far the relationship went has never been clear although most writers now accept that there was sexual contact of some sort between them. Geli's asides or brief comments on the matter certainly seem to indicate that she and Hitler were intimate and several Nazi officials reported on statements she had made to that effect.

Geli was his niece, an underage niece, and that in itself was trouble enough. Soon, however, rumours began to circulate about Hitler's strange sexual perversions. Geli was to comment on these to various people, notably William Stocker, an officer in the SA who was often on guard outside the flat in Munich. Whether by design or accident, Geli never told the full story, always stopping tantalisingly short when it came to detail. Stocker later spoke about what Geli had told him:

> Hitler made her do things in the privacy of her room that sickened her but when I asked her why she didn't refuse to do them she just shrugged and said she didn't want to lose him to some woman who would do what he wanted.[3]

According to Stocker, Geli was kept on a very tight rein but when Hitler was away, she would seize the chance for freedom. Then she would head off to the bright lights of Munich. Geli had encounters, Stocker claimed, with many people during these free times, including a violinist from Augsburg and a ski instructor from Innsbruck. When Hitler returned it was back to the same tight routine that she despised. Stocker claimed that he had said nothing about her illicit jaunts because he liked Geli. More than that, he rather fancied her himself.

Dozens of stories continued to circulate throughout Munich but how much of this was part of a campaign to blacken Hitler's name remains up for debate. Until the defeat of Germany and death of Hitler in 1945, it was all rumour and 'behind the hands' sneering. Then things changed as the full story of the Nazi atrocities became known and it was suddenly right to be critical, openly critical, about what had gone on during the Third Reich years.

Hitler perpetrated such horrors, such evil, that people were unable to consider or reflect upon him without regarding the man as a monster. All things were possible with someone like this and to present him as depraved and perverted in his private life simply added to the picture. Sexual depravity reinforced the stereotype and confirmed the malevolent nature that would have been needed to create the concentration camps and death factories.

Nothing could ever excuse Hitler's treatment of the Jews and other opponents during the seemingly endless years of the Third Reich. Such cruelty was beyond the understanding of most thinking individuals and so it was easy to heap the coals of perversion onto his back, not as an excuse but as a way of explaining away how he could come to create such evil. As the camps, mainly in Germany and Poland, were overrun by the Allies, so much had already been exposed – which really left only his private life. He might well have been as warped and disturbed as legend believes. Then again, he might not. We simply do not know. It is interesting to see, however, that the vast majority of the accusations of sexual depravity were delivered post-1945. The only formal accusations levelled before the end of the war came from Otto Strasser in the OSS investigation carried out by Walter C. Langer. If Langer's opinion that he was a coprophile is correct then it is easier to accept Hitler's bizarre behaviour. Otto Strasser believed – or at least was seen to believe – that Hitler's particular perversion where Geli was concerned was mainly in the field of undinism, sexual pleasure gained from water, particularly urine:

> Hitler would make her undress. He would lie on the floor. Then she had to squat over his face, when he could examine her at close range and this made him very excited. When the excitement reached its peak, he demanded that she urinate on him.[4]

Strasser's evidence has to be taken with a pinch of salt. His brother Gregor had been killed by Hitler during the Night of the Long Knives massacre and Otto himself barely escaped from Germany alive. He claimed that Geli had spoken to him about Hitler's unpleasant sexual desires but that seems unlikely. Geli, like many others with close connections to the leadership, had no sort of relationship with Otto. She knew that Strasser was on the left wing of the Party, was an openly acknowledged critic of Hitler and would do anything to portray him in a bad light. And that was all.

While Strasser's story was backed up by Puzi Hanfstaengl, both men were refugees from their own country and after being unceremoniously discarded, had little affection left for the Führer. Puzi had no love for Geli either – he called her 'an empty-headed little slut'. Both Puzi and Otto Strasser had a vested interest in making Hitler appear as debauched and unnatural as possible, an understandable if morally reprehensible position when they were living in a country at war with Germany. They were never likely to say or do anything that was going to upset the American government and organizations like the OSS. It is probably unwise to put too much credibility in the stories of Hitler's perversions. Something was amiss, that was for sure, but exactly what it was and how it affected the relationship of uncle and niece is best left to imagination.

The relationship between Hitler and Geli was a timebomb waiting to explode and almost from the moment she was installed in the Munich apartment a storm began to brew. Geli's attraction to Hitler, begun and developed during their time at the Berghof, had already begun to wane as soon as she experienced the delights of Munich and other men started to take her fancy. One of them was Hitler's bodyguard and chauffer, the highly dubious and enigmatic Emile Maurice.

Geli and Maurice were thrown into contact with each other on a regular basis – Geli wanted to go shopping, Emile would be delegated to drive her; Geli had a singing lesson, Emile would drive her and wait for her to finish. The idea was that Maurice would wait and watch, then report back on Geli's behaviour. It did not work out that way.

She and Maurice flirted, kissed and probably became lovers. Geli certainly thought she was in love with him and hoped that he was with her. He was a charming sort of man, on the surface at least, whose interests did not start and stop with street fighting and persecution of minority groups. He was relatively cultured, played musical instruments and had an almost poetical touch in his writings. There is no doubt that he was attracted to her: 'Her big eyes were a poem and she had magnificent hair. People in the street would turn round to take another look at her, even though people don't do that in Munich.'[5]

However, it was not long before Emile Maurice had more practical things to worry about than Geli's affections. When, towards the end of 1927 or the beginning of 1928, Hitler found out about their relationship, he went berserk and threatened his chauffeur with a gun. To Hitler, his friend and long-time Party comrade had committed the ultimate betrayal and blind rage took over. He brandished his pistol in Maurice's face. Maurice believed Hitler really was about to shoot him and had to run from the building in order to save his life. He was replaced in his post as chauffeur first by Julius Schreck and then by Erich Kempka. More significantly, Maurice lost his unofficial but much coveted position as an 'intimate' of Adolf Hitler.

Despite the fact that for a long while Maurice was out of favour with his old Party comrade, he was still allowed to retain his SA commission and was later to feature significantly as one of Hitler's official murderers during the Night of the Long Knives. Geli was sent to live with Frau Bruckmann for a short period in an attempt to curb her passions.

Late the following year Geli managed to slip away from Munich and went to spend time in Vienna with friends of her mother. During this short respite Geli managed to meet and fall in love with a violinist from Linz. There is no record of the man's name but, according to Angela he was sixteen years senior to Geli. Young Geli always did seem to have a thing about older men, possibly some form of searching for the father figure she had never known.

When she returned to Munich, Geli was angry and distraught to find that events had moved on in her absence. Hitler and her mother had forbidden any further contact between Geli and her violinist, a one-year period of separation being insisted on by Hitler so that the pair could prove their love to him and to the world.[6] In reality, of course, he was intent only on keeping the pair apart. Once installed again in Munich Geli was monitored even more closely by Hitler. For what seemed to her like forever – in reality just a few years – the situation remained the same. Hitler was in charge, even though he was now in the final throes of making his thrust for power. Geli had more or less forgotten her Austrian violinist but relations between the uncle and niece did not grow any easier. They were in fact quite strained.

Gone were the shopping expeditions and the wonderful little presents. Gone were the idle hours in the bustling Café Heck and the visits to the theatre. Neither of them could have been very happy with the situation but Hitler would not let her go. He had her in his thrall and was determined that matters would remain as they were. Now they would argue more and more, screaming matches that disturbed not just the peace of the apartment but were also heard by those who lived in close proximity on the other floors of the apartment block. He was not above grabbing her roughly, a trait that left bruises – except that nobody saw them because she was never allowed to go anywhere.

All that Geli wanted now was to escape the prison that Hitler had woven around her – all he wanted was to keep her there. The more she demanded freedom, the stricter Hitler became and the tighter the tensions grew. In September 1931 matters came to a head. In a surprising moment of leniency Hitler had acceded to one of her wishes and Geli was given permission to spend a few days with her mother at the Berghof. Hitler, however, was not happy; as soon as she was gone, he wanted her back with him in Munich. He telephoned and, no matter how much she wanted to remain with her mother, she trotted obediently back to Uncle Alf. The moment she arrived at the apartment violent quarrels began once again.

Geli wanted to go to Vienna for vocal tests but although the visit had been long planned, Hitler now refused to give his permission. He was afraid that she was intending to meet up with her Austrian violinist and at that moment the only safe place for Geli Raubal was where Hitler could control her, in the apartment at Prinzregentenplatz. She was insistent, he was adamant and the arguments ran on, becoming ever more violent and loud.

Finally, in the late morning of 17 September, Hitler stormed out, declaring he would be back in time for lunch. As it happened, he did not return until late afternoon. Geli had been waiting all that time, nursing her thwarted desires, and she, like Hitler, was now taciturn and bitter. When he informed her that he had to leave immediately for a speaking engagement in Nuremberg another argument broke out. It was again vitriolic and culminated, yet again, with Hitler storming out. As she had been so often lately, Geli was alone once more.

Frau Winter later reported that once Hitler had gone, Geli began wandering, aimlessly and listlessly, around the apartment. She opened drawers and rooted through the contents, as if desperately searching for something. She read Hitler's correspondence and she cried. There had been anger and recriminations; now there was depression as well. Frau Winter and Geli had always got on well but now, this night, there was no way the older woman could get through to her. At last Geli told Anni that she was going to go to the cinema to watch some movie or other. Anni Winter relaxed; the movies would be good for Geli. But she never went. Instead she locked herself into her room, coming out only once to rush into Hitler's room, then dash back into her own. In hindsight, that was when she probably picked up Hitler's gun.

The following day, 18 September 1931, Anni Winter took up Geli's breakfast but she could get no answer to her knock and call. The bedroom door remained firmly locked. Eventually Anni's husband, finding that the key was still in the lock on the inside, had no alternative but to break down the door. There Frau and Herr Winter found Geli Raubal dead on the floor. There was blood from a gunshot wound to her chest and Hitler's Mauser pistol lay by her side. There was no suicide note but to all of the staff it was clear that Geli had shot herself.

The first official to arrive on the scene was Franz Schwarz who as well as being a member of the Reichstag was also the Nazi Party treasurer. Frau Winter had telephoned him before she even phoned the police. When the police finally arrived, they were met by Schwarz whose first point was that Hitler had been in Nuremberg when Geli shot herself, making sure that the alibi was clear and convincing. The police officers nodded and noted the information.

As ever, once the news broke, fantastic stories abounded all around Munich. According to the rumours, as well as the gunshot wound Geli had a broken nose, she had cuts and bruises on her body, she had been dead for twenty-four hours when she was found. It was all the product of the dreaded rumour mill but it should have given the police a reason to investigate more fully. In truth, the Munich police and justice departments were heavily loaded with Nazi Party members. Pressure was applied to bring the matter to a quick conclusion.

By the time Hitler arrived, called urgently back from Nuremberg, Geli's body had been removed to the morgue. There was no formal autopsy, the apartment had been cleaned and to all intents and purposes it was as if nothing had happened. Hitler had raced back to Munich as soon as the news was relayed to him, picking up a speeding ticket on the way – or, at least, his chauffeur did.

The newspapers had a field day, blaming Hitler for the suicide. Or was it suicide? Had Hitler shot Geli and then gone off to provide an alibi for himself? And what better alibi than a police speeding ticket? The official Party line was that the death had been an accident. The gun had gone off when she was cleaning it. Nobody believed that but the thought of an accident was better than the possibility of suicide which, in turn, was considerably better than murder.

There were many points left unanswered. Most suicides shoot themselves in the head or mouth but Geli had pointed the gun at her chest. That was an unusual way to kill oneself; one could easily miss one's heart – if one could locate it in the first place. That was, in fact, what Geli had done. The fatal shot missed her heart and struck her in the lung. Her final moments would have been very painful and horrible as she bled slowly to death. No one in the apartment block had heard the gunshot. That was unusual in a building where dozens of residents, willingly or unwittingly, regularly listened to the arguments between Hitler and Geli. That night Hitler's apartment was deathly quiet and the expectation was that a loud gunshot would have echoed around the hallways.

When questioned by the police, Hitler stated that he knew no reason why his niece should want to kill herself. He denied that he and Geli had quarrelled before he left for Nuremberg. Whether or not Hitler knew of any reason for suicide, Geli Raubal must have been reduced to a very low and deadly level of sorrow and anguish. The emotional pain must have been so unbearable that she could clearly see no way out of her dilemma other than to take her own life. Always a lively, upbeat type of person, her 'downs' would have been equally as intense. Her decision to kill herself was undoubtedly brought about by Hitler's emotional abuse over an extended period of time. Whether or not this was compounded by physical and sexual abuse cannot now be proved. Geli and Hitler have both gone, only the stories remain.

And then there is always the possibility that it was not a suicide attempt at all, just a cry for help that had gone horribly wrong. Like many would-be suicides Geli was desperate for attention and assistance, neither of which she was given. The decision to put a bullet into her chest rather than into the head might be taken as support of this theory. It was not 100 per cent certain but a bullet in the brain would have been far more likely to cause immediate death than one into the body. But, of course, if nobody heard the gun going off then it hardly mattered where she actually shot herself. Death would have been inevitable and no rescue in the nick of time was ever going to work.

Hitler was distraught, devastated by Geli's death. He apparently thought about following her to the grave, committing suicide as she had done. He ranted and raved about ending it all and even made several gestures or attempts to shoot himself. Once it even needed the intervention of Gregor Strasser of all people to take the gun out of his hand.

For a while – a short while – he thought about giving up politics and retiring to the country. Finally, he took himself off to Lake Tegernsee to contemplate and reflect in solitude – a degree of solitude, it must be noted, that placed his minders and bodyguards just a short distance away, within hailing distance. He might be grieving but not to the extent where he made himself totally vulnerable and open to assault. So, it was guards at a distance but guards there were nevertheless. Despite the precautions, Hitler's behaviour was, at times, hysterical. Everyone, even his most extreme critics and opponents, had to acknowledge that he appeared to be overcome by grief.

When he did finally feel able to return to Munich – having missed Geli's funeral – Hitler set up a shrine in her room. It was to be left exactly as it was on the day she died and only he was to be permitted access. In death, as in life, Geli was to be his and his alone:

> He had become dependent upon her, having her around him. It was, however, a suffocating love, one that could never be properly fulfilled. Geli proved to be the most important love of his life.[7]

Hitler's grief, turned in on himself, faded only slowly but the daily grind of Party politics eventually intruded and took over. Within two years he had achieved the pinnacle of his desires and become Chancellor of Germany. Geli was never forgotten but it seemed as if he had managed to put her memory in the right place – a shrine and a sanctuary in his apartment at Prinzregentenplatz.

One of the strangest phenomenon to follow in the wake of Geli's death was Hitler's decision to become a vegetarian. He gave up all alcohol at the same time. He had never been a great lover of meat or beer and wine, sweet pastries being much more to his liking. Whether the decision to give up eating meat was as a result of her suicide is difficult to judge – the obvious question is why. Why would the death of his niece, beloved as she was, cause him to abstain? There might be no link at all but the change in dietary habits certainly took place around the time of the event. It is, however, hard to find a link between Geli's death and his vegetarianism. It is also difficult to know what would have happened if Geli Raubal had still been alive when Hitler was made Chancellor. Could she have functioned as First Lady of the Fatherland? More to the point, would Hitler have married her? In many respects perhaps Geli was better off dead.

Chapter 8

The Berghof Set: Eva's Domain

When Adolf Hitler became Chancellor of Germany in January 1933, Dr Joseph Goebbels, the grand puppet master and propaganda chief of the Third Reich, began the process of turning his chief from an ambitious and seemingly successful politician into a creature of almost mythical proportions. Goebbels set his bar high. He decided that he would create, in the form and person of Adolf Hitler, nothing less than a Teutonic messiah. The process began immediately, on 31 January 1933, the night of Hitler's appointment as Chancellor. Hordes of SA men, their eager and triumphant faces illuminated by flames from burning torches, marched around and around the Chancellery. For hours they marched, singing the Horst Wessel Song and other Nazi marching tunes, howling their support for the man who had taken them from grinding ignominy and made their lives bearable – the man who had given them a purpose.

Hitler stood by an open window, accepting their salutes, not caring that the stormtroopers were doubling around the block to make their numbers seem even greater. In the streets thousands of astonished spectators gazed at the spectacle in awe. In the wake of such a successful beginning it was clear that the event would have to be repeated – often.

That night kick-started an intense and much-faceted campaign. Over the next twelve months Goebbels orchestrated and ran Hitler through an extended process of massed rallies and beer hall speeches, taking care to emphasize the improved standards of living the Führer had provided for the people of Germany during the short time he had been in power. It was a fact that standards of living in Germany had improved under Hitler. Such improvements were not all down to the Führer and even those that did come as a result of his policies were likely to be short-lived. Goebbels took care to emphasize Nazi involvement, however, convincing men like Britain's David Lloyd George that Hitler was something of a miracle worker: 'He is a born leader of men, a magnetic personality with a single-minded purpose, a resolute will and a dauntless heart.'[1]

Hundreds of marching stormtroopers – preferably at night and by the light of flaring torches – added to the image of power and strength that the new regime had brought. And after that first night in January 1933 they were carefully marshalled so that nobody had to double back on themselves! Before long, SA strength was numbering in the region of three million members, larger than the entire Wehrmacht.

Public appearances were one thing but there was also a more subtle side to Goebbels's campaign. Part of his 'Messiah Vision' was ensuring that Hitler's private life was now no more; his private life had become a public life – up to a point at least. There was intense interest in Hitler, both from home and abroad. They may not have worried about whose shirts he wore or who designed his uniforms – that was very much a 1960s phenomenon – but people did want to know how and where he spent his leisure time. Enter the Berghof.

Hitler had fallen in love with the Obersaltzberg area of the Bavarian Alps in 1923 when Dietrich Eckart first introduced him to this land of deeply wooded valleys and stunning mountain scenery. As Eckart had found, it was an area that was perfect as a refuge from the world and a place to rejuvenate even the most jaded of souls. The village of Berchtesgaden was picture-postcard perfect and Hitler was to return on holiday several times over the next few years.

He first stayed at the Pension Moritz but then the family that owned the small hotel sold up. Hitler did not like the new owners and changed his base. He went first to Marineheim, then to the Deutsches Haus in Berchtesgaden. It was there, in the summer of 1926, that he sat dictating volume two of *Mein Kampf* and met Mitzi Reiter who worked in the shop on the ground floor of the hotel.

He was already looking for a more permanent holiday base in the region and from 1928 he rented a small chalet called Haus Wachenfeld just outside Berchtesgaden. It had been built by wealthy businessman Otto Winter (no relation to Anni) in the closing years of the First World War but he had had little time to spend there. Hitler bought the chalet in 1933 when Herr Winter's widow agreed to sell the property to the new Chancellor of Germany. Hitler was inordinately proud of the fact that he was able to make the purchase on the strength of increased sales of *Mein Kampf* which, thanks to his new high profile and the beginnings of Nazi dictatorship which made ownership of the book a somewhat advisable purchase, had become a bestseller. As well as being a published author, he was now, for the first time in his life, a property owner.

During 1935 and 1936 the small summer residence was extended and developed under the oversight and supervision of Party activist and self-serving Secretary Martin Bormann. The place was renamed The Berghof which translates as The Mountain Court and from the beginning no expense was spared. Bormann, with Hitler's blessing, used the success of the development to advance his own power and position as a confidant of the Führer. A large terrace was built, overlooking the valley, while a huge picture window, able to be lowered completely if needed, provided a spectacular view of Austria's Unterberg Mountain. The main hall was filled with Teutonic furniture – and with Hitler's enormous globe. Guest bedrooms were adorned with great paintings taken from the museums and art galleries of Germany and with several of Hitler's own watercolours.

This was Hitler's retreat and the place where he was happiest in the world. But, of course, there were other residents on the mountain. They were at best an intrusion, at worst a security risk and 'Mr Fix It', Martin Bormann, soon made sure that they knew the score. One after the other they were induced – paid or forced – to leave their properties. Some of them took longer to convince than others. The owner of the Hotel Zum Turken spent a month in Dachau concentration camp before he came to his senses and agreed to move on.

Other Nazi leaders soon copied the Führer and built themselves holiday homes or weekend retreats on the Obersaltzberg. Martin Bormann and Albert Speer both created grand residences but the house that Goebbels erected for himself was, as might be expected, palatial.

Barracks for the guards were also created, dozens of SS Leibstandarte (Hitler's personal bodyguards) and SA Brownshirts being permanently based close to the Berghof. Checkpoints and security fences soon closed off access to the house and to the Eagle's Nest, the tearoom built in 1938 on the top of the mountain above and behind the main building. An airstrip was carved out of the mountain but Hitler invariably arrived by train rather than fly in to his mountaintop idyll.

The 'Berghof Set' began to form as soon as the alterations and extensions, complete with new dining rooms and guest bedrooms, were ready for use. The term Berghof Set is, perhaps, something of a misnomer as this was never a formal group and the epithet has only been applied in hindsight. Yet it sums up the individuals involved, giving them a corporate identity and a power base that was envied by those not involved.

The personalities within the Set changed or rotated on a regular basis. They were, in the main, those closest to Hitler, people who could be relied on to be discreet and carry out the Führer's orders with the minimum degree of fuss. To be given an invitation to come and sit on the Berghof terrace, to listen to Hitler's diatribes and take afternoon walks to the Eagle's Nest or the smaller teahouse in the grounds, was a coveted treasure in the Third Reich.

Some people, like Eva Braun – who reigned quietly but effectively as Queen of the Mountain – were regularly in residence at the mountaintop dwelling. When Hitler was 'at home', she was there with him; when he was away, she usually spent much of her time in Munich at the small apartment he had bought for her. Only after 1939, as the war began to increase in intensity, did Eva allow herself to be persuaded to remain full time at the Berghof. It was safer, Hitler said. Other dignitaries came and went as their jobs or situations allowed.

The one group that was virtually always constant was the huge mass of tourists who began flocking to the Berghof once they realized that Hitler and his entourage were in residence. They might not be able to gain entry to the house and grounds but they could at least stand outside the gates and hope to see Hitler or one of his minions drive past. Actually, Hitler often appeared in front of or amongst the crowd, signing autographs for the children and soaking up the adulation. He was happy to give them this contact, as long as they left him alone for the rest of the day.

In April 1933 one little girl, Bernile Nienau, was chosen from the crowd to come into the Berghof to celebrate hers and Hitler's joint birthday with a dish of strawberries. Hitler always had a soft spot for children – quite apart from the Hoffmann-induced photo opportunities. He fussed over Bernile, stayed with her and helped her overcome the inevitable shyness. She loved it, all of the attention and the fuss. And it did not stop at that one meeting in 1933. Bernile Nienau became a great favourite, both with Hitler and the Berghof staff, and was a regular visitor – an honorary member of the Berghof Set, you might say – until Bormann discovered that her grandmother was Jewish.

To Bormann and other hardliners, this was unthinkable. A Jewish girl defiling the Führer's home – the spiritual heart of the Third Reich – was unthinkable and steps were immediately taken to end the arrangement. Despite Bormann's attempts to prevent Bernile visiting, Hitler was adamant – the girl could come as often as she wished and she continued to visit regularly until the days of the happy Berghof parties ended in 1944. Tragically, Bernile later died aged just 17, apparently from natural causes.

Regular female visitors to the Berghof naturally included the wives of nearly all the Nazi high officials. The men might have to discuss policy with Hitler but the women were able to sit and gossip, enjoy the scenery and the weather, and wait for the Führer to come along to bestow a little attention on them. Away from the rigours of government Hitler was a gracious host and life at the Berghof was, in the main, gentle and relaxing. Women were an important part of the routine. The two best-loved meetings or sessions were on the terrace during the day and gathered around the giant fireplace in the hall each evening.

Hitler, always a creature of the night, made brief appearances on the terrace. He tried to avoid the direct sunlight, which hurt his eyes, and was always more inclined to parade outside if the weather was overcast. The late-night soirée around the fire was always his metier when he would sit with Eva Braun waiting patiently and demurely at his side and regale the women of the Reich with stories and tales of his youth. Discussions around the fireplace often did not start until very late, a lot depending on Hitler's day and his timings. They usually followed dinner which was, nominally at 8 o'clock each evening but if Hitler wanted to see a film or if there was a crisis to discuss then the meal and the fireside gathering were pushed further back.

The conversation was not always stimulating or exciting, especially if things degenerated into one of the Führer's endless diatribes, and with the lateness of the hour many of the 'Hitler women' went to bed at two or three in the morning, dog tired and hardly able to stay awake. And yet their presence at the Berghof in the company of the Führer was a gift that most German women would have given their eye teeth for. The women of the Berghof Set might not love Hitler in the way that so many women of Germany did but they admired him, respected him and looked up to him with awe. After all, this was the man who could advance or destroy their husbands' careers – and their own standing as people of power – at the drop of a hat. Being part of the worshipping Berghof Set was a vital part of their lives. As everyone soon realized, what you did there was significantly less important than the fact that you were actually there.

Eva Braun was installed at the Berghof in 1936. As the Führer's mistress she had a position of honour, at least to the members of Hitler's inner circle. People not in the know thought she was just one of the secretaries:

> In 1936 Hitler brought Eva to the Berghof and made her part of this fantasy world … In the years from 1936 to 1945 Eva Braun was to spend more than two-thirds of her time on the Obersaltzberg.[2]

However, not everyone was kind or pleasant to Eva. It started with Hitler himself. In public he was as distant to her as the mountains he loved to look at across the valley. He rarely spoke to her and usually walked ahead of her whenever they went for a stroll. Only late at night around the fire and, more significantly when she could at last slip through the door connecting her room to his, did their relationship begin to assume different proportions.

Emmy and Hermann Göring were regular visitors, at least until Emmy committed a terrible faux pas. She was Göring's second wife, the corpulent ex-flyer and drug addict still in mourning when they first met. He was soon captivated by the beautiful actress and the couple were married in April 1935. To begin with, as the wife of the second man in Germany, Emmy served as Hitler's hostess at the Berghof, something that annoyed both Eva Braun and Magda Goebbels. Normally Eva was told to retire quietly to her room whenever the Görings came to the Berghof. Hitler was not sure how his old comrade would take to Eva and rather than cause offence to the commander of his newly reformed air force, Eva was forced to eat alone and spend her days wishing that it was time for the Görings to leave: 'Eva suffered these slights in silence, for she was well aware of her fragile position within the group … She knew she could be exiled from his presence on a whim.'[3]

One of the rare occasions when Eva was allowed to meet Emmy and Hermann Göring resulted in a dreadful scene. Emmy, always conscious of her status and like her husband a confirmed egotist, snubbed Eva, cut her dead. For one of the few times in her life Eva complained to Hitler. He was furious, bawled out Göring and demanded that such a thing should never happen again. Emmy was suitably chastened and her moments of glory as a central element of the Berghof Set were, thereafter, considerably reduced.

Being 'exiled' from the Berghof was a fate that no one wanted. Even so the potential punishment was always there, hovering over their heads as they simpered and smiled in the Führer's presence. Emmy Göring and Henny Schirach, victims of ego and humanity respectively, could testify to that only too clearly. Each in their own way had both spoken unwisely and while Hitler was open to discussion, he was unmoving over matters that really concerned him.

Annelies von Ribbentrop loved the Berghof. Wife of the ex-champagne salesman and diplomat Joachim von Ribbentrop, Annelies was a constant presence at the house. Ambassador to the Court of St James before becoming the German foreign minister who signed the non-aggression pact with Soviet Russia, von Ribbentrop was a self-important opportunist. He and his wife revelled in the atmosphere of the Berghof but she dominated him, causing Hitler to remark that he could see who wore the trousers in that particular family. Von Ribbentrop was one of the most sycophantic of Hitler's acolytes. As Göring once declared, he never had a thought that Hitler had not had first. This man who had once given the Hitler salute to King George of Britain was thoughtless but careful to do nothing that would upset his chief. The rest of the world could go hang.

Afflicted by health problems all her life, Annelies von Ribbentrop enjoyed the luxury and the majestic mountain scenery of the Berghof. Apart from making friends with the other dignitaries with whom she could mix and spread gossip, she gained considerable benefit from the clean mountain air. It worked well – von Ribbentrop grovelled, Annelies enjoyed the surroundings and the company.

That 'company' was wide and varied, including women like Lina Heydrich. She was the wife of Reinhard Heydrich, the stone-cold, unemotional deputy to Himmler who had been called 'The man with the iron heart' by no less a person than Hitler himself. Lina regularly took her place on the Berghof Terrace. The daughter of a minor German aristocrat, Hitler was drawn to her and she immediately reciprocated, placing him on a pedestal where she could be seen to worship and adore.

Reinhard Heydrich was assassinated by Czech commandos in Prague in 1942. Even though he blamed Heydrich's arrogance and stupidity for his own death, Hitler still had a degree of affection for Lina. He presented her with an estate at Jungfern-Breslau in Bohemia in belated but heartfelt appreciation of her – and Reinhard's – services to the Reich.

Some of the wives did not enjoy the atmosphere at the Berghof and so made only infrequent visits to the house. One of these was Bormann's wife Gerda. Increasingly indispensable to Hitler, Martin Bormann had built a large chalet for himself not far away from the Berghof and Gerda seemed to spend most of her time there. Safe within her own space, she devoted her time to rearing and looking after the ten children that she and her husband had between them. A devoted Nazi, Gerda stood a foot taller than the short, rotund Martin Bormann. She was a modest character and preferred to stay in the shadows. That suited Bormann perfectly, giving him the freedom to plot and plan his way to the top of Hitler's regime. Gerda knew that Bormann regularly took mistresses, the actress Manja Behreas being one, but in the best traditions of Hitler's belief system, she tolerated the relationship, even encouraged it. She wrote to him that he should ensure Manja had a child one year, while she would have one the next – 'that way you will always have a wife who is serviceable'.[4]

Heinrich Himmler and his wife Margarete (Margi) came occasionally but he was a more frequent visitor on his own. She was a cold, distant type of person, thoroughly detested by other wives in the Berghof Set and by the partners of SS officers. Margi enjoyed making them squirm, holding her power over them like a modern-day Sword of Damocles. Himmler found himself a home on the shores of Lake Tegern rather than on the Obersaltzberg and kept his distance from other Nazi officials. That deliberately contrived distance made the scheming Himmler seem more evil than ever and was totally in keeping with the slow but steady development of his own power base and alternative culture, the SS. The Himmlers had a strange marriage. Himmler and Margi had little in common with each other – apart from their interest in homeopathy and herbal medicine – and by the final years of the war had already separated. Such discord would not have been welcomed at the Berghof. Hitler could not afford to annoy Himmler too much as he had the power of the SS in his hands – much better, then, to let Heinrich and Margi go their own ways.

The couple who were even more unpopular than the Himmlers and therefore very rare Berghof visitors were Rudolf and Ilse Hess. She was judgemental and hectoring in her attitude and, in the opinion of Hitler, far too manly. In fact, she was clever, intelligent and able to see through the falseness and the glossy veneer of Hitler's persona – another reason for his dislike. Rudolf Hess suffered for this, finding himself increasingly side-lined by more ambitious men like his personal secretary Bormann. Whatever he thought of her, Ilse was the first person to award Hitler the unofficial title of 'Chief', a nickname that stuck with members of the inner circle. Whether or not Ilse meant the appellation ironically, it is doubtful if the other women ever realized.

And then there were the doctors and their wives. Theodor Morell was nothing more than a quack medicine man. He filled Hitler with amphetamines but in the days before the war he somehow managed to cure him of stomach cramps and a virulent leg rash. In truth Morell's medicines and cures were doing considerably more harm than good and might well have eventually killed Hitler had not events forestalled them. The Führer became obsessed by his treatments and ensured that Morell and his wife Hannelore were regular attendees at the Berghof. For several years they were one of the central components of the Berghof Set, always present and as far as Dr Morell was concerned, always on call for the Führer.

Hannelore, like the wives and mistresses of so many of Hitler's associates – Bormann and Göring amongst them – was an ex-actress. But a very rich one. As far as Hitler was concerned, she was a welcome addition to the ranks of the Berghof Set, not just because of her relationship with Dr Morell but also because of her acting background. The other women, however, did not like her. She had nothing in common with the Berghof wives and so, in desperation almost, gravitated towards Eva Braun. She and her husband inundated Eva with presents such as embossed jewellery cases, handbags and clothes. It was clear from her responses that Eva did not need the gifts and the other members of the Set looked down their noses even more at the rich but uncouth and unwelcome actress. In a spirit of fun, albeit perhaps with an edge of sarcasm, Hannelore Morell was given a nickname by the secretaries and other regular guests of Hitler: 'Wife of the Reich Injections Impresario'. It was poking fun at Frau Morell but also at the tradition or habit within the Third Reich of seemingly giving everyone titles – Reich Minister for Armaments, Reich Stage Designer and so on.[5]

Dr Karl Brandt, later executed as a war criminal because of his experiments in the concentration camps, had come to Hitler's notice when he helped treat the Führer's Adjutant Wilhelm Bruckner who had been injured in a car accident. Brandt's quick reactions and his ongoing care undoubtedly helped to save Bruckner's life.

Brandt was the fiancé of Anni Rehborn, a swimming champion and would-be model, noticed by Hitler when she posed for a magazine. He made contact with her and she duly became a regular guest at the Berghof. Inevitably Brandt came with Anni on some of her visits. He impressed everyone by his efficiency when dealing with Bruckner and as a reward was soon appointed head of the Health Department, a post he held almost to the end of the regime. After they were married, Anni Rehborn (Brandt) maintained her position as a member of the Berghof Set – albeit a peripheral and non-political one – and became very friendly with Eva Braun. In this set within a set she was joined by the wife of Albert Speer, another woman not really accepted by the Emmy Görings and Anneliese von Ribbentrops of this mountaintop world.

In addition to the regulars, occasional guests were sometimes given temporary, if unofficial, status as visiting additions to the Berghof Set. Very often these newcomers were dignitaries – royalty even – from foreign countries that were either allies or likely allies to the Third Reich. As long as Hitler and the Reich could benefit in some way, they were most welcome.

The Aga Khan, one of the richest men in the world, came to the Berghof, despite his ancestry and Islamic religion, and made a powerful impact on Hitler. The Führer was particularly taken by the Muslim ban both on drinking and the eating of pork. Britain's Neville Chamberlain also came but his 1938 visit was made with a single purpose – to prevent war between Germany and the British – and there was no time for socialising.

David Lloyd George, British prime minister during the Great War that had shattered Hitler's life, came in 1936 and was suitably impressed by the views and by the achievements of the Nazi Party in reducing unemployment. Lloyd George's view of Hitler was almost entirely positive but by then the Welsh Wizard was in his dotage and had only a few more years to live.

By far the most significant foreign visitors to the Berghof, however, arrived in October 1937. They were the Duke and Duchess of Windsor, exiled British royalty but still the most attractive and interesting couple in Europe. They had an air of mystery about them, this twice-divorced American woman and the man who had been born to be king but had chosen not to fulfil his destiny if it meant losing the woman he loved. The Duke had abdicated as King Edward VIII of Britain just nine months before. The abdication affair had shaken the British Empire to its core but, perhaps inevitably, it was a six-day wonder and by the autumn of 1937 Edward and Mrs Simpson – as she would always be known – were reduced to wandering aimlessly around the world. They had fine titles but very little purpose in life. Mrs Simpson made a great impact during her short stay at the Berghof. Dressed in a simple but chic blue dress and with her hair coiled tightly into a bun, she was the epitome of class and quality that Hitler so admired:

> In the evening he said, 'She would definitely have made a good Queen.' He saw in the Duke a friend of Germany and regretted that he had not fought the Establishment rather than abdicating, particularly since he could have relied upon the sympathy of the working class.[6]

Eva Braun was hurt by the fact that she was not presented to the Duke and Duchess. She should have expected it, given the way she was treated when distinguished visitors came to stay, but she had been captivated by the love story of the Windsors and by the fact that this man was prepared to give up his throne for the woman he loved. The obvious comparison to herself and Hitler must have made the lack of a formal presentation an even greater blow.

Lack of a formal position or role hurt Eva greatly. Arguably she was a simple soul, a 'pretty, empty-headed blonde', as Alan Bullock called her.[7] But she was not without talent and would have made guests and visitors very welcome. As it was, she was excluded from so many of the activities and the party atmosphere that visitors brought. And so, she had to find her own forms of enjoyment. In the winter she skied, although Hitler disapproved; in summer she swam and took long country walks. She always enjoyed physical activity and was good at outdoor pursuits but they hardly made up for her lack or recognition.

During the day and evening, when Hitler was otherwise engaged – usually when he was taking one of his regular early evening naps – Eva often showed her home movies, cine films she had taken in and around the Berghof. She had trained as a photographer and had a good eye for an outstanding image, a talent that took her out of the 'snapper' variety of camera operator. Only the most intimate friends were invited to these picture shows which invariably centred on Hitler – a sad but telling infatuation that remained with her until her final moments in the Bunker.

The Berghof Set was never more than an informal gathering of men and women, all of them fascinated by the Führer. When all was said and done, they were part of an essential support system for a man who, as time progressed, was clearly becoming more and more fractured and fragile. The Berghof Set may have begun life as a group of friends and acquaintances but as the world tottered and fell into war it had become so much more. To be a 'member' of the Berghof Set was a much-coveted dream and yet by 1942/3 it was clear that Adolf Hitler needed these people – the women in particular – far more than they had ever needed him.

Chapter 9

Passing Ships in the Night: Suzi Liptauer and Many Others

All of his life Adolf Hitler was a ladies' man. He charmed them, he made love to them – with his eyes if nothing else – and had the uncanny knack of making women believe, when he was in their company, that they were the only people who ever mattered to him. It was not something that Hitler practised, it came naturally. Undoubtedly, much of his charm arose from his position as, first, the red-blooded revolutionary and action man at the head of the Nazi Party, and then as Chancellor of Germany. Power is perhaps the greatest aphrodisiac in the world and as dictator and leader of the Nazis, Hitler had power in spades. Women were readily available for him. It was not just a question of female company being found and then provided if he wanted intimate contact, it was more a matter of whom he wanted and when. So many women flocked around him and in many cases literally fell at his feet. It would have been impossible for any man, even the strange and self-contained Adolf Hitler, to resist for long.

Hitler's interest was not always sexual, even with attractive girls like his younger secretaries or with members of the Berghof Set. It was often the same with passing contacts who might intrigue him or hold his interest for a few moments. At such times his concern was almost paternal.

In particular he had a strong fatherly affection for Eva Braun's younger sister Gretl. She had dropped out of school at the age of 16 and begun working as a clerk, like her sister, for the photographer Heinrich Hoffmann. Due to the photographer's friendship with the Nazi leader, that brought her into regular contact with Hitler. In 1935, when he bought Eva Braun an apartment in Munich, the expectation was that Gretl would move in with her. When, a few years later, the sisters took possession of a villa in Bogenhausen, again provided by the Führer, it caused their father to write a letter of protest to Hitler. What would people think, he asked? No matter how angry Herr Braun might have been, Hitler, of course, poured oil on troubled waters and pointed out that as long as Eva was present, that would prove appropriate and socially acceptable.

As a member of the Berghof Set, Gretl fitted perfectly into the mountaintop environment, enlivening the conversation and atmosphere with her easy charm and good looks. She clearly admired Hitler but there was never any trace of anything more. Gretl would have done nothing to upset or destroy her sister's world and consequently set her sights lower. She enjoyed flirting with the orderlies, in fact with any of the black-uniformed SS officers who just happened to be in attendance. She was young, pretty and full of life, enjoyed dancing and drinking but, in particular, she was addicted to cigarettes. Hitler, in his fatherly fashion, tried his best to persuade her to stop smoking. There were several intense debates and discussions on the subject as Hitler attempted to point out the dangers and social drawbacks of nicotine. It was not just the possibility of disease, he told the sisters, but there was also the smell and the taste of cigarette smoke on women's bodies and hair. Here he was certainly ahead of his time as most people, fuelled undoubtedly by Hollywood, thought of cigarette smoking as fashionable, even romantic. Hitler, who was a passionate anti-smoker, offered all three of the Braun sisters – Eva, Ilse and Gretl – a gold watch if they could manage to last one month without lighting up a cigarette. Eva was the only one to win the watch. Hitler then upped the stakes by replacing the prize of a watch with a villa. Generous as that was, Gretl refused to be drawn. A villa was, she declared, just one thing; smoking could give her twenty separate joys each day. Hitler did not, as might be expected, fly into a rage. He just accepted Gretl's view – such was his pleasure in her company.

Gretl fell for SS adjutant Fritz Darges but he was dismissed in 1944 and sent off to the Eastern Front after what was apparently an insubordinate remark. Gretl promptly turned her attention to the handsome but fickle Reichsführer Hermann Fegelein, the liaison officer between Hitler and SS chief Heinrich Himmler. To begin with it was her sister Eva who found Fegelein interesting and, possibly, sexually stimulating. She confided in her friend Marianne Schönmann, stating that Hitler had once told her that if she ever found another man attractive, she should make him aware of her feelings and he would allow her to go free. If she had met Fegelein ten years ago, she declared, she would have asked the Führer for exactly that gift.[1] How genuine Eva was about that remains unclear. She and Fegelein certainly enjoyed dancing together, something they did whenever Hitler allowed his inner circle to let their hair down. Hitler, who did not dance, watched and said nothing as Fegelein regularly lifted the diminutive Eva off the floor, raising her up until their eyes met and then keeping her in that position as they danced around the room. The dignitaries and guests kept their eyes partly on Fegelein and Eva, partly on Hitler. That was as far as things went. Fegelein would have been a fool to take it any further – to be cuckolded in his own backyard, so to speak, would have infuriated Hitler and meant an instant death warrant for the culprit.

Regardless of how she felt about the good-looking SS man, Eva was happy when Gretl and Fegelein became intimate. More than that, she was beside herself with joy when they were married in June 1944. Himmler and Bormann were the witnesses and the reception, which took place in the Eagle's Nest at the Berghof, lasted for three whole days. In a moment of self-deprecating irony Eva now showed that she was not just an empty vacuum, as so many believed, but a woman of some insight when it came to analysing her position: 'I am so grateful to Fegelein for marrying my sister. Now I am somebody. I am the sister-in-law of Fegelein!'[2] Clearly her situation, her lack of status and position within Hitler's inner circle was beginning to grate. She wanted more, even if her desires were confined to her diary.

There was undoubted affection between the Braun girls and Hitler. His regard for Eva is known, although perhaps not such common knowledge as might be thought. But the other sisters also occupied his mind. He wanted to do the best he could for them. In April 1945, with the Reich collapsing in ruins around him, Hitler initially chose not to execute Gretl's husband for desertion. Gretl was heavily pregnant; desertion was common enough, but even the fact that Fegelein had been caught, drunk and with another woman, failed to influence Hitler. He would not hurt Gretl and so Fegelein would be allowed to live. Then he learned that Himmler was trying to negotiate a separate peace and that Fegelein, as his liaison man, was aware of the treachery and had possibly acted as an intermediary. Then, not all the love and affection in the world could save the duplicitous Fegelein. He was duly executed and Eva Braun did not disagree with Hitler's verdict on the matter.

Eva Braun might have been the quiet secret of Hitler's existence but she managed to carve out a life for herself, particularly in the Berghof years.

Two women, perhaps more than any others – mainly because Eva chose them – helped her to fill her day. Marianne Schönmann, daughter of an opera singer from Vienna who Hitler had admired in his youth, was a regular attendee at the Berghof. Originally invited because of her Viennese connections, she became particularly friendly with Eva, even more than with Hitler. The pair often took long walks together and Eva confided many of her inner secrets to Marianne. It was Marianne who first introduced Eva to Hermann Fegelein and thus, inadvertently, set up the affair and wedding between him and Gretl. Despite her intense friendship with Eva, she maintained a fondness for Hitler and when she married architect Fritz Schönmann in 1937, the Führer was present at the ceremony.

Unlike many others, Marianne was able to joke with Hitler and once, upon learning that his favourite dish as a child was meatballs, offered to cook some for him – good Austrian food as she declared, much better for him than the vegetarian rubbish he normally ate. Unfortunately, the meatballs turned out hard as rocks. Marianne was crestfallen but Hitler smiled graciously and often laughingly reminded her of the disaster. She should use them, he suggested, as hand grenades or mortar bombs to defend her home.

The second great companion for Eva was her best friend from childhood, Herta Schneider. They had kept contact throughout the early 'Hitler years' and when her husband was away fighting with the army, Herta and her children became regular visitors to the Berghof. Hitler grew very fond of her daughter Ursula, Uschi as she was known, and Heinrich Hofmann, without either of the subjects knowing, managed to snap many pictures of the two together. Herta was nothing if not a great believer in the outdoor life and the need for Spartan living. On one visit to the Berghof she insisted that her baby was to be bathed only in cold water. The child, she declared, needed toughening up and freezing cold water was an ideal way to start. It was to Herta that Eva wrote one of her last letters. Just three days before her death and with the Red Army tanks closing in on the bunker, she put pen to paper for the last time: 'We are fighting here until the last but I am afraid the end is threatening closer … I am dying as I have lived. It is not difficult for me. You know that.'[3]

Herta remained at the Berghof until the last, hearing the news of Hitler's and Eva's demise in the building where she and her friend had spent so many hours. She had known of Eva's decision to die alongside Hitler and realized when, that February, she and her friend had said goodbye that it was for the last time. With Allied bombers regularly pounding the Obersaltzberg, she and Greta Fegelein/Braun, who was now close to giving birth, were forced to spend the final days of the war underground in the bunkers that Bormann had constructed but which, until that moment, had never been used. It might have been uncomfortable but it undoubtedly saved her life. It is doubtful that Herta and Marianne ever had much direct influence on Adolf Hitler. They were always a peripheral part of his life but they did perform one very useful function: they kept Eva Braun happy and for that Hitler was grateful.

Hitler's admirers, lovers, girlfriends – call them what you will – were many and varied. Some, like Eva and Geli, are now well known even though their names were largely unheard of at the time. Others were notorious in the 1930s but have now slipped below the radar. One of these was a beautiful young woman by the name of Ada Klein. Hitler saw her first at the Burgerbraukeller on 17 February 1925 when he was giving a rousing speech to mark the re-establishment of the Party after his period in prison. He noticed a pretty young girl standing on a chair so that she could see and hear him better and dispatched Emile Maurice to talk to her and find out who she was. Unluckily for him, Ada had left the hall before Maurice could get to her.

By pure chance a few weeks later Hitler bumped into Ada in a Munich street. They stopped and talked and it became clear that she was interested both in him and the Party. She had recently been recruited by Max Amann, the Party publicity chief, to work as a secretary on the racist newspaper *Volkischer Beobachter* and so they had much in common. After that first encounter the two met regularly at Party functions and became friendly. It was inevitable that an invitation to his Munich apartment and to the Haus Wachenfeld, predecessor to the Berghof, on the Obersaltzberg should arrive at some stage.

Significantly, they were often alone together; on one occasion Hitler took her to Emile Maurice's flat. The chauffeur admitted them to his quarters and then left after a few minutes:

> The door to the second room was open, and Ada saw a bed
> in it … He told her that he could not marry but also, 'You

make me more light headed than when I add the strongest
rum to my tea!' and 'It was you who taught me how to kiss.'[4]

Rum in his tea – it is one of the few times that Hitler ever acknowledged
the use of alcohol. Whether or not the pair were ever sexually
intimate, the relationship between Ada and Hitler lasted for two years.
She eventually realized that there was no future with Hitler and in
1936 married Dr Walter Schultze who became head of the Bavarian
Department of Health. After the war he was convicted of war crimes
because of his involvement in the Nazi euthanasia programme.

Hitler's other comment to Ada is interesting. Being taught how to
kiss properly by a beautiful Bavarian girl might not be significant in
the grander scheme of things but for Adolf Hitler it was a profound
experience. It makes Ada Klein as crucial a factor in his development as
almost any other of his female acquaintances.

Then there was the singer and actress Gretl Slezak. Daughter of the
famous tenor Leo Slezak, she managed to captivate Hitler for many
years. She wanted an even closer relationship but the acknowledged fact
of her Jewish grandfather prevented him from becoming too intimate
with her. However, he did use his influence to keep her performing
when many other opera stars with Jewish ancestry were banned from the
stage. A woman of great charm and humour, Gretl Slezak entertained
Hitler with tales of the goings-on in the world of opera. Always a
terrible gossip, he loved to hear the latest stories, especially when they
were told by someone of great charm, beauty and mischief like Gretl.
According to rumour, in 1932 Hitler painted a portrait of her, one of the
last-ever watercolours he produced. But in 1932 he was in the throes of
electioneering and it is highly unlikely that he had either the time or the
inclination to get out his paints and easel again. If such a painting did
exist it has never been found.

Jenny Haug was a young Party activist whose name was linked
romantically to Hitler at the start of the 1920s. An early member of
the NSDAP, Jenny was certainly very close to Hitler for a while and
she even claimed to have sewn the first Nazi swastika flag for the
Party. She accompanied Hitler on many of his speaking tours, usually
staying in the same hotel or apartment house. Hitler even bought a fake
wedding band for her to wear. He was very much in love with her, for a
while at least. In the rumour-strewn streets of Munich it was whispered

that the two were going to be married. Nothing came of the rumour and, in time, Hitler and Jenny drifted apart.

One of the more unusual women close to Hitler in the early days of the Party was the bizarre Sister Pia. Not a Catholic Nun, her real name was Eleonore Baur but she was always known, in the Party and in public, as Sister Pia. She worked for the Catholic charity Yellow Cross and had spent time in Egypt as a nurse. The nursing or caring appellation stuck and *Der Spiegel* went into print, calling her 'The Nurse of the Nazi Nation'. In 1920 she met Hitler on a Munich tram, was impressed by his nationalist views and became an early member of the Party. Violently anti-Semitic and racist, Sister Pia was the only woman to take part in the Beer Hall Putsch. She was wounded during the final firefight and fled the scene with Hitler. Some accounts say she took refuge with him at Puzi Hanfstaengl's house. The Beer Hall Putsch was an action for which she was later awarded the Blood Order, the highest decoration of the Nazi Party, one of only two women to be granted this award during the Third Reich. Something of a hero in Party circles, Sister Pia became welfare sister for the Waffen-SS at Dachau where she was a major figure in the administration of the camp. There is no evidence of Sister Pia ever carrying out atrocities at Dachau but she undoubtedly bullied both the staff and the prisoners – and developed a marked propensity for requisitioning or obtaining for her own use anything that was not 'nailed down'. She also often used prisoners to carry out work on her own house.

After the war Pia was arrested but released by a War Crimes Tribunal for lack of evidence. She was hauled back in front of a German-run De-Nazification Court and this time she was not so lucky. She was sentenced to ten years in prison for war crimes but was released early in 1950 due to ill health. Despite this supposed illness or debility, Sister Pia lived until 1981, dying at the age of 95. It has never been clear how close Hitler and Sister Pia really were. They certainly became great friends and she accompanied him on numerous picnics and days out in the country. They were also often alone together which, in Hitler-speak, could well mean a degree of intimacy between the two. Perhaps more interestingly, during the war years Sister Pia ran a brothel. It was an unusual establishment, being based on a train which rolled slowly across Germany and German-held territory. As the Madam, Sister Pia carefully controlled her clients, only officers of the Wehrmacht and SS being allowed access to the Polish and Ukrainian girls working in the mobile brothel. Hitler's comments or thoughts on this have never been recorded.[5]

One of the more interesting women associated with Hitler in the days after his return from the army was the enigmatic Suzi Liptauer. Little is known about her or about the intensity of their relationship but, reportedly, despite her beauty it appears that most of the passion and desire in the affair came from Suzi rather than Hitler. In the early 1920s they used to meet regularly, perhaps two or three times a week, always in the afternoons. That left the evenings for Party business, political speeches and recruitment rallies. It also left time for other liaisons whenever Hitler felt the need. Suzi was a native of Vienna and was a stunningly beautiful woman with dark blonde hair, blue eyes and a fabulous figure. She had what was called a Viennese charm that drew men to her. But she had eyes only for Hitler and seems to have fallen head over heels in love with him – not always a sensible thing to do. From the beginning of their relationship, which was clearly sexual, he was often unfaithful. It was a habitual problem with him, as if he couldn't help himself. Women were always there for him and whatever he felt about Suzi Liptauer, he was always a target. In the words of Hermann Esser: 'I saw him with a number of married women in the period 1920–23. I noticed that oftentimes Hitler was not the instigator in these love affairs but was, rather, the hunted.'[6]

For a while Hitler and Suzi did the normal things that young couples do. They went on drives or visits to the theatre, took picnics and went out for meals together. Above all, he took her to the apartments of other Nazi colleagues where they could be alone and undisturbed. He called these times 'interludes' and for a while Suzi was blissfully happy. But the more she saw and heard what was happening with other women the more depressed she became. Suzi was undoubtedly a victim of Hitler's amorous nature. According to friend and Party colleague, Hermann Esser, he avidly pursued women, as did many other men who had been through the war. He was, without knowing it, hugely attractive to women:

> It wasn't long before I realized Hitler's tremendous impact on the female sex. No one in the general public knew who he was in 1920 … but I noticed not only the waitress but several other young ladies were making eyes at him … He seemed oblivious to the attention of the girls.[7]

Finally, the affair ended. Suzi was jealous, immensely jealous, and had long been threatening to kill herself if Hitler ever became involved with another woman. When she heard of an affair between her lover and a woman by the name of Emmi Marre, she decided to make good on her threat. She checked into a hotel, took a sash and wound it around her neck in an attempt to hang herself. The chambermaids found her, unconscious but still alive, half an hour later. The potential scandal was quickly hushed up by the Party and Hitler, presumably out of guilt, went back to Suzi. Thereafter he took her more completely under his protection – in other words he had her watched by his stormtroopers and undercover members of the Party.

It was 1921 and the attempted suicide of Suzi Liptauer was the first in a string of other suicide attempts, some successful, some not, that would accompany Hitler throughout his career. There was a rumour doing the rounds in Munich at the time that Suzi had tried to kill herself after spending the night with Hitler and becoming disgusted by what she experienced. It was probably no more than a rumour. Suzi and Hitler had been intimate long before the suicide attempt and if she had been so upset by what went on that night, she would never have agreed to the renewal of the affair. More bad-mouthing of Adolf Hitler it would seem. The relationship was never the same second time around and, eventually, they drifted apart. She married an Austrian but Hitler never forgot her. He sent her flowers and chocolate for her birthdays and sometimes even little gifts of money.

With Suzi finally out of the way, Hitler resumed his affair with Emmi Marre, a statuesque and well-built Bavarian blonde. Apparently, her greatest pleasure was in darning his socks and making him tea. In other words, she mothered him even though she was only 18 years old. Hitler was happy to accept this until Emmi began to speak too vocally and too publicly about their relationship. She could not, Hitler said, learn to keep her mouth shut and so he ended the affair. Emmi was devastated: 'She wandered about, lost and lonely, bitterly crying that no man would ever be like her Wolfchen [little wolf.]'[8] She was certainly right about that. They met again in 1929 but by then the flame had gone. Hitler had other things on his mind and now they were just good friends.

Chapter 10

A Dream of Valkyrie:
the Mitford Sisters

He would probably never have acknowledged it but Adolf Hitler was a snob. He loved to rub shoulders with men and women who had titles or came from aristocratic backgrounds – one of the reasons Puzi Hanfstaengl and his family remained friends for so long. But it also meant that people like Unity and Diana Mitford, daughters of the English Baron Redesdale, were more than welcome in the Führer's inner circle of friends and acquaintances.

The Mitford family, from the father to the youngest girl, were a glamorous, bohemian group of individuals who were renowned, not to say notorious, in 1920s and 1930s Britain. They were an old established aristocratic family who could trace their origins back to the era of the Norman Conquest. One-time bandit reivers on the Scottish borders, by the early twentieth century the family had become 'respectable' and all of them moved easily and efficiently amongst the upper echelons of English society. The twentieth-century scion of the family, David Ormsby Freeman-Mitford, 2nd Baron Redesdale, was an old-fashioned Tory; his wife Sydney Bowles – first cousin of Winston Churchill – leaned even further to the right, her opinions bordering on outright fascism. Their seven children were nothing if not Catholic in their politics and social opinions.

Six girls and one boy, the Mitford children lived a pampered and privileged existence. The boy, Thomas Mitford, had distinct fascist leanings and when the war came in 1939, he refused to fight in Europe against the fascist forces of Hitler and Benito Mussolini. He was posted to Burma where he died in action against the invading Japanese soon after his arrival.

The girls were never going to be outshone by their brother and soon developed highly individual personalities. The writer and journalist Ben

Macintyre summed them up succinctly in a recent article in *The Times*: 'Diana the Fascist, Jessica the Communist, Unity the Hitler lover, Nancy the Novelist, Deborah the Duchess and Pamela the unobtrusive poultry connoisseur.'[1]

At one stage Unity and Jessica shared a bedroom. Being, politically, at opposite ends of the spectrum this sharing made for an interesting environment. The sisters apparently drew a chalk line down the middle of the room – on the walls of Unity's side pictures of Hitler and swastikas, on Jessica's hammers and sickles.

From an early age Unity, known in the family as Bobo, was determined to be different and many believe that she turned to fascism simply as a way of standing out in the crowd. It was, perhaps, a sure way of being noticed in a large family where parental attention and emotional support were limited. Her personality as a young girl was such that she was opposed to everything, particularly opinions and rules laid down by Baron Redesdale, her father. Opinions vary about Unity's appearance. Some say she was unattractive, others that she was beautiful. Hitler, when he met her, certainly thought her good looking and felt that she was the epitome of Aryan beauty. He was quite happy to use her as a way of making Eva Braun jealous.

Unity and Diana were always the most right-wing of the girls. Diana Mitford had married Bryan Guinness, heir to the Guinness family fortune, but with her right-wing leanings she soon left him for Sir Oswald Mosley, the charismatic but misguided leader of the British Union of Fascists (BUF).

Her father was furious when he learned that Diana was living in sin with Mosley and forbade members of the family to have any further contact with her. Unity, of course, promptly disobeyed and met Mosley at a party thrown by Diana. Unity Mitford duly became a very public and extrovert member of Mosley's Blackshirts.

Unity was a regular attendee at Communist Party meetings on behalf of the BUF where she would inveigle her way in past the 'heavies' on the door, then heckle, scream and shout at the speakers. She was more than happy to get involved in the scuffles that inevitably broke out and at BUF marches and rallies she wore her black shirt with intense pride.

However, it was not long before Mosley became unhappy, both with the publicity that Unity was garnering and with the way she was making an exhibition of herself. He was more than content when she and Diana set off to attend the Nuremburg Rally of 1933. The gathering with its thousands of SA troopers and the ecstatic reception for Hitler and his cronies astounded both girls who were soon in awe of Hitler and what he had managed to achieve in such a short time.

The sisters were back in Germany the following year, Unity openly expressing her admiration of Hitler the man and for Hitler the politician. She was supposedly in Germany to study but, in reality, she spent most of her time stalking the Führer and when she sat for several hours watching him eat and talk at the Osteria Bavaria café in Munich it was inevitable that sooner or later Hitler would notice her.

Her persistence worked. Hitler invited Unity across to his table where they talked, joked and laughed for nearly an hour. And then he picked up the bill. Hitler was enchanted by his new friend and as far as Unity was concerned, he had cast a spell over her, one that would last a lifetime. He was, she wrote in a letter to her father 'the greatest man of all time'. She, because she had finally made the acquaintance of Germany's leader, regarded herself as the luckiest girl in the world.[2]

To Hitler, Unity more than matched her middle name – Valkyrie. The Mitford family had German connections and Unity's grandfather had been a personal friend of Richard Wagner's. He had also translated the works of Houston Stuart Chamberlain, one of Hitler's great heroes. Hence the decision to award Unity the bizarre middle name. Her appearance, her personality and her aristocratic background were enough, once the initial introductions had been made, to guarantee Unity Mitford access to Hitler's inner circle. It was not all altruism and admiration on his part, however. He undoubtedly hoped that she would provide a 'way in' to British aristocratic circles. That was destined never to happen but in the mid-1930s with Hitler just beginning to flex his muscles, almost anything seemed possible.

For the next few years Unity Mitford moved easily between Germany and Britain. She had easy access to Hitler who genuinely believed that this English Valkyrie had been 'sent' to him. Their companionship was the fulfilment of destiny and so it was right that she should sit next to him at Party rallies or be given her own private box at the Berlin Olympics in 1936.

Unity became particularly friendly with the Munich Jew baiter Julius Streicher. In hindsight, it seems a strange alliance, the virulent and coarse Streicher and the pretty aristocratic Unity, but like Streicher,

Unity had a fierce hatred of anything connected with Judaism. She accompanied Streicher, always the most unpleasant of a very unpleasant band of high-ranking Nazi officials, to the Youth Festival in Hesselberg where she stood before the thousands of eager young Germans and gave a virulent anti-Semitic speech. She also wrote articles for Streicher's paper *Der Sturmer* where she was insistent that her full name be attached to each piece she produced: 'I want everyone to know I am a Jew hater ... The English have no notion of the Jewish danger.'[3]

Unity's antics caused public outcry in Britain but she carried on regardless. The British security services opened a dossier on her, monitoring her behaviour and movements around Europe. Even at home – perhaps particularly at home – her exhibitionism was a cause for concern. When Unity turned up at a Labour or Communist rally, violence was never far behind. She, of course, loved it.

Incidents like the time she gave the Hitler salute to the British consul in Munich – in its own way as shocking as von Ribbentrop's greeting to the king – were well documented and it was not long before her letters and baggage were being intercepted and examined by MI5. They were usually found to be full of Nazi propaganda.

So wild and outlandish were Unity's statements that, inevitably, many people considered her to be a threat to national security. The more sober, realistic representatives of the government soon declared her to be no more than an out-of-control socialite. She was hysterically fanatical in her support for Adolf Hitler but she was never likely to offer a threat to the security of Britain and the British Empire. However, that might be, the security agents were adamant that in the increasingly likely event of war between Britain and Germany there should be some restriction of her movements. She was not the type of person who should be allowed to roam freely around the country.

In Germany she was thought to be far more important than that. Hitler presented her with an engraved swastika badge, complete with his signature on the back, and when the Anschluss occurred in 1938, she stood beside him on the balcony in Vienna as he received the adulation of the Austrian crowd.

There was no doubt that Hitler and Unity were very close but whether or not the relationship went beyond friendship remains unclear. As with so many of his female companions, Unity was valuable to him – particularly in light of her Englishness and her supposed connections –

but whether they had a more intimate relationship remains unknown. The one thing that is clear is the fact that however close they might have been, Unity did not influence any of Hitler's decisions. She might argue, shout and debate all she liked but Hitler was set on his course. No amount of urging on Unity's part would ever cause him to waver and placate Chamberlain. If there was any hesitation, it would have to come from Chamberlain and the British, not Hitler.

On a personal level he certainly played her against Eva Braun, leaving his insecure mistress jealous and angry. Eva was helpless, being reduced to making bitchy remarks about her rival – if rival she was – about Unity's appearance, her rather sturdy legs in particular, in her private and secret diary.

For her part Unity would undoubtedly have slept with the man she adored but there is no record of this ever having happened. At this stage in his life Hitler had progressed past the womanizing of his early days. He was now dedicated to Germany and, besides, he always had Eva Braun to fall back on should he require solace. Even so, Hitler gave Unity a degree of laxity that hinted at a friendship which was far beyond the normal relationships between the Führer and his women. When she met for dinner or coffee with Hitler and other Nazi leaders, Unity was the only one allowed to talk politics. To everyone else the subject was banned but the Führer tolerated Unity with a leniency that amazed everyone. Unity Mitford loved Britain but felt that the country was being irrevocably damaged by the evil influences she so detested and urged Hitler to ally himself to her homeland. Sometimes she was quite wild with her remarks but Hitler tolerated her outbursts – and did absolutely nothing to keep the British government happy with the state of affairs.

Meanwhile, the other Mitford girls continued with their lives. Nancy became a novelist of some note and a historian, producing *The Sun King*, a more than respectable biography of Louis XIV. Several of her books were later filmed for television or movies. The communist sister Jessica spent most of her life in the US but not before a period in Spain lending assistance to the opponents of General Franco during the Spanish Civil War. She immigrated to the USA where she and her second husband became members of the US Communist Party and, during the post-war McCarthy witch-hunts, refused to testify in front of the tribunal. She later resigned from the Communist Party in protest against the policies of Joseph Stalin. Pamela was, for a brief while, the object of unrequited love from poet John Betjeman but otherwise lived an unremarkable life in the country. Deborah married the Duke of Devonshire and settled down to creating the perfect stately home out of the chaos that had once been Chatsworth House.

That left Diana. Always the most beautiful of the Mitford girls, she was presented at court and seemed to be destined to a life of luxury and wealth after her marriage to Bryan Guinness. It was not to be. She had become a rabid fascist while still very young and begun her affair with the BUF leader Sir Oswald Mosley as early as 1932. Her 1936 marriage to Mosley, kept secret for some time, took place in the home of Dr Goebbels outside Berlin. Adolf Hitler was the guest of honour. Friendship with Hitler and her connection with the British Union of Fascists meant that Diana was always well treated whenever she travelled to Germany. In 1936 when she arrived in Berlin for that year's Olympic Games, Hitler sent a plush Mercedes to meet her and take her to the stadium.

She was never as close to Hitler as Unity but she did become very friendly with Winifred Wagner and with Magda Goebbels. Whenever they met, the three of them would sit together venting their spleen against the socialists, the communists, the Jews and whoever else had annoyed them – the analogy of Shakespeare's three witches is hard to avoid. Diana's relationship with Mosley and her right-wing beliefs might have given her credibility in Nazi Germany but they caused major rifts within her family. Her father disowned her and for a long while she was persona non grata in aristocratic and upper-class circles where she might have expected some form of support.

Politically, Diana Mitford was about as far removed from the communist Jessica as it was possible to be and by the end of the 1930s, she had become permanently estranged from her sister. They rarely spoke again after Diana's marriage to the man whose political beliefs Jessica detested.

The 1920s and 1930s were a boom time for the communists across Europe as the Great Depression bit deeply into the lives of the working classes. Communism seemed to be one way out of the crisis, particularly to people like Jessica. In her own way she was as dogmatic and convinced about her beliefs as Unity and Diana. If that meant the destruction of family ties, so be it.

Jessica was not the only sister to annoy Diana. When Nancy Mitford wrote the novel *Wigs on the Green*, satirizing Mosley and his beliefs,

Sir Oswald was furious. Diana, naturally, took his side and it was inevitable that publication of the book led to yet another permanent falling out between Mitford sisters.

Hitler, meanwhile, was happy to take Diana into his confidence. In August 1939, while Neville Chamberlain of Britain, Edouard Daladier of France and other politicians were still hoping to maintain the peace, he sat on a couch alongside her and whispered into her ear that war between Germany and Britain was now inevitable. It was a warning that she took to heart but never, at any time, did Diana attempt to pass on Hitler's words to the British government. Such a warning would probably have been immaterial to Prime Minister Chamberlain whose views and policies were already set but, as a principle, it would have been the right thing to do.

As the war approached MI5 prepared a secret report on Diana. Only released to the public in 2002, the report was scathing in its conclusions: '[Diana] is said to be far cleverer and more dangerous than her husband and will stick at nothing to achieve her ambitions. She is wildly ambitious.'[4]

Unity might have the ear of Adolf Hitler but in the eyes of the British secret service it was clearly her elder sister who was more dangerous.

The outbreak of war in September 1939 was both devastating and disastrous for Diana and Unity Mitford. Their dreams of an alliance with Germany were smashed to smithereens and their world of cardboard credibility was instantly sent up in smoke. Freedom of speech during peacetime was one thing. In time of war it was something entirely different. Once their ultimatum to Germany over the invasion of Poland was ignored, the British government was going to take no chances with the representatives of the British Union of Fascists. Both Diana and her husband were arrested and interned under Defence Regulation 18B. There was no trial for either and the BUF was quickly and efficiently dissolved. Diana spent three years in Royal Holloway Prison. Initially she was held on her own but later she was allowed the company of her husband. They were released in 1943, partly because of Oswald Mosley's ill health and partly because they were no longer considered a threat to security. The couple spent the rest of the war under house arrest, without passports, and under close observation by the police.

For Unity Mitford a more complex and disabling fate lay in wait. As war inched ever closer, both in Germany and Britain, she continued to proclaim her faith in National Socialism. She took every opportunity to oppose the left-wing theories and activists that she saw as being totally destructive to her country. She was provocative in the extreme and was once knocked to the ground by Labour supporters when she tried to disrupt their meeting in Hyde Park. Only the swift intervention of the police prevented her from being dumped unceremoniously in the Serpentine.

Somehow, she had always managed to be present whenever Hitler made one of his dramatic land grabs in these frenetic years – the Anschluss with Austria and the re-occupation of the Rhineland being two prime examples. On occasions like these she was usually at the front of the crowd, eyes aglow with an almost sexual pleasure, and Hitler always seemed to notice her.

By the early summer of 1939, Unity had become totally disillusioned with Britain, its politicians and the way the country seemed to be drowning in its own disharmony. Already at odds with her parents, she disowned her family and moved permanently to Munich, clearly mapping out where her real loyalties lay. Her timing was disastrous. Far from being able to spend more time with her, Hitler now took the opposite tack and shied away. It is easy to see why. Despite her beauty, her idealized Aryan looks and her move to Germany, Unity Mitford was still English. Germany was about to engage in a life or death struggle with the British Empire and Hitler could not be seen to be favouring someone from the very country he would soon be fighting. He was also extremely busy, running and planning for a military campaign that would culminate in the conquest of Europe. He had little time to entertain emotional, not to say hysterical young girls like Unity Mitford.

When war between Britain and Germany did finally break out, Unity was devastated. She had pleaded with Hitler for restraint and diplomacy and hoped it would not come to this. But now her worst nightmares had come true. Despite several urgent messages to Hitler begging him to meet her one more time to discuss the situation, Unity was to be disappointed. The Führer did not even bother to reply. Sadly, she realized that she had put herself beyond the pale:

> Her intrigues had left her with no country to call her own. She had forsaken Britain to become an enemy alien living in Germany. Neither side now wanted her for she was a security risk to both.[5]

Despite her nationality and her potential risk, Unity was certainly not a prisoner in Germany. She had complete freedom of movement although the local police and the Gestapo did keep her under close surveillance. Slowly but surely the pressure mounted on a girl who had never had real control over her emotions. Seemingly rejected by Hitler, alone and isolated in her flat in Munich – once the property of a Jewish family – Unity was simply unable to cope. Despite all her hopes Britain and Germany were finally at war; she was possibly even guilty of high treason. It was not to be contemplated.

One day she drove to the English garden in the city and sat on a park bench. Pulling out the pearl-handled pistol given her by Hitler himself, Unity Mitford breathed in what she believed was going to be her final breath and shot herself in the head. The noise of the shot alerted the shadowing Gestapo officer who immediately picked her up and took her to hospital. By now she was bleeding profusely but the wound, though serious, was not likely to be fatal. However, an operation to remove the bullet lodged perilously close to her brain proved unsuccessful and she lay, drifting in and out of consciousness in her hospital bed. Hitler sent flowers, insisting that she have the best possible treatment but could not spare the time to visit his Aryan beauty. For two months she remained in the Nussbaumstrasse Clinic, recovering slowly and only partially from her wound. Finally, with the war now raging across the globe, in December 1939 it was decided that she should be moved to neutral Switzerland.

Lord Redesdale was informed of Unity's whereabouts and told that he should make arrangements to have her brought back to England. He turned to his family for help. The logical sibling to make contact with Unity was Diana but she was already locked up in Holloway Prison and so it fell to Deborah to make the journey across Europe to Berne in Switzerland. Accompanied by her mother, Deborah endured the dangerous journey to Berne. Once there she arranged for Unity to be brought back to England by hospital train. They arrived in January 1940. Every jolt on the rails, Deborah later said, was agony for her sister. Both she and her mother had been shocked by Unity's appearance:

> The person lying in bed was desperately ill. She had lost
> two stone, was all huge eyes and matted hair, untouched
> since the bullet went through her skull. The bullet was still

in her head, inoperable the doctor said. She could not walk, talked with difficulty and was a changed personality, like one who has had a stroke … she was a stranger, someone we did not know.[6]

There was a public outcry at Unity's return, many people calling for her to be arrested and tried as a traitor, or even incarcerated, without trial, alongside her sister under Defence Regulation 18B. Controversy continued to follow her and there were even rumours that she was carrying Hitler's child. The rumours, like the calls for her arrest, came to nothing.

Incontinent, childlike in her attitude, Unity was lodged with her mother – now divorced from Lord Redesdale – in a small cottage close to the family home at Swinbrock in Oxfordshire. Physically, she recovered from her ordeal, putting on weight and gradually learning to walk and talk again. On the other hand, improvements in her emotional and mental state were slow and she never really progressed beyond the mental age of a 10-year-old child. However, she was able to get out and about and even make a visit to see Diana and Oswald Mosley at Holloway Prison in March 1943. Whatever she felt about Hitler – and that remains unclear – Unity never lost her affection for the Nazi Party or for right-wing politics. Unity Mitford lived on until 1948. She had been on a family holiday on the Scottish island of Inch Kenneth when she was taken ill and removed to hospital in Oban. There she died from meningitis caused by cerebral swelling around the bullet that was still lodged in her brain. She was just 33 years old.

Unity Mitford, Hitler's English girl, as she was called, had led an adventurous life, one that had seen her mix with the elite of British and German society. She had been admired and she had been reviled, she had loved and seen her dreams of happiness come to nothing. Sadly, she had neither the fortitude nor the maturity to cope and eventually it all tore her apart. Her relationship with Hitler remains shrouded in mystery although it is clear that he enjoyed her company and was prepared to put up with many of her foibles, at least for as long as his interest lasted. He was always inclined to endure comments from her that would have enraged him had they come from anyone else but when he had had enough, he simply discarded her and moved on to other things.

'I fear I bring women no happiness,' Hitler declared in the wake of Unity's suicide attempt. As far as Unity Mitford was concerned it was an accurate statement.[7]

Unity's sister Diana lived, briefly, in Ireland after the war but spent most of her declining years in France where she and her husband Sir Oswald became friendly with the Duke and Duchess of Windsor. Diana was briefly reconciled with her sister Jessica while they were both nursing their sister Nancy who was living at Versailles and suffering from Hodgkinson's disease.

After Nancy's death Diana and Jessica never spoke again. Oswald Mosley died in 1980, Diana in 2003 at the age of 93. She had become a writer and a reviewer of note, someone with an impressive turn of phrase and a quirky sense of humour – she never cultivated such delicious strawberries, she declared, as the ones she grew in the garden of Holloway Prison

Diana was to condemn Hitler for the atrocities committed during the years he was in power but still admitted a fascination with the man and with fascism in general. Just as Jessica was to cast aside the communism of her youth in the wake of Stalin's atrocities, Diana put the fascism of her dandelion days behind her.

It is perhaps inevitable to wonder whether or not Unity Mitford would have grown out of her adolescent fascination with Hitler and the Nazis. Her early death prevents any answers but where she would have stood and what she might have thought of it all remains one of the great imponderables of Hitler's life and times.

Chapter 11

Closer Yet: Traudl Junge, Hanna Reitsch and More

Out of all the women with whom Adolf Hitler consorted, in particular after he had become Chancellor of Germany in 1933, there can be little doubt that it was his secretarial staff who knew him best. His secretaries worked with him every day, and most nights too, sat with him, drank tea with him and ate with him. They also gossiped with him on a regular basis. They were the eager recipients and observers of his charm and his fury. They knew him in his public persona and in his private, more intimate moments. They knew him like no others. Because of the closeness of the contact, most especially during the last few years of the Third Reich, Hitler's secretaries were given a unique opportunity to see the man at work. It is doubtful that they were ever able to influence his decisions or his thinking on matters of state, at least not in a major way, but his attitude to these women was revealing of a gentle and caring side of his personality. And even if one or more of them was able to achieve only the minutest fraction of change in his attitude or behaviour then they are worth looking at and recording.

Almost without exception Hitler's secretaries found him to be charming. He was, they said, the most understanding of employers – hardly the picture you would expect of a mass murderer and the architect of one of the biggest genocides the world had ever known. None of them ever expressed any personal knowledge of the horrors of the concentration camps. It was rose-tinted spectacles, perhaps, or maybe just a matter of personal survival, but the fact that several of them remained with him in the Bunker until the end gives some indication of the respect and affection with which they held him.

One of the longest-serving and therefore one of the closest to Hitler – who always preferred to have people around him that he knew well – was Johanna Wolf. Like many of Hitler's closest staff she was a native of Munich and until she began to move around the country in her capacity as the Führer's private secretary, she had spent most of her life in the Bavarian city. A committed National Socialist and Party member, Johanna Wolf spent several years working for Hitler's great friend and fellow NSDAP member Dietrich Eckart. He had introduced her to Hitler in the early days of the Party and a mutual admiration quickly grew between the two. On Eckart's death in 1923, just a few weeks after the Beer Hall Putsch, she found herself a job with Dr Alexander Glasser of the Bavarian Diet. This lasted until 1929 when she began to work for another of Hitler's colleagues in the Nazi Party, Gregor Strasser. Having also carried out occasional secretarial work for men like Rudolf Hess and Obergruppenführer Wilhelm Bruckner, when Hitler became Chancellor, Johanna Wolf was appointed the Führer's senior personal secretary. It was a compliment to her efficiency and to her confidentiality and was a post she held until the final days of the regime in the Führer Bunker.

Wolf and Hitler grew close, both of them fuelled by the same ideals and philosophies. He called her his Little Wolfin (She Wolf) because of her fascination with wolves and their way of life. She was recognized by most of the staff around Hitler as perhaps the best means to get to the Führer – grab the ear of Wolfin, people began to whisper, and your message would soon come to the attention of the one man who really mattered in the Third Reich. In that way Johanna Wolf may have been quite an effective influence on Germany's leader, not as someone who had original ideas of her own or even as a dissenting voice, but as a filter and a conduit. At the very least, her influence would allow different or new ideas to be presented to the Führer. They would then gain a hearing although where they went from there would largely depend on Hitler's mood of the moment.

Interestingly, Johanna Wolf was one of the few people close to Hitler who, after the war, did not write about her time with him. She was, she told journalists who tried to inveigle her into writing articles, exposés and books, a private secretary and what went on between her and Hitler would remain private. It was a stance that she took with her to the grave.

Her affection for Hitler was noticed and accepted by all. Traudl Junge, the Führer's last private secretary, wrote movingly about the parting of the secretary and her boss a few days before his suicide on

30 April 1945 – even though she was mistaken about the number of years they had worked alongside each other. Junge says twenty-five – in actual fact it was just sixteen:

> Fraulein Wolf and Fraulein Schroeder, the other two secretaries, were among those who left. Fraulein Wolf had tears in her eyes when she said goodbye, as if she sensed that she would never again see Hitler, who had been her boss for 25 years.[1]

Hitler's Little Wolfin had wanted to stay and to die alongside him. Hitler persuaded her that she should leave because she still had her 80-year-old mother to look after. Otherwise there is no doubt that Johanna Wolf would have ended her life in April 1945 alongside the man she idolized.

Christa Schroeder was the second long-serving member of Hitler's staff. She began working for the Nazi Party in 1930 as a stenographer in the SA but Hitler noticed her and, more importantly, liked what he saw. Consequently, she was transferred to his private staff in June 1933.

She worked predominantly at the Reich Chancellery in Berlin until war broke out in 1939; then she became one of the Führer's mobile or peripatetic secretaries and accompanied him on his various travels around the region. He enjoyed her company, listened to her opinions and often amused her with stories and jokes.

Once, in the pitch darkness of the Eastern Front during the early stages of the Operation Barbarossa and when, it must be noted, all was going well for the Wehrmacht, she realized that she had left her flashlight in Hitler's room:

> I asked the manservant to fetch it. He returned empty-handed. 'Where could it be then?' I asked. Hitler, in jovial frame of mind, defended himself with a smile. 'I have not stolen it. I may be a thief of lands but not of lamps.'[2]

Between 1941 and 1944 she was based mainly at the Wolf's Lair, Hitler's base near Rasentburg in East Prussia, before returning to Berlin where she found herself established in the Führer Bunker. Highly efficient and hardworking, Schroeder was also someone who believed in speaking her mind. She did not tolerate fools gladly and was known even to contradict Hitler when she felt he was wrong. Normally Hitler smiled at her comments, putting them down to her direct personality, but if he felt she had gone too far he would sulk with her rather than tell her off – as he did when she argued for allowing the troops on the Eastern Front to smoke, in complete contrast to his long-held views on the use of tobacco. It was the one comfort they had, Schroeder said. It was bad timing on her part. The Russians were pressing hard, driving the Wehrmacht back, and Hitler was in no mood to discuss or put up with such trivialities. For the first time in his career as a war leader, things were not going as he wanted. This time the Führer was not for turning and his sulking fit lasted almost to the end of the regime.

Smile or sulk, it did not stop Christa Schroeder making her point but, inevitably, the more she disagreed with him the more her standing in Hitler's eyes was diminished. He was not the man to stand being corrected, at least not on a regular basis and certainly not by a woman. It was a two-way process and eventually she became disenchanted with him, particularly after the clear failure of the Russian campaign. He was no longer willing to enjoy a joke or even to laugh, something that Christa had always felt was one of his strengths.

Like many of the staff gathered around Hitler, Christa Schroeder eventually became very depressed and fatalistic. She knew that such emotions were, partly, due to the environment and the excessive workload that Hitler piled onto them but she was also well aware that his attitude and personality played a large part in people's feelings:

> Hitler's influence was felt everywhere: either nobody had a private opinion or feared to express it. Whoever dared was cold shouldered ... After Stalingrad Hitler could no longer relax to music. Then we spent the evenings listening to his monologues ... On most topics we knew what was coming next and so the evenings required endurance.[3]

She would do her duty to the end but there can be little doubt that Hitler's orders for her and Johanna Wolf to leave Berlin on 20 April were welcomed by Christa Schroeder. Even the Wolfin could see that the final curtain was only a few days away from being lowered on the Third Reich. Knowing her likely fate once Berlin fell to the Soviets, Schroeder had resolved to end her life with a cyanide capsule she had managed to acquire. Anything was better than being taken prisoner and being abused by the Russians. This last-minute reprieve took the decision out of her hands.

Hitler was always insistent that at least one of his secretaries should be present to take dictation and to type his letters at all times of the day and night. This meant that his whole secretarial staff had to accompany him and be on call wherever he went. And that really did mean *wherever* he went. That might be the border lands of Poland and Russia, the forests of Eastern Prussia, the city of Berlin or the relative calm of the Obersaltzberg. Inevitably, the amount of work he laid down before them put an immense strain on the two women. Both Johanna Wolf and Christa Schroeder were, at various times, forced to spend time undergoing what was euphemistically called 'the cure' at health centres or spas – rest periods where they could relax and forget the insistent calls to duty that Hitler threw at them. In order to help out with the workload, it was decided that further secretarial help was needed.

First there was Gerda Daranowski, known to everyone on Hitler's staff as 'Dara'. She came from Berlin and was originally employed in the Reich Chancellery. An attractive and pleasant young woman, she was the very opposite of Christa Schroeder: where Schroeder would challenge, Dara was more accepting and avoided confrontation. Hitler was attracted to Dara although there seems to have been no intimacy between them. He simply liked having her around. She was a light-hearted soul and that was something the Führer needed more and more as the conduct of the war went from bad to worse.

Eva Braun noticed the attraction and was jealous that Dara seemed to have such a firm hold over her lover. She was, however, powerless to do anything about it. Whatever Eva thought, it is unlikely that Daranowski had any real influence over Hitler, not even in the subtle manner of Johanna Wolf. She was more concerned with placating her boss, keeping him happy and thus safeguarding her own position. She would never have challenged any of the Führer's views or ideas but, instead, used her obvious femininity to make him feel good about himself. Like most men he enjoyed being flattered and to have a pretty, vivacious young woman pandering to him did, at the very least, reinforce his opinion of himself.

Dara had joined Hitler's personal staff in 1937 and from the beginning made an excellent impression not just with Hitler but also with the many officers who thronged around him. She was, for a short while, involved in an affair with Erich Kempka, Hitler's chauffeur – some reports say they were actually engaged. It did not last and before long Dara had formed a deep relationship with Colonel (later General) Eckhard Christian of the Luftwaffe. With Hitler's approval they were soon married.

Shortly after the marriage in 1943, Dara left Hitler's employment, naturally wanting to spend more time with her husband. It was a mistake as the couple soon found they had little in common and before the year was out, she had returned to the Führer's side. Hitler was more than pleased to have her back. He had missed her.

Both before and after Dara returned to the fold, the pressure on Hitler's secretaries increased to an intense level and it was soon decided that yet another typist/office worker was required. After a series of interviews and tests, Gertrude (Traudl) Humps was employed. She was just 22 years old, pretty and with a personality to rival that of Dara Daranowski. Traudl joined Hitler's staff in the winter 1942/3. At that time Hitler had based himself at the Wolf's Lair in East Prussia. It was a bleak, heavily forested area with few facilities for staff but she loved it and enjoyed every minute of being in the company of such distinguished men as Martin Bormann, General Alfred Jodl and Field Marshal Wilhelm Keitel – and, of course, Adolf Hitler.

It was a degree of naivety that would come back to haunt Traudl Humps in the years after the war. At the time she had simply taken a job with the leader of her country, an opportunity that, as someone remarked, any young girl in the Third Reich would have jumped at. Only much later did the regrets surface:

> How could I have been so naive and unthinking … In 1942, when I was 22 and eager for adventure, I was fascinated by Adolf Hitler, thought him an agreeable employer, paternal and friendly, and deliberately ignored the warning voice inside me, although I heard it clearly enough.[4]

Only after the revelation of his crimes against humanity did Traudl's guilt really hit home. Whether she was deceiving herself – as so many supporters of the Nazi Party managed to do – is irrelevant. How she felt about Hitler and the regime at the time of her employment is what really matters when examining her role as Hitler's youngest and final personal secretary.

Several observers have remarked that there was an element of 'slyness' in the personality of Traudl Humps and that in her daily contact with Hitler and the rest she was doing little more than playing a role. On that particular matter the jury, as they say, is still out. To begin with Traudl took over the work of the absent Dara. Regardless of whether she was playing a game or whether what Hitler saw in her was genuine, she was the perfect secretary for the Führer and he immediately fell for her charms:

> Blond hair, blue eyes and slim figure made her the perfect type of woman that so pleased him. She was also so similar to Eva Braun that the two of them looked like sisters … The final detail which sealed her advancement to the position of secretary was her father. He had been decorated with the Nazi Blutorden [Blood Order] awarded for the part he played in Hitler's failed putsch in 1923.[5]

Once again, there was nothing sexual about the relationship between Hitler and Traudl Humps. As with Dara, he simply liked to have her around. He enjoyed the company of beautiful young women; their charm, enthusiasm and energy seemed to revitalize him. Traudl Humps was no exception and Hitler took a decidedly paternal interest in her life. He would have loved nothing more than to see her settled down with a good Aryan boy. It was almost preordained and Traudl soon became infatuated with one of the Führer's adjutants. Hans Junge was a member of the SS Leibstandarte, Hitler's personal bodyguard, a handsome and captivating young man who immediately swept her off her feet. Soon they were going on long walks together and everyone knew that romance was blossoming. Hitler approved of the relationship and urged that the couple marry quickly. This they did, in June 1943, a hurried affair as Junge was about to leave Hitler's staff and join a front-line fighting regiment.

Traudl Junge, as she now was, continued to work for the Führer. She and Hans had spent almost no time together but with him now posted away from the Berghof it was logical for Traudl to continue in her employment with Hitler. Their father–daughter relationship was effectively and quickly re-established.

She and Eva Braun also became close during this time – after all, Traudl was married and clearly offered no threat to Eva's position as the Führer's mistress. The affection between the two women seems to have been genuine enough and lasted right through until the double suicide of Hitler and Braun in Berlin. In the final days Eva even gave Traudl her glamorous and much-prized fur wrap, stating that she would have no further use for it, not where she was going.

It was Eva Braun's brother-in-law, Hermann Fegelein, who broke the news to Traudl Junge of her husband's death. Hitler had known of the tragedy for a few days, having been informed in his capacity as head of state that Hans Junge had been killed in the Normandy campaign. However, he had not been able to steel himself and make the announcement – a clear indication of the fatherly affection he held for the pretty young secretary. The marriage, as with so many wartime matches, was something of a mistake. After the initial shock of Hans's death had worn off, Traudl Junge was able to make an accurate analysis of her relationship with him and her short-lived marriage. She realized that she and Hans had rushed into their union and, as a result, from that time onwards she became far more independent and less likely to get herself tied down:

> Hans Junge and I had no opportunity at all of coming intellectually close. I never had deep, probing conversations with him and I didn't know nearly enough about his interests. We never even made plans for the future.[6]

With the Third Reich beginning to crash down around their ears, planning for the future was something that very few of Hitler's inner circle were able to do. It was more a matter of taking each day as it came and hoping against hope for a miracle.

Hitler had become a vegetarian soon after the death of Geli Raubal. He gave up alcohol – with which he had always been abstemious anyway – at the same time. This change in diet was meant to aid him but Hitler did not look after his health. He ate poorly and irregularly and as a result was often afflicted with stomach and skin problems. He had particular problems with flatulence and bad breath, hardly surprising considering the nature of his diet. He sought relief in the winking needle and the regular pill-popping of his physician Dr Morell. To begin with these remedies were successful but given the makeup of the medicines he used, Morell's cures were actually more dangerous and troublesome than they were helpful. There is little doubt that if he had continued taking them, they would eventually have killed Hitler. For his flatulence Morell prescribed enormous amounts of something called Dr Koester's Anti-Gas Pills, little doses of death containing, amongst other constituents, strychnine and Atropine. Hitler was also given pills to reduce his weight, sleeping pills to help him cope with insomnia and injections of pulverized bull testicles to prevent impotence.[7] Hitler swore by Morell's cures but as the Russian campaign turned from success to failure, his stomach problems returned with a vengeance. Morell's remedies now seemed to be having no effect but when Marshal Ion Antonescu of Romania told him of a cure he had tried for the same problems Hitler was hooked.

Antonescu, like Hitler, was an autocratic dictator (later executed for war crimes) who for years had experienced severe intestinal pains, particularly when he was under stress. The only relief he had found came from Frau Marlene von Exner, a dietician from a clinic in Vienna. Under her direction, Antonescu declared, his stomach problems had totally disappeared. Hitler was intrigued and asked Frau von Exner to join him at the Wolf's Lair. Almost immediately her new diet and food preparation began to work. She cooked Hitler's meals herself and within a matter of days he was actually enjoying his food again – something he had not done for years. He particularly loved the delicious puddings she made him, the apple pies and other Austrian delicacies appealing to his notorious sweet tooth.

It was not just her food that Hitler enjoyed. Marlene von Exner was a beautiful woman with a sparkling personality that only added to the appeal of the nightly conversations between Hitler and his women. The young officers on his staff were also taken with Marlene but when one of Bormann's adjutants, an SS officer by the name of Frederich Darges, fell in love with her and asked permission to marry her, Hitler was not overly pleased at the prospect of losing his new dietician.

As Darges was an SS man any prospective bride was required to prove her Aryan line of descent. A grandmother of Marlene, it was discovered, had been a foundling, an orphan who had been dumped on the state. Her racial purity could therefore not be confirmed. There might well have been Jewish ancestry in Marlene's background, nobody was able to say, and much to Hitler's – and Darges's – fury she was dismissed from her post.

Once again Adolf Hitler was without a dietician. His stomach issues immediately returned and for a while he was consumed by all of the old problems of intestinal pain and flatulence. Dr Morell saved the day by bringing in Constanze Manziarly who was then working at a sanatorium near the Berghof. As Frau von Exner had done, Constanze prepared his meals herself – in the kitchen her predecessor had designed – and Hitler's health problems ceased almost immediately. He was quite taken by her charm and her skills, declaring with childish delight that he now had 'a cook with a Mozart name'.[8] He was referring, of course, to Mozart's wife Constanze. Constanze Manziarly became a full member of the 'female corps' around Hitler from 1943 onwards, travelling with him to the Berghof and his other bases. She was another statuesque woman, in her early twenties. She was not only a beautiful brunette, she was also a gifted and skilled pianist. She took immense care with the preparation of Hitler's meals and he often invited her to share dinner or lunch with him. After all, he reasoned, she should be able to share and enjoy what she had created.

Once again Eva Braun grew madly jealous of this new addition to the inner circle, particularly when it often meant that she was relegated to eating alone as Hitler and Constanze sat together over one of her new creations. Yet again she could do nothing except vent her spleen to Hitler – not always the best or wisest thing to do. The regular evening or late-night tea sessions continued, wherever the group found itself, but it was the gatherings at the Berghof that were always looked forward to by everyone. An air of peace and security pervaded Hitler's favourite residence and there was no doubt that his female staff were instrumental in establishing this comforting and comfortable environment.

It could be argued that Hitler would have been better off using his time to plan the defences of his capital, the war against the Soviets and so on. Perhaps so, but he gained immense pleasure from these nightly discussions and presumably used them to recharge what was left of his emotional batteries. The war was lost anyway.

Part of this female inner circle and yet not part of it – mainly because she was so often away – was Hitler's favourite pilot Hanna Reitsch. He had his own personal pilot, Hans Baur, with whom he got on very well and trusted implicitly but Hitler had always had an affinity with pretty girls and Hanna Reitsch fitted that bill perfectly. He never flew with her but he avidly followed her exploits and gloried in her fame.

Born in 1912, Hanna Reitsch undertook her initial flight training in gliders and then powered aircraft while she was a medical student. However, flying was in her blood and she soon gave up medicine to concentrate on becoming a pilot. After gaining her wings, she became a stunt pilot for the UFA film company and then began testing aircraft for the Luftwaffe. She was one of the test pilots on the prototype of the Junkers Ju 87 Stuka dive-bomber and also for the first jet-powered Komet fighter. She managed to claim over forty endurance and altitude records during her career and became the first female helicopter pilot on the experimental machines designed in Germany in the late 1930s.

She was fearless and highly skilled, perhaps too much so. A serious crash in one of her test aircraft saw her hospitalized for five months but by the end of the war she had recovered sufficiently to begin flying once more.

Reitsch had a great desire for publicity and, being slim, blonde and pretty, Goebbels and the Nazi propaganda machine were happy to oblige. She was the perfect size, shape and character for a hero of the Reich and it was not long before she was a household name in Germany. During the early days of the war Hitler awarded Hanna Reitsch the Iron Cross First Class, an event that was greeted with great jubilation in the country. She was one of only three women to win this coveted award during the Second World War.

She went on to volunteer as a pilot for the experimental V-1 manned rocket scheme, a project that was eventually dropped – just as well as it would probably have killed her. The volunteer pilots named themselves the Suicide Group, which provides a fairly accurate picture of the project and the desperation that German military leaders had reached in the final stages of the war.

In October 1944 Hanna happened to be in Stockholm when she was given a booklet outlining the horrors of the death camps. On her return to Germany she immediately presented the booklet to Himmler. He, of course, denied the accusations but Hanna Reitsch, despite her support of the Nazi Party, was not convinced. Himmler, she said, must refute the claims; otherwise the good name of Germany would be polluted for ever. Himmler, of course, did nothing.

The final days of the war saw Hanna fly a tiny Fieseler Storch into Berlin, landing on the roadway near the Brandenburg Gate. Accompanied by her lover, General Robert Ritter von Greim, a renowned airman who had just been appointed head of the Luftwaffe in place of the disgraced Hermann Göring, Hanna Reitsch knew she could be flying to her death. She had no way of knowing how close the Russians now were to the Bunker or if the improvised roadway-landing strip was still open for use. The whole enterprise was one of exceptional courage and daring. The Storch was under fire from Russian aircraft and AA guns almost the whole way into Berlin and then, with Tempelhof and the other city airports now in Russian control, the landing strip was littered with rocks and debris around which Reitsch had to manoeuvre and taxi the plane. Greim was wounded in the leg by enemy fire, while Hanna arrived at the Führer Bunker unscathed. Her motive behind making this desperate flight into Berlin was simple: to persuade the Führer to leave the city and to fly out with her in the redoubtable Fieseler Storch. Hitler, of course, refused. He had already decided he would die in the capital. She made the same offer to Magda Goebbels. She would take the six Goebbels children out with her, she declared, not realizing that Magda had deliberately brought the children to the Bunker for the last act. Again the offer was refused.

In the end Hanna Reitsch left Berlin under heavy fire from the nearby Russian forces, the only addition to her luggage being the two cyanide capsules Hitler had given her before they parted.

Hitler was, by then, a shell of his former self. His hands and legs shook and he gazed at people through near-sightless eyes. He was stooped and dragged his left leg when he walked, partly as a result of the failed assassination attempt at the Wolf's Lair and party because of the rapid onset of what appears to have been Parkinson's disease. Reitsch could see, only too clearly, the disintegration of the man she admired more than anyone else in the world. It did not stop her trying to save him but she must, in her inner being, have realized that he had reached the end. When she left the Bunker on 28 April, flying the last plane to leave the beleaguered capital, she knew that she had seen Hitler for the final time. With her world crashing down around her, she considered using one of the poison capsules that Hitler had given her. After all, she had little to live for but, eventually, she decided against it and held onto the containers as a keepsake. There are those who believe that when she finally died in 1979, it was not as a result of a heart attack – the official cause of death – but because she took one of the suicide capsules. There was no autopsy and the theory cannot be proved.

Hanna Reitsch was a Nazi and a supporter of Adolf Hitler to the end; she had an enormous affection for Hitler and would have done almost anything for him. Flying the Führer out of Berlin to the safety of the Berghof or somewhere similar was, to her, a logical move. The alternative was to fight and die alongside him – and that was also something she was quite willing to do. Hitler had no desire to see her die. His future was set but Hanna Reitsch, like many others of his inner circle, still had life to live. She must go, leave while there was still time. It did not best please her but obedient to the end she did as her Führer asked. As she told the American interrogators after her capture: 'It was the blackest day when I could not die at my Führer's side … We should all kneel down in reverence before the altar of the Fatherland.'[9] By altar of the Fatherland she meant the Führer Bunker where Hitler shot himself in April 1945. It was rhetoric, grand rhetoric, and should be viewed in the context of the times. Ultimately it was more bravado than intent. Hanna Reitsch remained in awe of Adolf Hitler until the day she died. She was brave, fearless even, in all of her activities and escapades. How much she knew about the murder of millions remains questionable but there can be no doubt that she was the epitome of an inner-circle woman, someone who held Hitler's ideals firm in her bosom. She remained a Nazi to the end.

Chapter 12

The First Lady of Germany: Magda Goebbels

Adolf Hitler was both hated and loved by millions but it is doubtful if any of them – not the inmates of Dachau or Auschwitz or even his greatest acolyte Eva Braun – held him in such awe as Magda Goebbels. Wife of Hitler's propaganda chief Joseph Goebbels, Magda was a strikingly beautiful woman with chiselled features and glowing masses of dark-blond hair. She was universally regarded by everyone, high officials and the public alike, as the First Lady of Nazi Germany, a role into which she had been cast by no less a person than Hitler himself.

The role, unofficial as it was, had originally been filled by Emmy Göring, second wife of the Luftwaffe chief, but Magda soon usurped her. In theory, it was something of a 'nothing job,' simply appearing in public, smiling at the right time and not doing anything that was ever likely to upset Hitler's apple cart. It was a position she gladly undertook as her right; for nearly fifteen years she did her best to live up to the Führer's expectations.

Magda made more of the job than that, however. From the beginning she was determined that as First Lady in a singularly male-orientated regime she would contribute something, minimal as it might be, to the running of the country. She would play her part, making herself indispensable to the man she regarded as the saviour of her beloved country. Magda was unashamedly open about her admiration for and devotion to Adolf Hitler. This same woman who announced to the world that she would never wear clothes designed by any Jewish costumier also went on record to state that her main reason for marrying Dr Goebbels was that it meant she could be closer to Hitler: 'Of course, I love my husband, but my love for Hitler is stronger; I would be willing to lay down my life for him.'[1]

Nobody has been able to say, unequivocally and without question, whether or not her love was of a physical, sexual nature or whether it was an idealized and spiritual emotion that reflected Hitler's own feelings for Germany. Many have speculated but none has been able to prove or disprove the hypothesis – which makes the matter so much more intriguing. In a regime that relegated women to a lower-grade ranking Magda certainly had a desire and a will to serve both the country and the Führer. Hitler exploited that will and unashamedly used her. To ask how much further the relationship went is not exactly a rhetorical question even though the answer is always likely to remain something of a mystery.

Erich Kempka, Hitler's long-serving chauffeur, was a man always able to come up with a telling comment to summarize any debate. Being so close to the top people he was well placed to observe and make judgements about their lives. He once described Eva Braun's brother-in-law, Hermann Fegelein, as having 'his brains in his scrotum' – true and memorable. But his comment on Magda was colourful, incisive and probably even more accurate: 'When Magda Goebbels was around Hitler one could hear her ovaries rattling.'[2] Unfortunately, he did not go on to say if Hitler reciprocated the feelings and whether or not his testosterone levels took a sudden leap whenever Magda appeared.

Magda Goebbels's origins were fairly humble. Her mother, Auguste Behrend, was a housemaid and although Magda was born out of wedlock, she was soon legitimized by her father. His name was Oskar Ritschel and as an engineer from the Rhineland, he was reasonably well off, which enabled her to be well educated in Belgium and, thanks to her father's situation, at the prestigious Holzhausen Ladies' College in Germany.

Within a relatively short period of time her mother married Richard Friedlander, a wealthy Jewish businessman and it was not long before Magda was wearing a Star of David on a chain around her neck. Inevitably she mixed with Jewish people, children and adults alike. She fell in love with a Jewish boy by the name of Victor Arlosoroff and, although she remained a gentile, together they dreamed of leaving Germany and creating a Jewish homeland in Palestine. The relationship was no more than a teenage romance, however, and eventually the young couple drifted apart. Arlosoroff eventually changed his first name to Chaim, found a Jewish partner and in 1924 moved to Palestine.

He was soon recognized as one of the major Zionist leaders in what was later to become Israel but was shot down and murdered by unknown assassins while out walking one evening. Cynics might say that this curious accident – which took place just as she and Victor/Chaim were beginning to achieve prominence – prevented the world from learning about Magda Goebbels's Zionist past. Certainly, Magda's life after her split from her Jewish boyfriend took her on another path and in another political direction altogether.

Magda's brief dalliance with Jewish culture was not long lasting but it did give her a greater insight into the ways of Jewish people than many other Nazi officials. Although her mother and her husband soon divorced, Magda's stepfather made a point of continuing to care for and look after her during what was clearly a difficult time of her life.

Not long after the end of the First World War Magda met wealthy businessman Gunther Quandt on a train when she was returning to school after a holiday. For him it was a moment of sudden and thrilling ecstasy, something that would change his life forever. In a matter of minutes Magda had captivated the older, somewhat austere Quandt and they were married in June 1921. Five months later her first child Harald was born. The marriage did not last long but Magda did manage to fit in a number of trips, courtesy of Quandt's money and business enterprises, to the US, Latin America and several European countries. The death of Magda's much-loved stepson Helmut really marked the end of the relationship and the divorce settlement enabled her to establish an independent lifestyle for herself. In particular the award of a 50,000-mark lump sum enabled her to set herself up in a luxurious seven-room house in Charlattenburg in the western part of Berlin. From there she held court and established a reputation as a woman of taste and refinement.

She was much sought after by would-be husbands, one of whom was the nephew of US President Herbert Hoover. When she refused him the young Hoover, also called Herbert, was so upset that he crashed his car, with Magda in it, and Magda was hospitalized with broken bones and other injuries.

Post-war Germany was a land sharply divided. It was a time of high tension and violence where the gun, knife and jackboot were as much a part of political argument as debate and discussion. In the bitterness of defeat in the recent war and the perceived injustice of the Treaty of

Versailles semi-militarized Freikorps battalions clashed with the police and communist agitators in a bloody, seemingly never-ending series of street fights. At opposite ends of the spectrum, communists and socialists to the left, monarchists and nationalists to the right, there seemed to be no answer to the problem. It was exactly the type of environment in which small political parties like Hitler's NSDAP grew and thrived.

For several years Magda had been moving steadily to the right wing of politics and in 1930, after attending a Nazi Party rally, she found herself caught up and enthralled by the event's main speaker, Dr Joseph Goebbels. It was a landmark moment for her. Hardly the best looking of men, Joseph Goebbels was exceptionally short, walked with a limp – the result of osteomyelitis in childhood, although he claimed it was a war wound – and had a head that seemed out of proportion with the rest of his body. He was a writer and journalist, an unsuccessful novelist, and stood in total contrast to the strikingly attractive Magda. But while he might look like the runt of the litter, once he stood before a crowd and opened his mouth to speak, Joseph Goebbels had his audience caught in a vice-like grip that few could resist. It was clear to everyone that he passionately believed in the manifesto that he was proclaiming. He might not possess the raw fury and passion of Hitler but his words were carefully chosen to exert maximum effect on the listeners. If Hitler was all emotion, Joseph Goebbels was logic personified. And that was the element of his personality to which Magda responded. From the moment she first heard him declaim in public the flowing oratory, Joseph Goebbels held Magda spellbound. She was not interested in his physical appearance but when he spoke her whole world seemed to light up and she was caught in the trap of charm and promise that had already ensnared so many.

Soon after that initial contact Magda took the next step. She duly joined the Party and before long she had begun to carry out secretarial duties for Goebbels – then Gauleiter of Berlin – and his deputy. It was soon clear that Joseph and Magda Quandt, as she still termed herself, had become an item. He had taken to calling her 'a lovely woman' and promising to himself, in his diary, that he would doubtless fall in love with her. True to his word he was soon recording his boundless love for what he termed 'this beautiful creature' but qualifying the statement with the observation that she, too, seemed to be in love with him.[3]

The road to marriage was a rocky one for Joseph and his would-be bride. To begin with he was a serial womanizer and vacillated between opting for a full-time steady relationship with Magda and a life of free and easy adultery. Probably because of his physical deficiencies he seemed to have an innate desire to prove his manhood by bedding as many women as he could. Magda was no saint but Joseph Goebbels seemed to have taken the role of Don Juan to the extreme. That was not the only problem. He might feel free to seduce whomever he wished but that was his right as a man with normal sexual urges and a libido to satisfy. It was, as he would have put it, simply how he was. The same leniency did not extend to the woman to whom he had already professed his undying love and admiration. And therein lay another problem.

He was insanely jealous of Magda's affection for Party chief Hitler. She and Hitler had certainly become very close and the Führer made no secret of how fond he was of this voluptuous and dynamic woman. He knew that he could not marry – the old problem of being wedded to Germany – but the idea of having Magda close at hand remained enticing. Therefore, let her marry little Joseph and, as a consequence, she would always be available and nearby. Eventually the decision was made. She was too useful to be allowed to just slip away and despite all the difficulties, Joseph and Magda Goebbels were married on 19 December 1931. Adolf Hitler was chief witness.

Once Adolf Hitler became Chancellor at the end of January 1933, Goebbels set about making himself invaluable to the Führer and to the regime. He was intelligent, ruthless and consumed by bitter anti-Semitism that was rivalled only by Hitler. But more importantly, alongside Hitler, he was one of the few men in the Party who understood the value of propaganda and the new technological devices by which it could reach out and draw in the entire German population.

Magda did her best to aid and abet her husband's rise. As unofficial First Lady, she needed to provide an example for all the women of the country and quickly set about creating the image of a perfect Aryan wife in a perfect Aryan marriage. Having six children was part of the process, blond-haired, blue-eyed children who, together with Magda and Joseph, looked and behaved like the ideal German family – on the surface at least.

It was all part of reinforcing Hitler's belief that the women of Germany should know their place – producing numerous children for the Reich, children who would help defend the country in time of need. Or, as it turned out, play their part in exporting the murderous ideals of the Nazi Party. Magda, imperious and distant as she might be, could always be relied upon to play her part. She felt it was an important element in the role of First Lady – her sacred duty, almost – to always look as attractive as she possibly could and thereby present an idyllic image for the women of Germany. Public appearances saw her with carefully manicured nails, hair beautifully styled and always clad in exquisite tailormade dresses. And the women of Germany loved her, doing their best to emulate her behaviour and look just like her.

She acted as 'agony aunt' for hundreds of those women who would write in to her at Goebbels's new Propaganda Ministry asking for advice on matters as wide-ranging as sexual deviancy, furnishing a home and how to make the man of the house feel comfortable and in charge. Of course, like so much of Hitler's Germany, it was all a sham.

Joseph Goebbels continued with his philandering and Magda retained her unbridled love for the Führer. It was a house held together with straw and inevitably, at some stage it was a structure that was bound to crack. Joseph and Magda were strong personalities and the marriage was, at best, tempestuous. Magda's response to her husband's infidelities was usually to ignore them. They were, she knew, temporary infatuations and besides, she was not above the occasional dalliance herself.

If, however, any of Joseph's affairs seemed to be growing a little too serious then her reaction was either to sulk or to withdraw from public appearances. Her absence from the public stage was something Hitler and the Party did not need and several times it required the direct intervention of the Führer to bring her back into the fold. Magda, always susceptible to Hitler's charms and having made her point to both her errant husband and to his most recent paramour, would slip quietly back into the old routine.

Hitler brokering a settlement between two of his favourites usually seemed like the best solution, one that really hurt no one. Nothing, however, quite prepared either Hitler or the Goebbels family for the events of summer 1938. Early that year, what started as just another fling for Joseph Goebbels began to escalate into something a great deal more significant. As head of the German film industry, Goebbels had immense influence and like Hitler, he was happy to exploit that influence to meet and become intimate with the actresses who depended on him for their livelihood. The 'casting couch' at Goebbels's ministry was often red hot from use. Most people involved in the film industry knew what was going on and accepted it as part of making the grade in a very lucrative industry. But what began as a brief flirtation with the beautiful Czech actress Lída Baarová gradually developed into a full-scale affair.

To begin with Magda tried ignoring the stories that were inevitably fed back to her. That had worked in the past but not this time. As the relationship developed, she summoned Lída to her house and told her that she was quite prepared for her to continue seeing Joseph as long as the affair did not interfere with her family or with her position in the regime. Unfortunately for Magda she had not appreciated that Lída's ambitions which went far beyond becoming a great star of stage and screen. She had also underestimated her husband's rampant sex drive. Joseph and Lída simply shrugged and took her at her word. They began spending long weekends together at Goebbels's country house but, more worrying for Magda, they began to openly appear together in public. Film premières and Party receptions soon saw the First Lady of Germany elbowed aside. She was being replaced in the public eye by Lída Baarová.

Gossip flared into open debate and eventually Magda, who with pressure and stress mounting had now left the family home, felt that she had no recourse but to seek help from the Führer. She went to him, sobbed on his shoulder and fluttered her eyelids at him. The result was as expected. Hitler was furious. Apart from his feelings for Magda, he needed his ideal Aryan family to symbolize the peaceful and harmonious nature of Nazi Germany. He would not tolerate even the faintest hint of a divorce scandal – particularly now when he was about to put the finishing touches to his plans to invade Lída Baarová's home country of Czechoslovakia. Goebbels was summoned into the Führer's presence at Berchtesgaden and given an ultimatum. If he wanted to retain his job there would have to be an immediate reconciliation between him and Magda. Lída Baarová was to be jettisoned. Goebbels, ever the pragmatist and career Nazi, caved in and meekly agreed.

When, shortly afterwards, German tanks rolled unhindered over the Czechoslovakian border, poor Lída found that she had gambled and lost more than she had ever bargained for. Her country had been conquered, her high-profile Nazi had abandoned her and she was quietly dropped from the rota of German film stars: her country, lover and profession all gone in a flash.

The only one to gain from the Baarová affair was, perhaps inevitably, Magda Goebbels. Her position as the only woman able to stand alongside

Adolf Hitler, if not as his equal then at least at his right-hand side, was now unchallenged. It had been a close-run thing but Magda was nothing if not a cunning and totally dispassionate player of court politics.

Over the next few months Hitler and Magda grew closer than ever while Joseph watched and simmered. He was powerless and he knew it. Magda had played him at his own game and won.

She enjoyed her victory and became even more open in her admiration and love for the Führer. Just as significantly, everyone at Hitler's 'court' knew what had happened and revelled in the humiliation of the treacherous propaganda minister:

> After he had finished whispering in her ear, Hitler put both his hands on her shoulders. That was when I saw the explosive look they exchanged. I certainly never saw Magda Goebbels look that way towards her husband.[4]

It was an emotion of such depth that Magda took it to the final hours in the Führer Bunker. And then she was willing to sacrifice not just her own life but those of her six children and her husband as well.

As war approached Magda and Joseph Goebbels gradually became close again. There was undoubtedly love there and now that she had his undivided attention Magda was not afraid to show it. The prospect of war merely quickened their heart rates. It was the ultimate test of pride and passion for Magda and Joseph – and for the whole German nation. Just a year after the Lída Baarová affair, Magda gave birth to Heide, her sixth and final child with Joseph Goebbels, the reconciliation child as she was called. It was a sign, a symbol that everything was all right once again. Joseph and Magda Goebbels had picked up the reins of their marriage. He suffered a short period of isolation from the inner circle but Goebbels was too valuable to Hitler to remain in limbo for long. As far as Magda was concerned it did not stop Hitler regarding her favourably. She remained one of the few people to whom he turned to for advice. Sometimes he even acted upon her suggestions.

When war broke out Magda immediately trained as a Red Cross nurse. It was, she told the nation, her way of giving something to the war effort that was necessary if Germany was to survive and prosper rather than decline and die. She also began to set several further examples for German wives and mothers to follow. Whenever her presence was required at the Chancellery or any other government enclave, she took a tram into the city rather than a Party car. Being chauffeured was considerably more convenient and more fitting with her position as First Lady but it would use up valuable fuel that was sorely rationed. The gesture was not missed by the people. Food was rationed or restricted and Magda immediately saw this as another way of improving her status with the people. She started to serve up frugal and very basic meals to her house guests, casting aside all the luxuries that she had become so used to enjoying. The message was simple: if I can do it so can you.

Personal sacrifice took on another dimension later in the war. Harald, her son from her first marriage, was wounded while fighting in Italy and taken prisoner by the Allies. He was, at least, Magda consoled herself, safe from harm in the hands of the British.

It all increased the strain she was under. She was intelligent enough to see what was coming, particularly after Hitler committed the country to a war on two fronts by invading Russia in 1942. Despite the initial successes in the Soviet Union and eastern Poland Magda was only too well aware of the dangers, not just to the country as a whole but, in particular, to her and all of her family. She was constantly worried and her health began to deteriorate. Increasingly, she began spending more and more time in hospital and health spas undergoing treatment for depression, facial tics, twitches and other mannerisms, and for nervous exhaustion. There was even a suggestion that, at one stage, she had suffered a heart attack. Whatever was medically wrong with her, the strain took an enormous toll and slowly reduced the once-immaculate Magda Goebbels to a mere shell of her former self. In many respects her decline was symptomatic of the German state and of the women who had always adored Magda and adhered to her doctrines of German womanhood. It was small comfort. Increasingly she became dependent on alcohol and tobacco, always taking care to hide the addictions from Hitler. Soon the shadows on her face, the lines on her cheeks and the bags under her eyes began to lengthen and grow as the reality of German defeat edged, like a nightmare, closer and ever closer.

Magda knew what her fate – and the fate of her husband – would be if they were ever captured by the Allies. Falling into Russian hands was the ultimate fear of all German women with stories of rape and brutality commonplace. For Magda there was the added pressure of being the wife of one of Hitler's most trusted lieutenants.

After discussing the matter with Joseph, long and painful discussions that lasted until the early hours of the morning, Magda decided that as the end approached, she would join him in the Führer Bunker and remain in Berlin until the final moments of the regime. Then she and Joseph would take their own lives. Their six children – Helga, Hilda, Helmut, Holde, Hedda and Heide – would stay with them and face exactly the same fate. It meant that once they had entered the Bunker, Magda Goebbels and the children would never emerge again. They would die there alongside Joseph and her beloved Führer.

At the time nobody, only Joseph and Magda herself, had any idea of the fate that awaited them and their offspring. The occupants of the Bunker, however, must have suspected what she had in mind. Why else would anyone decamp to such an awful place and at such an awful time? But nobody quite had the courage or the temerity to put their concerns into words. The six children, as children do the world over, played happily in their new environment, oblivious that their own mother would soon be ending their brief lives. The children were, Magda wrote in a letter to her son Harald 'too lovely for the world that lies ahead'.[5] The prospect of ending their lives sickened her but Magda Goebbels was nothing if not a determined woman. Once she had made up her mind nothing on God's earth would make her change it.

Magda and the children arrived at the Führer Bunker on 22 April 1945, just a week before the final act. They had spent the previous few weeks at their house outside Berlin, watching and waiting as the Russian troops inched ever closer. Joseph had been in the Bunker with his Führer all that time but knew, now, that the moment of truth was near. He telephoned Magda and told her it was time to join him. On their way into the underground warren that was Hitler's last refuge Magda and the children passed a city that had been destroyed by bullets, shells and bombs. It was barely recognizable, even to this Berliner. Soon the group of refugees came face to face with the man the children regarded as a favourite uncle. He, like the country he had led and ruined, was a shell of his former self and was already preparing himself for death.

Hitler welcomed the children who, if nothing else, brought a little light and happiness to the Führer Bunker. He tried, briefly, to persuade Magda to leave and take the children with her. This, he told her, was no place for them. It was no use. Magda Goebbels had made her decision and now she would stay in the Bunker, alongside the man she worshipped and adored.

Chapter 13

Curtain Down, Last Love: Eva Braun

Eva Braun lived with Hitler as his mistress for fourteen years. She had made his acquaintance some time before that. And yet almost nobody in Germany or, for that matter, in the wider world had any idea that she even existed. It was, as Traudl Junge said, 'the best kept secret of all … no one was obliged to keep quiet, we just instinctively avoided talking or gossiping about it.'[1]

Secretary Junge was being a little disingenuous or, at best, was talking about the situation based on her own limited knowledge as one of Hitler's clerical staff about the relationship as she and the other secretaries saw it. For years there had been a deliberate policy of keeping Eva's presence in the Führer's life totally secret. They travelled in different cars, sat apart at dinner and in many cases the mistress was excluded from high-powered debates and dinners. Hitler was aware of it and in agreement with the clandestine arrangement. Married to Germany, that was the line, and he would do nothing to spoil the image.

Eva Braun was born on 6 February 1912, the second daughter of schoolteacher Friedrich Braun and his wife Franziska. Brought up as traditional Catholic girls, Eva and her sisters Gretl and Ilse lived with their parents in Munich where they were confirmed into the Catholic Church, attended Sunday services and regularly took communion. Eva was educated at a convent boarding school outside Munich where some of the teachers and nuns found it difficult to engage her in the learning process. She was reasonably clever but she was also terribly lazy and with a propensity to become unruly if things did not go exactly the way she wanted.

The Brauns were not rich but they were reasonably well off and lived a comfortable life in Bavaria. Eva, always demanding of attention, quickly became the central attraction in the family. She was a pretty girl, determined and always ready for a joke or piece of fun. She had the ability to wrap people around her little finger and so she managed to get through school without exerting herself too much. The only subjects that she really enjoyed – and excelled at – were PE and sport. If she ever had ambitions they were limited to physical activities. Eva always wanted to do well at sports – not just do well, but be the best. She liked to come first in swimming or skiing races and to perform at the highest level in gymnastics, for which she had a particular penchant. For a while she had ambitions to become a film star but in the Germany of the 1920s acting was a career that was open to only a few. It was a shame because Eva Braun certainly had the style and the looks to do well on the cinema screen.

From the beginning she always liked to appear elegant, constantly brushing her hair and sometimes changing her clothes two or three times a day. This was a trait that accompanied her into adulthood when, thanks to Hitler, she had more than enough money to spend on fashion and little else to do with her time. Always interested in the arts, on leaving school Eva took up an apprenticeship with Heinrich Hoffmann in his photographic studio in the city. Hoffmann had already become the official photographer for the Nazi Party and was on first-name terms with Adolf Hitler. It was only a matter of time before Eva and the future leader of Germany made each other's acquaintance.

On their first meeting at Hoffmann's studio in 1929 Eva was disconcerted because Hitler kept looking at her legs. She was not worried about the direction of his gaze but did wonder if the hem of her dress, which she had just shortened, was straight! Eva did not recognize him even though there were dozens of images featuring him around the studio. He was introduced to her as Herr Wolf.

Despite some disapproval from her conservative father – who considered the ex-soldier and street-corner agitator a dangerous man – Eva began seeing Hitler on a regular basis. They went on walks and picnics but to begin with there was nothing sensual or sexual about their meetings. They were friends and that was all.

It was inevitable that Hitler should talk about politics and his plans for the future. Eva could barely understand his political diatribes and later, when the rumour mill got into full stride, there were stories doing the rounds that she had to look up in a dictionary many of the words he uttered. It did not stop the friendship slowly starting to grow, to move on from mere comradeship to, first, special friendship and finally to intimacy.

It was after the death of Geli Raubal in the autumn of 1931 that things took their most compelling turn. Whatever he felt for Geli, Hitler had continued to meet with Eva throughout the period of his attachment to his niece. It was not something that either Geli or Hitler himself ever worried about – after all, his relationship with Eva was purely platonic. Eva was a much-needed companion during his relationship with Geli. It was obviously a time of emotional torment for him and Eva was a constant in his life, perhaps the only one, totally different from the mercurial Geli Raubal. After Geli's unexpected and violent death, he needed Eva and her constancy even more. It might be, perhaps, simplistic to say that he needed someone to console him in the wake of his niece's death – in the way that his mother would have done. Simplistic but true – at various times in his life even Adolf Hitler needed consolation and a friendly face. Eva Braun could be guaranteed to provide both of them.

Quite when companionship morphed into intimacy, when sexualized encounters between the two became common, is not known. The line between friendship and loving in any relationship is at best blurred. With Hitler and Eva, it was doubly so. Part of the trouble in dating the advance in the relationship derives from Hitler's motives. A friendly, welcoming face, a warm hand upon his arm, that was one thing but there was a lot more than that to his choice of Eva as a mistress. She was a girl who fitted perfectly with his credo that the more significant the man, the more insignificant his partner. Hardly the most intellectual of women, Eva Braun was exactly what Hitler wanted in a companion. She was someone who would not challenge him, someone who looked good in the eyes of his closest comrades and, perhaps most important of all, someone who clearly admired, even adored, him – and was not afraid to let people see how she felt. She preened when in his company and although by the summer of 1932 she was still living at home it was not long before she was staying the odd night or two at his apartment – the same apartment where Geli had shot herself.

Eva coped rather well with the plethora of photographs, the drawings and busts of Geli Raubal, icons that were plastered all over the apartment in what was clearly a shrine to the dead girl. Many would have been disconcerted, demanding that the images be removed but Eva adopted a pragmatic approach. As far as she was concerned Geli was dead; her memory might remain but that was all and she could not stand between herself and her lover. Eva now had Adolf Hitler and nothing would change that. Or would it?

In the run-up to the elections of 1932 and with the Nazis now serious contenders for supreme power in Germany Hitler was inordinately busy. He flew all over the country, the first mainstream political leader to use air transport, making speeches and attending rallies. He had little time for Eva Braun and weeks passed without contact between them. Always emotional, Eva sat at home or in the apartment and fretted. At last she came to the decision that he was no longer interested in her. Politics and, who knows, other women seemed to have taken him over. Life suddenly seemed worthless. Her response was to take her father's pistol and shoot herself in the chest. Discovered by her sisters, Eva was rushed to hospital where she survived but only just. Hitler flew to her side, appalled by what she had done but, faced by the prospect of losing her – as he had lost Geli Raubal – he was suddenly aware of just how much he wanted her. Eva's suicide attempt might have been genuine. It might also have been a gesture, an attempt to pull him back to her side. She was to repeat the performance later in the relationship, that time with sleeping pills. Now, however, near death but secure in the knowledge of his love, she basked in the attention that was thrown at her, from Hitler in particular. After all Eva had always wanted to be centre stage and, as she lay in her hospital bed swathed in bandages, pale, ghostly and more beautiful than ever, there was no way she could be more of an object of Hitler's desire than this.

Debate has raged for many years about the nature of the relationship between Hitler and Eva Braun. Was it platonic, was it sexual? The answer to that seems to be that it was certainly an intimate and highly personal coupling. So sexual, yes, it probably was. Evidence comes from many sources. To begin with her bedroom and his at the Berghof had connecting doors so that it was easy to move from one room to the next without detection. It is hardly concrete proof but is a good basis with which to start. During all the years that Eva stayed with Hitler in his apartment in Munich she would reportedly set off with a small overnight case whenever he called. The case was nicknamed by Eva and by her staff as 'BuKa', the 'screwing kit'.

Eva's maid Margarete Mittelstrasser, later wife of the house manager at the Berghof, obviously knew her well and was even more graphic in her descriptions of what went on between them: 'When he came to her and she had her period, she got something from the Doctor to get rid of her period. And it was usually me who fetched it from the Doctor. I went myself.'[2]

After the war Dr Morell gave evidence to a commission of inquiry, stating that Hitler's sex drive decreased rapidly during the years of conflict. This was partly due to the depressing war situation and partly his declining health. Eva, he stated, approached him and asked him to prescribe something to rejuvenate her lover's sexual appetite. She herself once alluded to sexual encounters between herself and Hitler. Pointing to the couch on which British Prime Minister Neville Chamberlain had sat during the Munich Crisis of 1938, she apparently smiled and said, 'If only he knew what has gone on there on that couch.'

It was the secrecy which surrounded Hitler and Eva that caused the problem. If he had come out with it, directly and without debate, no one would have minded that he had a mistress. Many important men had found themselves lovers, illicit or compliant, and while Hitler wanted to sustain the idea that he was wedded to the country, nobody would have denied him a little love and affection.

Partly the idea that he was always available lay behind the decision. By being free of any relationship it meant that, to the adoring millions there was still a chance that he might someday choose one of them as his partner.

By insisting that Eva be kept out of the limelight, Hitler hurt her terribly. All she wanted was to be recognized as the partner of the man she regarded as being the greatest power for good that the world had ever seen. She would never receive that recognition until the very end – and then, of course, it was far too late. It was doubly distressing for Eva when she could see her younger sister Gretl married to Hermann Fegelein while she remained the hidden, unknown mistress. It was not right, she felt, particularly as she had been instrumental in the coupling of Gretl and Fegelein.

Eva was not above making the odd critical comment to Hitler. She liked jazz and would occasionally play jazz records for him on the phonograph at the Berghof: 'Apparently Hitler once said, "That's nice, what are you playing?" To which she retorted, "Your friend Goebbels has just banned it."'[3]

Jazz was one thing, recognition was another. Eva knew exactly how far she could go and challenging Hitler about her status or place in his life would have been a step too far.

It meant many lonely days for her once Hitler installed her at the Berghof. Hitler was often away on state business and only rarely showed her affection or attention in public. On the one hand she was delighted, queen of all she surveyed; on the other most visitors to the grand house, not realizing who she was, thought of her only as another secretary – and a pretty junior one at that.

The lack of physical contact between the two was noted by all of Hitler's secretaries and staff. They simply accepted it as the way they were. So that when there was sudden and unexpected contact between them it was something worth recording. And sometimes, as when Eva told Hitler she would not leave him in the Bunker but would die alongside him, it was the physical contact that made them react in ways that surprised everyone:

> He kisses Eva Braun on the mouth, while the officers stand outside waiting to be dismissed. I don't want to say it but it comes out of its own accord; I don't want to stay here and I don't want to die, but I can't help it. 'I'm staying too,' I say.[4]

Until that moment, just a few days before he and Eva died, Traudl Junge and none of the others had ever seen Hitler kiss his mistress, let alone on the mouth.

The final stages of the war saw Eva Braun marooned at the Berghof. Hitler knew that she was safe there, away from the bombing of Berlin. And if the American and British aircraft should ever drop bombs on the Obersaltzberg area the air raid shelters that Bormann had created, deep below the mountain, were guaranteed to keep her safe. Eva, however, was not happy. The Berghof without Hitler was no more than a jumbled collection of buildings. She knew the dangers of being in the Bunker but that was a risk she was prepared to take. She wanted to be with her lover and, if necessary, die with him. She duly began to make arrangements to leave the Berghof for Berlin.

Several observers, however, felt that her motives were rather different, that Hitler was not the main reason for undertaking such a hazardous trip. Anna Plaim, chambermaid and manager at the Berghof was one of those who harboured suspicions about her true motives: 'To be honest, I think the Berghof really bored Eva. I suspect she'd have preferred to have more male company.'[5]

Plaim's comment may have applied in peacetime but in a time of war and discord they hold little credibility. For Eva the Berghof was Hitler and Hitler was the Berghof. If he was missing from the equation then nothing would ever work out.

Eva Braun arrived, unexpected and unannounced, at the Führer Bunker in the early spring of 1945. Hitler had paid his last visit to the Berghof in July the previous year and apart from a brief visit to Berlin early in the year, he and Eva had not seen each other for over six months. It had been a period of sheer purgatory for her, particularly when the 20 July bomb attempt on his life caused her such grief and anguish. The assassination attempt, planned and carried out by army officers, failed by a hairsbreadth to kill the Führer. There had been other assassination attempts in the past but this one came closer to success than anyone ever dared believe possible. The bomb, concealed in the briefcase of Count von Stauffenberg, the intended messenger or harbinger of doom, was accidentally moved behind the table leg where Hitler was shielded from the blast. While others died in the explosion Hitler suffered only a ruptured eardrum and other minor injuries. He was, however, shocked and frightened by the experience. Eva's immediate reaction on hearing news of the assassination attempt had been to drop everything and rush to the Wolf's Lair where she could hold and protect her man. Only Hitler's insistence – and the ludicrous gift of his torn and tattered trousers, held together only by the waistband – kept her safe at the Berghof.

They may have brought Eva up short but neither the bizarre gift nor his orders to remain in Bavaria were enough to keep her there for long. She would join him, not at the Wolf's Lair but in the Bunker where he had now set up his headquarters. The journey to Berlin was dangerous, Russian and American forces hurling shells and incendiaries against any form of German transport that moved. The city was, by then, almost totally surrounded. If Eva had left it a few more days she would probably never have got into the beleaguered citadel.

When she did finally arrive, Hitler's appearance shocked Eva. She had not expected to find the worn, emasculated and exhausted man who came to greet her. He was shaking continually and his bad breath had escalated into an appalling case of halitosis that he seemed unwilling or unable to do anything about. None of his ailments, however, had any effect on Eva. She managed to hide her shock, knowing that she loved him and would continue to love him through good and bad. As far as she was concerned the important thing was that they were together again.

Hitler was equally as delighted to have her in his presence. However, pleased as he was to see her, he knew that the dark and depressing Bunker was no place for Eva Braun. She must move on, quickly, while there was still time. The look on Eva's face told Hitler that whatever he said was no more than a waste of breath. He had already decided he would die there in the Bunker and now Eva pledged that she would perish along with him. He had no willpower left to argue and accepted her decision with as much magnanimity as he could muster. It is not difficult to see why Eva was so determined to die alongside the Führer. The simplistic view is that she could not bear the thought of life without him. There is undoubtedly an element of truth in that but her insistence on staying and dying with him certainly went far deeper.

Both Eva and Hitler had always been intrigued and fascinated by films. When they were in residence at the Berghof they regularly watched two or three movies a night and the core of the matter, the truth about her decision, probably lies there:

> Perhaps Eva Braun saw her destiny with Hitler in terms of a cinematic finale. Her last letters are untainted by melodrama and yet she had found a magnificent role – the heroine who after suffering years of humiliation and neglect in the shadow of the man she loves is vindicated in an ending where her devotion is finally acknowledged.[6]

Whatever the reason might have been, everyone could see that Eva Braun had come to Berlin in order to die alongside her lover. She moved into the room next to Hitler's and, finally acknowledged as an important part of the Führer's life, began to take on the role that had been waiting for her all along – First Lady of the Reich. Immaculately turned out, elegant to the last, she continued with her routine of changing her dresses and skirts several times each day and spoke easily and softly to Hitler's secretaries about what was to come. She was not afraid and regretted nothing. She was ready.

There was still a little time before the Red Army closed in. Eva and the other women in the Bunker, conscious of being taken prisoner by the Soviets and wanting to do anything to avoid that particular humiliation, practised their pistol shooting in the courtyard of the foreign affairs ministry. The women did well, surprisingly so, and in a spirit of light-hearted fun that totally belied the situation, even challenged those officers remaining in the Bunker to a shooting match.

Otherwise she sipped tea, ministered to the Führer's needs and reminisced with the secretaries. Traudl Junge had become a particularly close friend and now they spent a considerable amount of time together. They had little else to occupy them.

Above all, according to those who were able to leave a record of the final days in the Bunker, Eva emanated a sense of quiet dignity. In contrast to the ribald partying from some of those in occupation, she moved serenely around the rooms and corridors and impressed everyone with her calm courage and willingness to face the inevitable.

It was all so casually done and in the last few weeks, once it was finally accepted that the military situation was hopeless, a sense of unreality descended across the Führer Bunker. Men and women drank, smoked, gossiped and had sex; a few made the break for freedom. Mostly people just sat there and waited for the end.

Eva's final days were probably the happiest of her short life. She spent them not in the shadow of the Führer but alongside him as he strode – perhaps shuffled might be a better description – onwards towards death. They were a couple at last.

Chapter 14

The Furies: Women of Germany

During what was a relatively brief period of power there can be no doubt that Adolf Hitler managed to affect not just the lives but also the subconscious desires of millions of Germans. Using a whole range of techniques, he was able tap into their deepest emotions, dredging up the hidden ideals and secret dreams of the German nation – of German women in particular. And yet it is still one of the strangest manifestations of Hitler's time as Chancellor that the regime he created should have held such an enormous appeal for women.

The Nazi Party began its existence as a male-dominated organization promoting a male-centred way of life. Throughout its wild days as a street-fighting, rabble-rousing sect on the fringe of credibility nothing ever really changed. Of course, there were women in the Party, many of them, but most occupied subservient roles. In the main they were content to watch as the stormtroopers battled with the communists outside their windows. They would bathe the wounds of the SA men, they would distribute Nazi Party leaflets and they would raise funds whenever they were able. And then, at the insistence of Adolf Hitler, respectability and power arrived at the door of the Party. For the Nazi women, however, nothing seemed to change.

Almost from the moment Hitler took control of the country in January 1933, the concept of male dominance was transferred from being the main principle of a single political party to a position where it became one of the guiding lights of the nation. It remained that way until the final moments of the Nazi Party and its ultimate destruction in the ruins of Berlin.

The general consensus of opinion regarding this phenomenon is fascinating but a little confusing. Not only was the female vote at the 1932 elections instrumental in bringing Hitler to power, but the support of those women – who voted for the Nazis in their hundreds of thousands – was also in direct contrast to the basic tenets of Nazism:

> The Weimar Republic is popularly regarded as the heyday of emancipated women [in Germany] ... The Nazi Party was a dedicated opponent of female emancipation, the ultimate in male chauvinism, firmly committed to a view of women as inferior, whose main task in life was to bear children and look after the home.[1]

Nazi mythology was both simplistic and misguided, yet it was to underpin German life until defeat in 1945. It demanded a growing population, complete with sufficient living space, which would fight the wars intended to unite the Volk in one empire, under one ruler. That was a role for strong, Aryan males and was an inherently misogynistic approach where, on the surface at least, the only role for a woman was as a housewife. Remain behind as the men march off to war, keep the home fires burning and produce more little soldiers to fight the good fight – that was the theory and was, in the main, something that the women of Germany managed to do, at least until the final years of the war.

The bedrock that enabled this to take place can be found in the days and weeks immediately following Hitler's appointment as Chancellor in January 1933.

Barely a month after Hitler was made Chancellor, the Reichstag building, the symbolic heart of German democracy, was destroyed by fire. It was 27 February and the razing to the ground of the German parliamentary building gave Hitler the means and the opportunity to implement the dictatorship that he had always wanted and planned. The Reichstag Fire, depending on your view, was either deliberately started by Nazis or was a most welcome piece of happenstance. Rumours that Hermann Göring was behind the arson attack began to circulate almost from the moment the first flames were seen. He was to later admit his involvement in what was to be one of the most seminal moments of the regime but how much truth there was in his statement remains a matter of conjecture.

Either way, Göring had a readymade 'patsy' and the fire was immediately identified as part of a communist conspiracy to bring down the new German state. A simple-minded young Dutchman by the name of Marinus van der Lubbe was arrested, convicted and later executed for the crime.

Van der Lubbe had a history of arson and when questioned by the police admitted to lighting the fire that February evening. Even so his fire, started with four packets of firelighters and his hastily discarded shirt, were hardly significant enough to burn down the whole edifice – enter Hermann Göring ready to fan the flames.

Göring or van der Lubbe – or Göring and van der Lubbe together – Hitler was now presented with the opportunity he needed. The safest way to avoid the looming threat from the left was, the Nazis thundered, to rule without benefit and interference of parliamentary judgement. Stifle their voice, the Nazi propaganda alleged and you stifle the threat.

Consequently, in the wake of the Reichstag Fire, President Hindenburg, at the behest of Chancellor Hitler, announced an emergency decree suspending civil liberties. It meant the ruthless pursuit and persecution of communists, from rank and file members to their leaders and their Reichstag deputies. Mass arrests took place across Germany. By 15 March over 10,000 were in custody and within a matter of days after the fire the Nazis, instead of being in a position of parity with the communists in the Reichstag, were suddenly presented with a huge majority.

A series of Enabling Acts were hurried through parliament, meeting now in the Kroll Opera House in place of the burnt-out Reichstag. With most of the communist delegates either kicking their heels in concentration camps like Dachau or lying low, out of Nazi reach, their seats remained empty. With Göring as Reichstag president and the hall filled with Nazi Party delegates, there was nobody to challenge any aspect of the Nazi ideologies which were now installed as law.

Over the next few months other opponents, the Social Democrats and the rest, quickly followed the communists into political oblivion. Trade unions were shut down, not needed now that the Nazi Party was looking after workers' rights. Just as significantly, all political opposition to the Nazis was banned. In what had now become a one-party state, democracy simply shrivelled up and died.

The Reichstag duly became toothless. It met on only twenty occasions between 1933 and 1945, doing nothing more than rubber-stamping Nazi decrees. The new Enabling Acts and the other legislation that followed gave Hitler complete control of government. Under the terms of the new political establishment he and his Party could now do more or less whatever they wanted.

One of the first significant steps was to take control of the education and development of the youth of the country. It was not long before the curriculum for girls in German schools was changed in order to streamline it with the Nazi doctrine of male superiority. As might have been expected, the doctrine and the new curriculum encouraged the brotherhood of male compatriots at the expense of their female equivalents. Traditional subjects such as Latin and the sciences were, for adolescent girls, totally removed from the syllabus. In their place came a series of courses on the German language, mythology, history and, most significantly of all, domestic skills. Housekeeping thus became the main focus for women's education, as befitted their role in the new regime. For the women of the Reich there were more draconian policies to come as Hitler now stated publicly that he intended to take 800,000 women out of the workforce. They would be replaced by men. It was a brutal way of reducing unemployment.

By the end of 1933 the Law for the Reduction of Unemployment was offering significant financial encouragement for married women to remain at home rather than go out to work; that same year the Law for the Encouragement of Marriage awarded newly married couples an initial sum of 1,000 marks and a further gift of 250 marks for every child born thereafter. The pressure on women to remain at home and bear children for the Reich continued to mount. Soon the award of Motherland Crosses became commonplace. Women would receive a bronze cross when they had given birth to four children, a silver cross for six and gold for eight or more. Other benefits included more blatant incentives such as cheap theatre tickets, being given the right to 'jump queues' and significant tax concessions.

As Hitler embedded his dictatorship the professions, in particular the civil service, were purged of women. In a country that had led the way in female emancipation – 3,000 women doctors, 36 Reichstag deputies, over 13,000 professional women musicians – it was a cruel and mindless decimation.

From 1936 onwards women were forbidden to become judges and were not allowed to undertake jury service; nor were they allowed to become Reichstag deputies – not that it meant a great deal with the Reichstag already reduced to a shell and a sham. By the end of 1933 an astounding 15 per cent of teachers – almost all of them women – were made redundant while only 11 per cent of university places were now to be awarded to women. The process, known as *Gleichschaltung*, also included the mass burning of books considered unsuitable for German students and members of the general public.[2]

Single women were permitted to work but only 'outside' the professions, thus confining them to jobs such as factory hands, secretaries, care workers and nurses. Social controls included encouragement of traditional German peasant fashions – flat shoes, hair worn in plaits, no makeup or short skirts – and women were expressly forbidden to smoke in public.

As might be expected such restrictions did not apply to people like Magda Goebbels, Eva Braun or the rest of the Berghof Set – even though Hitler disliked the use of makeup and smoking. He would have dearly liked to end them both amongst his close female companions but that, as the Braun sisters had demonstrated, was a step too far.

On the face of it such restrictive rules and policies about their lives and the way they lived them should have been enough to alienate all intelligent, thinking and feeling women. In fact, the very opposite occurred. The message that was sold to the German people was not that women were secondary and subservient to men; they simply had a different role to fulfil in order to make Germany great again.

With the benefit of hindsight, it is clear that Hitler's timing was immaculate. As the country began to slowly but significantly improve its economic situation, support for the Nazis took a huge leap forward. From the early days of his tenure in power Hitler began, in the eyes of the German people, to right the wrongs of the Versailles Treaty. It was subtly done: increasing the size and strength of the Wehrmacht, secretly laying the foundations of a new air force and circumventing the terms of the treaty by building heavily armed pocket battleships, all of Hitler's military developments were gleefully accepted and applauded by the German people.

When he moved on to taking back territories such as the Saar Basin and the Rhineland there was unlimited joy in Germany. Incorporating Austria (the Anschluss) and Czechoslovakia into the Reich took the popularity of the Party to immense heights. Who was going to argue about the role and status of women when the German nation was beginning to be strong again?

And at the head of the Party which had achieved this success stood one man, a figurehead, one charismatic leader who had promised all of this and, more importantly, had delivered on his promises. Within a very short time of his coming to power, Hitler's bullish approach had made him Germany's most popular leader since the end of the First World War. The woes of the nation and the decadence of the Weimar Republic were forgotten.

None of this happened by accident; there was a steady and highly effective publicity machine at work. Goebbels and his propaganda ministry pumped out a steady stream of pro-Hitler news and information, extolling his achievements and dedication to the nation. It was backed up by posters, news snippets and thousands of postcard views of the Führer at work and at leisure.

Women undoubtedly found Hitler attractive but that was perhaps more to do with the aura of power that emanated from him than it was ever to do with his looks. He seemed to ooze strength and control. Power is undoubtedly an aphrodisiac and the feeling of being safe and protected from harm lay below any romantic fantasies the women of Germany might have held: 'Trust in Adolf Hitler gave a sense of security. One woman told the American reporter Nora Wall, "He is my mother and my father. He keeps me safe from harm."'[3]

Given the nature of the German defeat in the First World War and the economic crisis that had enveloped and then decimated the country in the late 1920s, a desire to feel safe and protected was understandable. If that was the root cause of Hitler's popularity – and it seems likely that it was – then the desire for safety and security simply overwhelmed any ability to maintain rational views about the other, less savoury things going on in Nazi Germany. The key was belief, belief in the promises Hitler made and the way in which those promises were being delivered:

> I believed the National Socialists when they promised to
> do away with unemployment ... I believed them when they
> said they would reunite the German nation which had split
> into more than forty political parties.[4]

Above all, people believed Hitler when he promised to negate the terms of the Treaty of Versailles which had been dictated by the victors of the war and imposed on the German nation. There was only one way to achieve that and, consequently, the people of Germany followed blindly as Hitler led them down the path to war.

For German success in the 1930s read Hitler success. His appearance at Party rallies and speaking events was usually met with near-hysterical outbursts of screaming and cheering from adoring female adherents who clearly worshipped him. The resemblance to modern celebrities is inevitable but even the movie idols of the day, the Rudolf Valentinos and Clark Gables, never received such adulation.

Thousands turned up just to watch him arrive at a function or drive past in a motor cavalcade. They would never meet him but they could at least say 'I saw Hitler today.' It is not too much of a generalization to say that as far as many of the women of Germany were concerned, Hitler was their night, their day and the reason to feel proud, once more, of being German.

Their influence, however, went far deeper than merely turning up at public events and screaming – crucial as that might have been for Hitler's public image. He knew, and played on the fact, that it was the women, the mothers and wives of Germany, who effectively gave Nazism its anchor in the world. Despite the misogynistic nature of the German state in the 1930s, the traditional middle-class fears of poverty and depression that emanated from these women simply fed Hitler's power:

> They were the ones who incrementally brought Nazism home. They indoctrinated their children in anti-Semitism. They were the ones who would tell their children to stop playing with Jewish children down the block.[5]

It was an insidious but effective process that left Hitler without any effective opposition for most of the decade. It was inevitable that things were never going to last. Hitler's glide towards war meant that by 1936 there was a major shortage of workers who were needed to shore up the country's economy and provide guns, shells and other necessary items for the army. The idea of using slave labour was still several years away and the only available untapped source of willing workers lay in the women of Germany.

Gertrud Schultz-Klink, the Reich Women's leader – until the end of the 1930s a position that had always been something of a sinecure – was one of those who attempted to rationalize what was really a sudden and remarkable change in government policy. Until then Hitler had been clear: the role of women was in the home; now he was making an about turn: 'It has always been our chief article of fact that women's place is in the home – but since the whole of Germany is our home, we must serve her wherever we can best do so.'[6]

The change of heart, necessary as it was, led to an increase of nearly 50 per cent in the female workforce as women were drafted in to take the place of men who could now be released for military service. It may be a generalization but in the main women were pleased to go into the factories and onto the farms, happy to do their bit to prepare for the war that was clearly coming. The creation of a Women's Labour Service in 1939 brought even more women into the workplace. Now all women had to do twelve months' voluntary service before they could begin work proper. Most of them were placed on farms, the German equivalent of Britain's Land Army girls. Any grumbling from within the ranks was soon eliminated by blinding military success in Belgium and France.

The NS-Frauenschaft (NSF), the political organization for Nazi women, had been created in 1931. Behind the grand-sounding title, its main thrust was still housekeeping and the place of women in the home. Overall, it had little effect on the running of the Party but the NSF did offer courses in how to use German-made products rather than fall back on imported ones. Later the women of the NSF helped in the war effort by providing refreshments for troops in transit at railway stations and other lonely spots.

The war, inevitably, changed everything and by 1945 there were 500,000 women auxiliaries serving in the Wehrmacht. They were employed as telephonists, clerks, nurses and so on. This was a revolutionary change for the army, one of the more conservative elements of Hitler's Germany, but by the closing years of the war such a move had become both necessary and inevitable.

The SS-Gefolge, the women's wing of the SS, was never particularly large but, from 1942 onwards, due to a shortage of camp guards approximately 3,700 women were trained at Ravensbrück concentration camp. Most served as camp guards in places like Auschwitz and Belsen and the names of brutal individuals like Irma Grese and Ilse Koch, the so-called 'Bitch of Belsen,' became infamous when, after the war, details of their sadism and cruelty were made known. Such women were hardly typical of Hitler's support base. They were thugs, pure and simple, who would have filled or carried out the roles regardless of the party in power.

Hitler's popularity did not diminish during the early days of the war as success followed success and the tide of German military might swept everything before it. Only after 1943 when an overextended Wehrmacht came face to face with the reality of Soviet power did attitudes begin to change.

By the early months of 1943, with casualties in the East rising by the day and women suddenly realizing that the sons they had so glibly encouraged to march away to war were never going to come back, the government had become hugely unpopular. This was a sudden and total swing in attitudes but was one that, strangely, never affected Hitler. He was still regarded as someone above the other leaders and dislike seemed to focus on obvious targets like Göring and Goebbels.

However, while Hitler still retained his position and continued to demand the respect of German women, this was garnered now through memory rather than actions. The death toll on the Eastern Front, the humiliation of the Stalingrad surrender and what was clearly a losing battle in the Atlantic had effectively eliminated everything but blind hope. German casualty figures eventually reached 4.8 million but, despite the unpopularity of the Nazi government and the hopelessness of the situation, at no stage was there any concerted campaign to end the war.

Throughout 1943 and 1944 Goebbels's propaganda machine was working overtime, churning out the Party message, while the system of informers in every apartment block and on every street – set up long before by Hermann Göring when he was in control of the police and Gestapo – ensured that anyone critical of the regime would be quickly reported and dealt with. Arguably a cowed and beaten population had, therefore, little or no heart to object to anything that was demanded of them.

Above all, however, no one ever really supported the idea of bringing the war to a conclusion. The soldiers at the front would fight on to the end, only certain members of the officer class, fronted by von Stauffenberg, ever attempting – unsuccessfully – to force the issue of a negotiated peace.

The people at home knew that all manner of sacrifice would be needed before victory was assured. Surrender, sue for peace – never!

That, everyone believed – or, more accurately, everyone had been indoctrinated to believe – would lead only to German annihilation.

And so, the women of Germany, like their men, buried their heads in the sand and carried on. They would fight to the last, even though there was now a dogged, black sense of humour across the land. In the face of ever-increasing rationing and constant Allied bombing raids, humour was one of the few avenues of solace left to the German people: 'When will the war end?' went one joke. 'Not until fat Göring can finally fit into skinny Goebbels's trousers.'

Hitler and the other leading figures seemed to disappear from view after the summer of 1944. It did not help their popularity but the war situation was by then critical and nobody had the inclination to gather together and celebrate what was now clearly a doomed regime. As a result, there were no longer any rallies or great speeches. The war was suddenly too close and the only Party dignitary who retained any sort of profile was Propaganda Minister Joseph Goebbels. That was his job, his role, to keep up morale: appearing in public and broadcasting on the radio was expected of him. Nobody really believed what he said but they listened and wondered why the Führer was not doing anything to improve the situation. It was a far cry from the days of unadulterated worship.

And so, the women of Germany, Hitler's furies who had screamed their devotion for the man who had led them to this, suppressed their concerns and concentrated only on living until tomorrow.

They scavenged for food, picked up rubble to clear the roads, repaired their houses and wondered, dimly, when their men would be coming back from the war. In far too many cases that was something that would never happen.

Chapter 15

Final Act: In the Bunker

The last weeks in the Führer Bunker were a curious mixture of fear, mild hysteria and fatalism. Everyone knew that the end was close and while most of those incarcerated in Hitler's Berlin stronghold were eager to seize any opportunity to escape, they were also realistic. Sooner or later they all expected that they would die.

Hitler had retreated to the Bunker in January 1945. It had been intended as a temporary refuge but, as it turned out, this was to be his last residence. By this time, he had little interest in personal comforts and his accommodation in the Bunker was at best sparse, in reality quite frugal. It hardly matched the style and comfort expected, by others at least, of the leader of the German Reich. His sitting room was little more than a narrow, unwelcoming alcove filled to overflowing with his writing desk, sofa and chairs. They took up nearly all of the space, making it difficult to move around. His bedroom lay to one side of the sitting room, his bathroom on the other.

On the wall above the desk the Führer had hung his portrait of Frederick the Great, the symbolic and talismanic Prussian emperor. Frederick was Hitler's role model, a man who had braved many disappointments and come back more than once from the abyss. The painting had accompanied the Führer wherever he went during the war years and had become symbolic of the miracle that Hitler and so many of his staff hoped would now occur. Despite the portrait's splash of colour, the atmosphere in the tiny, cramped room was oppressive. Hitler seemed not to notice.

By 20 April, Hitler's 56th birthday, Berlin was almost entirely surrounded by Red Army troops, over two million Soviets now beginning to fight their way into the city suburbs and streets. Soon they were within a mile of the Führer Bunker and the sounds of gunfire and shelling were incessant. Within a few days they were even closer and the only way into and out of the city was to risk a highly dangerous flight by aeroplane.

Despite the shelling, a party to celebrate the Führer's birthday was held in the Bunker. The great and the good of the Third Reich, from Göring and Albert Speer to Joachim von Ribbentrop and Joseph Goebbels came to celebrate with him. Nobody had the enthusiasm to enjoy the occasion very much. It was a depressing evening and Hitler, with Eva Braun on his arm, retired early.

Once he had gone Eva reappeared, clad in a new silver-blue dress, and gathered together as many people as she could. She led them up to the old sitting room on the first floor and there, without Hitler and to accompaniment of a battered record player, they partied:

> Eva Braun wanted to dance! Never mind who with, she whirled everyone away in a desperate frenzy, like a woman who has already felt the faint breath of death. We drank champagne, there was shrill laughter, and I laughed too because I wanted to cry.[1]

By dawn the following morning most of those who had come to pass on birthday wishes had disappeared, crouched low in fast motor cars that sped down the only highway left open or on the final trains into and out of the city. They were lucky to make it out. Göring and Himmler were gone before daylight and von Ribbentrop, after one last attempt to persuade Hitler to leave Berlin, slipped away like all the rest. Dr Morell hoisted his vast bulk out of the Bunker and, now discharged and dismissed by Hitler, fled to the West. Much against their wishes, Christa Schroeder and Johanna Wolf, the Führer's long-serving secretaries, finally acceded to Hitler's orders to leave him and the city. A few hours later they flew out of Berlin. The faithful – and the not so faithful – were leaving their master.

There were new arrivals, notably Magda Goebbels and her six children. The youngsters filled the corridors, the sound of their voices echoing around the cavernous tomb. They ran everywhere and got under everyone's feet playing with their toys. Nobody minded. The adjutants and the clerks strode around the place as if they were engaged in vitally important tasks but in reality, they had nothing to do. There *was* nothing to do, apart from sitting and waiting for the Russian to arrive.

Jodl and Keitel paid their last visit to the Bunker and then headed south at a considerable rate of knots. Speer came one last time to inform Hitler that he was leaving Berlin. Hanna Reitsch flew in for a brief visit and left when she realized she could not persuade Hitler to leave. And then the news came of Göring's treachery.

The Reichsmarschall had sent a telegram from Bavaria where he had now taken refuge, expressing his continued loyalty but, more significantly, his concerns about the Führer's inability to lead the nation from the centre of the beleaguered capital city. In light of this problem and as Hitler's duly nominated successor he would now, he stated, take over control of Germany. Hitler, prompted by the insidious and ever-present Martin Bormann, flew into a violent rage, removed Göring from all offices and ordered him arrested. And yet, despite the tantrum, Hitler maintained a degree of admiration for Göring whom he considered a man of steel, someone always prepared to seize the main chance when it was offered.

Göring's words had, if nothing else, shaken Hitler out of the terrible lethargy that had enveloped him for several days. It was not long, however, before he retired once more into his world of introspection and regret. Easily and apparently painlessly, he slipped back into a monosyllabic series of responses. He shuffled around the Bunker without purpose, his eyes averted and cast down to the floor.

The remaining secretarial and clerical staff, now just Traudl Junge and Dara Christian for the Führer, and Else Kruger for Bormann, found it harder and harder to understand what he was saying. He mumbled incoherently and sometimes allowed his sentences to drift away into unfinished whispers. He was a shell of his former self, a broken man. Although he urged them all to abandon their posts in the Bunker and flee to the American lines, all three secretaries, along with dietician Constanze Manziarly, refused to leave. Eva Braun had already made it clear that she was intending to stay and Hitler could do no more than gaze at them all in admiration. Almost in tears they left the Führer and sat together discussing the future. None wanted to be captured by the Russians and talk soon turned to what they thought was the best way to end their lives. Hitler had advocated a quick shot through the mouth into the brain but that did not appeal to Traudl Junge:

> She was horrified by this suggestion as was Eva Braun.
> 'I want to be a beautiful corpse,' said Eva. 'I wonder if it
> hurts very much?' she remarked, looking at the little brass
> phial of cyanide in her hand.[2]

The cyanide was one of several capsules given to Hitler by Heinrich Himmler but then news of an unbelievable betrayal of the Führer by the man who was considered the most loyal of all his acolytes caused everyone to ask the question – are these the real article or will they simply render us unconscious so that we can fall into Russian hands? Even Hitler had his doubts, hence his seemingly callous decision to test the poison on Blondi. The dog died in minutes, reassuring the Führer that the cyanide was effective and would work when ingested.

Hitler had managed to pull himself together and give vent to his spleen when news of Himmler's betrayal arrived in the Bunker. The SS leader, Hitler was informed, had been attempting to negotiate a peace settlement with the Americans and British, using the Swedish Count Bernadotte as a conduit. His negotiations were fruitless, achieving nothing apart from raising the Führer's ire. It was his last outburst of temper. Göring's attempted seizure of power had shaken Hitler but, really, he expected nothing less from the self-seeking Luftwaffe chief; the betrayal of 'faithful Heinrich,' as Hitler called him, was the last straw. Truly, now, it was all over.

The end came quickly. Just after midnight on 29 April, Hitler and Eva Braun were married in a simple civil ceremony. It was a symbolic gesture on Hitler's part. His 'marriage' to Germany was over and he could now officially bind himself to the woman who had been by his side for the last fourteen years. Eva was overjoyed with the decision, even though she and Hitler both knew that the marriage would be short-lived; for a while at least, she could finally stand alongside Hitler as his wife.

Legend declares that Eva began to sign the wedding document with her name Braun before realizing her mistake, crossing out the letter B and writing Hitler. It was the first time in her life that she was able to call herself by that name and so the clichéd story smacks of the truth. True or not, it was the type of foible that made the tragedy of the ceremony somewhat more bearable for her friends and family, the sort of thing you might expect from little Eva.

The ceremony was followed by a wedding breakfast where Hitler spoke only about the past with no interest or hope for the future. He interrupted the meal to take Traudl Junge to his private sitting room where he dictated his last will and testament. It was a two-part document, one part private, the other political. The general tenor was one of death over capitulation. Earlier that day Hitler had heard the news of

Mussolini's death. The Italian dictator and his mistress Clara Petracci had been captured and shot by partisans. Their bodies were then hoisted into the air to swing in a mixture of warning and retribution above the jubilant crowd. That humiliating end, Hitler decided, would never happen to him. He would kill himself and then his body, and that of his new wife, would be cremated.

Futile as the gesture may have been, with Heinrich Himmler and Hermann Göring now discredited and condemned as traitors, Grand Admiral Karl Dönitz was nominated to assume control of the new Reich government. The rest of the document was a rant – Germany and the German people did not deserve to be saved, they had betrayed him and his ideals.

There was a degree of rationale in choosing Dönitz to succeed him. Himmler, Göring and the rest were tainted figures in the eyes of the Allies; Karl Dönitz, despite his lethal U-boat campaign, was a warrior, someone who had fought a relatively clean war. If anyone could obtain reasonable surrender terms Dönitz would have been about the only candidate. Even so, in the short term, until Dönitz could assume control, Joseph Goebbels would carry out the duties of Chancellor.

The following afternoon, with the Red Army almost at the doors of their final refuge, Hitler and Eva bade farewell to everyone in the Bunker, went into their room and prepared for the inevitable end. The few remaining officials of note and the staff of faithful secretaries and aides waited outside the door:

> It may have been ten minutes, but it seemed an eternity to us, before the shot broke the silence … The Führer had shot himself in the mouth and bitten on a poison capsule too. His skull was shattered and looked dreadful. Eva Braun hadn't used her pistol; she just took the poison.[3]

As Hitler had ordered, over 200 litres of petrol had been obtained by the chauffeur Erich Kempka and brought to the Bunker, ready for the immolation of the two bodies. It was all done without undue emotion but Kempka found the situation almost unbearable, particularly with regards to his friend Eva. He was standing outside the sitting room when the bodies were carried out and taken upstairs to the Chancellery garden.

Hitler's manservant Heinz Linge and Dr Ludwig Stumfegger, who had taken over from Morell, carried the body of the Führer between them. Eva was held in the pudgy arms of Martin Bormann. He was trying hard to appear solemn:

> This shocked me almost more than the sight of the dead Hitler. Eva had hated Bormann. He had caused her a great deal of aggravation. His intrigues for power had long been clear to her. Now in death her greatest enemy carried her to the pyre.[4]

Without a word Kempka moved forward and took Eva's lifeless body from Bormann's arms. The 'funeral cortège' went slowly up the stairs and out into the garden. There, as Russian shells tore into the ruins of the Chancellery and mortar bombs rained down onto the once-pristine gardens, the bodies were placed into a shallow depression in the ground. Fuel was tipped over the two corpses.

Erich Kempka, who had earlier rejected the idea of using hand grenades to ignite the funeral pyre, lit a long length of rag and when it was burning brightly tossed it into the open grave. Eventually the bodies of Hitler and Eva also began to burn.

Setting fire to the corpses was not an easy task, made even more difficult by the artillery bombardment. More and more petrol had to be found and poured into the grave. It was not until 7.30 that night, five hours after the suicide, that the bodies were considered sufficiently burned. By then the Russians were perilously close.

When Adolf Hitler shot himself that April afternoon in 1945, the greatest tragedy of all was still waiting to happen. It was the final act in the opera that Hitler and the Nazis had orchestrated and was now about to end in a bloodletting worthy of Wagner himself. Nobody knew what she had in mind when Magda Goebbels brought her six children to the Bunker. Many wondered about her motives, some guessed, but it soon became clear to everyone that this was not just a farewell visit. Neither she nor the children would ever leave the Bunker again.

Traudl Junge and Hanna Reitsch – until her departure on 28 April – played with the children and read them stories to entertain them, anything to keep the looming threat of their fate away from their minds. In the main it worked but Helga, the eldest, seemed to sense something out of the ordinary. She said nothing but there was, everyone remarked, an air of sadness about her that was difficult to define.

Several people, in a final attempt to circumvent Magda's intentions, offered to take the children out of the Bunker and get them to safety. There were so many: a simple, unnamed chambermaid, Hitler himself, chauffeur Erich Kempka, pilot Hanna Reitsch and even Armaments Minister Albert Speer. There were several more but Magda refused them all. The children, too good and pure to live in a world without National Socialism, would die with her and Joseph.

The day after Hitler's death Magda prepared the children. That evening she dressed them in long white robes that were symbolic of sacrifice and purity and then put them to bed early. Rochus Misch, the Bunker wireless and telephone operator, was probably the last person, apart from Magda, to speak to any of them. Always a favourite with the children, Misch was in the radio room when 4-year-old Heide appeared in the doorway. 'Misch, Misch,' she warbled, 'You're a fish.' Then Helga pushed her up the stairs to their bedroom and Misch never saw them again.

Reports of how the Goebbels children were killed vary. It now seems likely that SS dentist Helmut Kunz gave each of them an injection of morphine, Magda telling them that they needed to relax and sleep well before they went on a long journey the following day. Then, when all of them were unconscious, Magda crushed cyanide ampules in their mouths. Rochus Misch later claimed to have seen Dr Stumfegger mix and administer a sweetened drink of poison to the six children. It is entirely possible – anything that would make them drowsy would have helped in the final act.

As it was, when the bodies were later examined by the Russians, it was discovered that Helga apparently had a broken jaw; she had awoken just before death, the Russians declared, and her mouth had had to be held open, and then closed, while the cyanide capsule was crushed between her teeth. It might perhaps have been Russian propaganda but if true it would be a terrible and terrifying end.

Magda and Joseph Goebbels did not survive their children by long. Magda spoke to no one and apparently played Patience for a while, waiting for her husband to summon her.

It is tempting to view Magda Goebbels as nothing more than a murderer, callous to the end and more interested in a pack of playing cards than in the fate of her children. That is far too simple a response and while not seeking to excuse what was an inexcusable act, the horror of what she had done must have haunted her final moments. Her emotions remained hidden but the strain, according to people like Misch and Kempka could be seen on her face.

When Goebbels was ready, he and Magda went out into the Chancellery garden where Joseph shot his wife and then put a bullet into his own head. The bodies were burned but there was not enough petrol to carry out the job effectively and their charred, half-destroyed corpses were soon discovered by the Russians. The bodies of the children were found in the bedroom where they had died. Laid out on a white sheet on the floor their corpses were photographed by the Russians, looking, as someone declared, like sleeping seals against the ice.

The fate of the other Bunker residents, in particular the few remaining Hitler women, varied. Traudl Junge, Gerda 'Dara' Christian (née Daranowski), Bormann's secretary (and mistress) Else Kruger and dietician Constanze Manziarly joined one of the escape groups that attempted to flee the Bunker after Hitler's death. They left the relative safety of the underground lair on 1 May. Led by General Wilhelm Mohnke, the group included Bormann, Erich Kempka and many other high-profile Nazis. Together they braved the bullets and shells, heading for the safety of the American forces outside the western perimeter of the city.

In the chaos of rubble and destruction it was inevitable that the group should gradually lose touch with each other as Russian tanks and troops kept them continually diving for cover. The four women tried to stay together. They encountered Russian soldiers scavenging for souvenirs and beer but for the first night at least managed to stay relatively safe from the abuse and violation they all feared.

Constanze Manziarly, apparently the image of the ideal Russian woman with a full figure and plump cheeks, disappeared on the second day of the escape. She went off to find civilian clothes to replace the Wehrmacht jacket she had been wearing. She was last seen being led into a U-Bahn tunnel by two soldiers: '[She] just had time to call back to Traudl Junge, "They want to see my papers," before she disappeared with the Russians. No one saw her again after that.'[5]

What happened to Constanze Manziarly is not known. It is unlikely that she ever re-emerged from the tunnel and may well have been killed by the Soviet troops. She did have in her possession one of Himmler's cyanide capsules and it is more than likely that this fearless woman ended her own life rather than endure rape and beatings at the hands of the Russians.

Traudl Junge had an adventurous time of it. After losing touch with her two friends, she managed to avoid capture and make it out of the city. After a month on the run, she managed to reach the Elbe but with no way to cross the river to the American lines she was forced to return to Berlin. There she was eventually arrested by Soviet police. Interrogated by both the Russians and British, she was released in December 1945 and spent the next few months living in squalor in the Russian sector. She caught diphtheria and almost died. However, on her recovery she found that her mother had 'pulled strings' and arranged for her to move to the safety of the British sector of Germany.

She worked as a secretary in what eventually became West Germany and after a while decided to publish her memoirs. She did not seek to excuse her time with Hitler or to explain away the evil nature of his regime but knew that she would have to live with her conscience for the rest of her life. Matching the monster with the caring, paternalistic employer she encountered and recognized was never going to be an easy task:

> Today I mourn for two things: for the fate of those millions of people who were murdered by the National Socialists. And for the girl Traudl Humps who lacked the self-confidence and good sense to speak out against them at the right moment.[6]

Over the years Traudl Junge became a regular guest on documentaries and TV programmes about the Nazi regime. Her book *Until the Final Hour* was made into a successful film under the title *Downfall*. She died in February 2002.

Gerda Christian and Else Kruger, the two other secretaries to leave the Bunker with Traudl Junge, were both caught by Red Army troops on 2 May. Christian was questioned but soon released and went to live in Dusseldorf where she died in 1997.

Else Kruger found herself being interrogated by the British. In a strange twist of fate worthy of any romantic novel she fell in love with her British interrogator, married him and went to live in Britain. She returned to Germany after her husband's death in the 1970s and died herself in 2005.

Christa Schroeder and Johanna Wolf, the two secretaries who had been ordered out of Berlin by Hitler before his death, were originally thought to have died in their escape attempt. There was a problem boarding the plane at Staaken: the aircraft they were supposed to have used, complete with their luggage and personal belongings, took off without them. The two secretaries were eventually crammed onto a Junkers transport plane bound for Salzburg. It was a hazardous flight. Snow flurries and rain made the take-off difficult and the trip to Salzburg was traumatic, passing low over burning towns and villages. They eventually arrived at their destination and were bundled onto a bus that would take them to the Obersaltzberg. On this journey they learned of the fate of their original aircraft, as Christa Schroeder later recorded:

> The Ju 52 which took off from Staaken, and on which we were booked, crashed at Bornersdorf near Dresden. One of the two female bodies burnt to a crisp was identified as me because my trunk was stored in the cargo hold.[7]

The true identity of the two women who were killed in the crash remains unknown. It was a time of chaos and confusion in Germany and nobody was particularly interested in things like procedure. They could have been girlfriends of the aircrew, journalists or just frightened women trying to get out of Berlin. Whoever they were their journey ended in disaster.

Schroeder and Wolf arrived at the Berghof to find Eva Braun's mother and sister (Gretl now heavily pregnant) and Eva's friend Herta Schneider already in residence. They were soon joined by Dr Morell and other refugees desperately seeking safety. The Berghof was subjected to heavy bombing from the Americans during the last days of the war and the women spent most of their time in Bormann's famous bunker.

Johanna Wolf left the Berghof on 2 May, travelling to Bad Tolz where her aged mother was then living. She was arrested a few weeks later and held prisoner until June 1948, the length of her incarceration presumably having something to do with her long record of service with Hitler.

She stuck to her decision never to write about her time as the Führer's secretary. Although she was never implicated in any of the horrors of the regime, she refused to make money or gain a degree of absolution from her memories. She died in Munich aged 85.

Christa Schroeder did write a book about the final days of the Nazi regime, a work that is still regarded as an invaluable source of information. It is an unapologetic tome and undoubtedly reflects the character of Christa Schroeder and, almost as a by-product, of Adolf Hitler. The book, printed in England as *He Was My Chief*, does not always make comfortable reading but, as far as we can tell, it remains an accurate picture of life in the closing months of the Third Reich. Christa Schroeder would not have wanted it any other way. Like Johanna Wolf, Christa Schroeder was arrested after leaving the Berghof and held captive by the Americans until 1948. After her release she settled in Munich, worked as secretary for a construction firm and died in 1984.

Gretl Braun, sister of Eva, had been in Berlin until January 1945 when she and Eva left for the safety of the Berghof. Eva later returned to the Führer Bunker alone while Gretl, heavily pregnant, remained in Bavaria. She gave birth to a daughter whom she named Eva Barbara in memory of her sister. Tragedy seemed to run in the family however as, sadly, Eva Barbara committed suicide in 1971 after the death of her boyfriend in a road accident. Gretl had heard the news of her husband's execution for desertion while she was still at the Berghof. The fact that a few hours later she became Hitler's sister-in-law did not save Hermann Fegelein – reports vary about whether or not Eva pleaded for his life. Gretl remarried in 1954 and died in 1987.

Even in death Hitler remained, for some, a figure of envy. He might be gone but his possessions – and those of his colleagues – were still around and now they were 'fair game'. Within days of his death the Berghof was looted by local residents, along with the nearby houses of people like Albert Speer. Anything moveable was taken away: vases and cutlery, pictures and bed linen, it was all purloined. Even the furniture that had once graced the Berghof rooms was removed, much of it being acquired by staff from the Berghof:

> After clearing the Berghof kitchen of rubble, house administrator Mittelstrasser made off with a loaded lorry.

His wife followed him a few days later after extensive packing. They were not heard from again.[8]

Eva Braun's dog Negus, an evil-tempered terrier that no one liked – apart from Eva – was left to roam and scavenge in the ruins of what had once been his home. No one had the desire or inclination to look after it – or, for that matter, put it out of his misery. There is no record of the dog's eventual fate; presumably it crawled away to die somewhere in the grounds. It may have been a cruel end for the animal but many who had fallen foul of the dog thought that there was undoubtedly something ironic, possibly even symbolic, in its fate.

Conclusion

*'Fate wasn't fickle. When the time did come for a killing,
she always gave him a signal: till then he must wait.'*
Richard Hughes, *The Fox in the Attic*

No one in their right mind would ever call Adolf Hitler a decent human being. He was the guiding light behind a brutal programme of mass murder, the founding father and leader of a cult that became a political party that became a government. He was undoubtedly one of the most evil men who ever lived.

Yet Hitler was also a man of many contradictions. Not in the big things – his virulent and unexplainable hatred of the Jews, for example, or his rabid desire to find living space in the east; they were constants in his life, constants that would lead him to some of the greatest and vilest actions in human history. Nothing and nobody would ever change those. But there were also moments and occasions in his life when the public image of him as a mad, ranting demagogue fell away, revealing an altogether softer and more pliable side to his character. The continuing fascination with Hitler as a man is largely due to these two, diametrically opposed sides to his nature.

How he could control or manage the switch from raving bully to understanding and considerate friend and manager remains a mystery. So too, is the answer to the obvious question – which of those two faces was the real Adolf Hitler? There may well be no answer to that. A mass murderer can also be a family man with values and standards just as a kindly and caring human being can go out and kill, seemingly without reason. It may not be obvious but there will *always* be a reason, a motive, deep within the psyche of the individual. Finding it, particularly with someone like Adolf Hitler, remains the key.

Almost without exception, Hitler's secretaries and personal staff regarded him as a good, caring and paternalistic employer. Members of the Berghof Set loved to be in his company when he would be funny, understanding and compassionate, entertaining the company with his wit and charm. They would have scratched out each other's eyes to get close to him. The people of Germany, the women in particular, had similar opinions and thought of him as a saviour.

If it was all an act then it was a damned good one. To a large extent acting a role, giving each individual – Party members, women of Germany or foreign diplomats – what they wanted, was part of Hitler's success. It was certainly part of his charm and one that, with his women in particular, was hugely successful.

He may well have been playing out a role when he sat and talked to his secretaries but he did not need to. There was nothing to be gained. That was simply part of his desire and ability to perform, even in private – the consummate and compulsive actor never quite went away.

And yet, no matter how he felt about the women in his entourage and no matter how well he was playing his part, he was still capable of sudden shafts of anger if anyone challenged him or disagreed with him overly significantly – as Christa Schroeder, Henny Hoffmann and Gretl Braun found to their cost. And once crossed or contradicted, Adolf Hitler was not the type of man to change his mind easily. Forgiveness was simply not in his armoury.

Right to the end of the Third Reich Hitler's women retained a huge influence on him. Perhaps they did not wield that influence in the typical or traditional way, helping to change his mind or pointing him in one direction or another, but they did provide him with comfort and security which were crucial for a man who for large parts of each day was consumed by hatred and by a single main idea – the glory and the greatness of the Aryan people. If nothing else the acceptance by his women gave him time and space to think and plan and plot.

The two concepts, comfort and security, invariably work or mesh together. If properly handled, both in the giving and in the eventual taking away, they can go some significant way towards creating a stable human being. The 'taking away' is crucial – everyone has to be able to stand alone at some stage in their lives, without parents or relatives to hold them up. Too sudden, too unexpected, and the taking away becomes little more than a drop.

Hitler's need for security can be traced back to his childhood when his mother offered so much – and yet so little. She gave without asking for anything in return, protecting the child she was terrified of losing. Klara Hitler died young so there was no opportunity to wean him, figuratively, from his mother's breast. Her death smashed away the care and compassion he so desperately needed and left him bereft and rootless in the world.

In many respects nobody was ever more important to Hitler than his mother. His love for her never wavered and, after her early death, he spent much of his life searching for the structure that Klara Hitler had once provided for him. His need for substitute maternal figures – Winnifred Wagner, Helene Bechstein and the rest – gives a clear indication of his desire for a surrogate mother to hold and help him through difficult times. That was something that no young and nubile actress or socialite could ever offer.

Kindly and caring, Klara Hitler was a woman who reflected traditional Austrian peasant values but, it can be argued, she did her son no good whatsoever when she spoiled him and gave him everything he desired. Her early death cut away the care, compassion and security he so desperately needed and cast him adrift upon a roaring sea of unhappiness that he was never quite able to calm.

It is one of the great speculations of history to wonder how Klara Hitler would have felt at the way her little boy turned out. Conversely, of course, is to ask yet another question – would he have become the monster he did if Klara had lived? It is, of course, unanswerable.

Notes

Introduction

1. *Daily Express*, February 2009

1. Popular Opinion: Myth and Truth

1. Hans Baur, *I Was Hitler's Pilot*, Frontline Books, Barnsley, p. 38
2. Christa Schroeder, *He Was My Chief*, Frontline Books, Barnsley, p. 117
3. Adolf Hitler, *Mein Kampf*, Jaico, Mumbai, p. 50
4. Baur, p. 40
5. Dorothy Thompson quoted in Walter C. Langer, *The Mind of Adolf Hitler*, Basic Books, London, p. 40
6. Herbert Dohring et al, *Living with Hitler*, Greenhill Books, London
7. Walter C. Langer, *The Mind of Adolf Hitler*, Basic Books, London, p. 168
8. Ibid, p. 172
9. Ian Kershaw, *Hitler 1889–1936 Hubris*, Allen Lane, London, p. 46
10. Schroeder, p. xix
11. Ibid, pp. 37-8
12. Ken Ford, *Women Close to Hitler*, KFMB, London, p. 31
13. Langer, p. 33

2. A Loving, Dysfunctional, Dangerous Family: Klara, Angela and Paula

1. Adolf Hitler, *Mein Kampf*, Jaico, Mumbai, p. 22
2. Christa Schroeder, *He Was My Chief*, Frontline Books, Barnsley, p. 173

3. Hitler, p. 29
4. Walter C. Langer, *The Mind of Adolf Hitler*, Basic Books, London, p. 116
5. Hitler, p. 29
6. Ibid, p. 31

3. Dreams of Love: Stephanie Isak and Charlotte Lobjoie

1. August Kubrizek, *The Young Hitler I Knew*, Greenhill Books, London, Chapter 3
2. Ibid
3. Ken Ford, *Women Close to Hitler*, KFMB, London, p. 21
4. Christa Schroeder, *He Was My Chief*, Frontline Books, Barnsley, p. 135
5. Ibid, p. 126

4. Women of the World: Society Ladies at Large

1. Ken Ford, *Women Close to Hitler*, KFMB, London, p. 25
2. Guido Knopp, *Hitler's Women*, Sutton Publishing, Stroud, p. 154
3. August Kubrizek, *The Young Hitler I Knew*, Greenhill Books, London, p.115
4. Geoffrey Wheatcroft in *The New York Times*, 11 March 2007
5. https://en.wikipedia./org/wiki/Winnifred_Wagner

5. The Silver Screen: Renate Müller, Leni Riefenstahl and Others

1. Christa Schroeder, *He Was My Chief*, Frontline Books, Barnsley, pp. 127-8
2. Walter C. Langer, *The Mind of Adolf Hitler*, Basic Books, London, p. 88
3. Quoted in Guido Knopp, *Hitler's Women*, Sutton Publishing, Stroud, p. 223
4. Ibid, p. 223

5. Traudl Junge, *Until the Final Hour*, Phoenix, London, p. 231-2
6. Langer, p. 171
7. Ibid
8. Ibid
9. Proceedings of De-Nazification Trial, quoted in Knopp, p. 143

6. Young Love: Mitzi and Henny

1. Ken Ford, *Women Close to Hitler*, KFMB, London, p. 39
2. John Simkin article on Spartacus Educational website, September 1997
3. www.en.wikipedia.org/wiki/Maria_Reiter
4. Guido Knopp, *Hitler's Women*, Sutton Publishing, Stroud, p. 13-14
5. en.wikipedia.org/wiki/Henriette_von_Schirach
6. Walter C. Langer, *The Mind of Adolf Hitler*, Basic Books, London, p.88
7. Traudl Junge, *Until the Final Hour*, Phoenix, London, p. 88

7. A Forbidden Affection: Geli Raubal

1. Ken Ford, *Women Close to Hitler*, KFMB, London, p. 43
2. Ian Kershaw, *Hitler 1889–1936 Hubris*, Allen Lane, London, p. 353
3. John Simkin article on Spartacus Educational website, September 1997
4. Ibid
5. Ibid
6. Christa Schroeder, *He Was My Chief*, Frontline Books, Barnsley, p. 128
7. Ford, p. 51
8. Traudl Junge, *Until the Final Hour*, Phoenix, London, pp. 88, 203

8. The Berghof Set: Eva's Domain

1. David Lloyd George, in *Daily Express*, 17 November 1936
2. Guido Knopp, *Hitler's Women*, Sutton Publishing, Stroud, p. 21-2

3. Ken Ford, *Women Close to Hitler*, KFMB, London, p. 71
4. www.britannica.com/biography/Martin-Bormann
5. Traudl Junge, *Until the Final Hour*, Phoenix, London, p. 128
6. Christa Schroeder, *He Was My Chief*, Frontline Books, Barnsley, p. 168
7. Alan Bullock, *Hitler: A Study in Tyranny*, Pelican, London, p. 396

9. Passing Ships in the Night: Suzi Liptauer and Many Others

1. Christa Schroeder, *He Was My Chief*, Frontline Books, Barnsley, p. 144-5
2. Ibid, p. 145
3. *Daily Express*, 11 June 2013
4. Schroeder, pp. 134-5
5. www.ww2gravestone.com
6. Hermann Esser in *Revue* magazine, 1 and 8 November 1949
7. Ibid
8. Ibid

10. A Dream of Valkyrie: the Mitford Sisters

1. Article in *The New York Times*, 2 March 2007
2. www.wikipedia.org/wiki/Unity_Mitford
3. Ibid
4. BBC News Online, 13 August 2003
5. Ken Ford, *Women Close to Hitler*, KFMB, London, p. 104
6. Deborah Mitford, letter in *The Guardian*, 8 December 2002
7. Guido Knopp, *Hitler's Women*, Sutton Publishing, Stroud, p. 15

11. Closer Yet: Traudl Junge, Hanna Reitsch and More

1. Traudl Junge, *Until the Final Hour*, Phoenix, London, p. 161
2. Christa Schroeder, *He Was My Chief*, Frontline Books, Barnsley, p. 87

3. Ibid, p. 105
4. Junge, p. 3
5. Ken Ford, *Women Close to Hitler*, KFMB, London, p. 110
6. Junge, p. 238-9
7. Walter C. Langer, *The Mind of Adolf Hitler*, Basic Books, London, p. 235
8. Schroeder, p. 121
9. www.enwikipedia.org/wiki/Hanna_Reitsch

12. The First Lady of Germany: Magda Goebbels

1. Magda Goebbels quoted Guido Knopp, *Hitler's Women*, Sutton Publishing, Stroud, p. 51
2. Erich Kempka, I Was Hitler's Chauffeur, Frontline, Barnsley, p. 13
3. Guido Knopp, *Hitler's Women*, Sutton Publishing, Stroud, p. 66
4. Hermann Esser in *Revue* magazine, 1949
5. Quoted Guido Knopp, *Hitler's Women*, Sutton Publishing, Stroud, p. 54

13. Curtain Down, Last Love: Eva Braun

1. Traudl Junge, *Until the Final Hour*, Phoenix, London, p. 177
2. Guido Knopp, *Hitler's Women*, Sutton Publishing, Stroud, p. 30
3. Ibid, p. 25
4. Ibid, p. 163
5. Anna Plain quoted Herbert Dohring et al, *Living with Hitler*, Greenhill Books, London
6. Antony Beevor, *Berlin*, Penguin, 2003, p. 253-4

14. The Furies: Women of Germany

1. Richard J. Evans, 'German Women and the Triumph of Hitler' in *The Journal of Modern History*, Vol. 48, No. 1, March 1976
2. www. johndclare.net/Nazis
3. johndclare.net/Nazi_Germany3.htm

4. Melita Maschmann, quoted on Spartacus-Educational.com/GER women.htm
5. Claudia Koonz, article in *The New York Times*, 1987
6. John Simkin article on Spartacus Educational website, September 1997

15. Final Act: In the Bunker

1. Traudl Junge, *Until the Final Hour*, Phoenix, London, p. 160
2. Ken Ford, *Women Close to Hitler*, KFMB, London, p. 122
3. Junge, p. 190
4. Erich Kempka, *I Was Hitler's Chauffeur*, Frontline, Barnsley, p. 78
5. Junge, p. 219
6. Ibid, p. 245
7. Christa Schroeder, *He Was My Chief*, Frontline Books, Barnsley, p. 180
8. Ibid, p. 190

Bibliography

Books

Baur, Hans, *I Was Hitler's Pilot*, Frontline Books, Barnsley, 2013

Beevor, Antony, *Berlin*, Penguin, London, 2003

Bullock, Alan, *Hitler: A Study in Tyranny*, Pelican, London, 1962

Carradice, Phil, *Night of the Long Knives*, Pen and Sword, Barnsley, 2018

Carey, John (editor), *The Faber Book of Reportage*, Faber, London, 1987

Davidson, Edward & Dale Manning, *Chronology of World War Two*, Cassell, London, 1999

Dohring, Herbert et al, *Living with Hitler*, Greenhill Books, 2018

Dunstan, Simon & Gerrard Williams, *Grey Wolf*, Sterling, New York, undated

Ford, Ken, *Women Close to Hitler*, KFMB, London, 2013

Hitler, Adolf, *Mein Kampf*, Jaico, Mumbai, 2018

Hughes, Richard, *The Fox in the Attic*, Chatto & Windus, London, 1961

Junge, Traudl, *Until the Final Hour*, Phoenix, London, 2013

Kempka, Erich, *I Was Hitler's Chauffeur*, Frontline Books, Barnsley, 2012

Kershaw, Ian, *Hitler 1889–1936 Hubris*, Allen Lane, London, 1998

Kubrizek, August, *The Young Hitler I Knew*, Greenhill Books, London, 2006

Langer, Walter C., *The Mind of Adolf Hitler*, Basic Books, New York, 1972

Knopp, Guido, *Hitler's Women*, Sutton Publishing, Stroud, 2006

Schroeder, Christa, *He Was My Chief*, Frontline Books, Barnsley, 2012

Periodicals

Daily Express, 17 November 1936, February 2009, 11 June 2013

The New York Times, 2 March 2007, January–December 1987

The Guardian, 8 December 2002
Journal of Modern History, Vol. 48, No. 1, March 1976.
Revue magazine, 1 & 8 November 1949

Websites

en.wikipedia.org/wiki/Henriette_von_Schirach
en.wikipedia.org/wiki/Maria_Reiter
en.wikipedia/org/wiki/Winnifred_Wagner
Spartacus Educational – various issues
www.britannia.combiography/Martin_Bormann
www.enwikipedia.org/wiki/Hanna_Reitsch
www.johnclare.net/Nazis
www.wikipedia.org/wiki/Unity_Mitford
www.ww2gravestone.com

Index

INDEX

207